THE WORLD WAR II READER

ALSO AVAILABLE

The Crossing
Moses
The Immigrants
by Howard Fast

The Man
by Irving Wallace

When Hell Froze Over
by E.M. Halliday

Helmet for My Pillow
by Robert Leckie

The Way of the Gladiator
The Hellfire Club
by Daniel P. Mannix

Samurai!
by Saburo Sakai
with Martin Caidin and Fred Sato

Fork-Tailed Devil: The P-38 Story
by Martin Caidin

COMING SOON

Thunderbolt!
by Robert S. Johnson with Martin Caidin

THE WORLD
WAR II
READER

EDITED BY THE EDITORS OF
World War II MAGAZINE

ibooks
new york
www.ibooksinc.com

DISTRIBUTED BY SIMON & SCHUSTER, INC

An Original Publication of ibooks, inc.

An ibooks, inc. Book

ibooks, inc.
24 West 25th Street
New York, NY 10010

The ibooks World Wide Web Site address is:
http://www.ibooksinc com

Material originally appeared in *World War II, MHQ: The Quarterly Journal
of Military History,* and *Aviation History* and is used with permission.

To subscribe to *World War II, MHQ: The Quarterly Journal of Military
History, Aviation History* or any of the other PRIMEDIA History Group
publications, call
1-800-829-3340 or 1-904-446-6914 (foreign)
or visit www.thehistorynet.com

Photos courtesy the National Archives, the Department of Defense, and
the Naval Historical Center.

Editor: Dwight Jon Zimmerman
Cover Design: J. Vita

ISBN: 0-7434-2387-9
First ibooks printing June 2001
10 9 8 7 6 5 4 3 2 1

Share your thoughts about *The World War II Reader* and other ibooks
titles in the new ibooks virtual reading group at www.ibooksinc.com

Contents

CONTENTS

1943

1944

1945

CONTENTS

Introduction

By Robert Leckie

It has been by war more than peace that our nation and our institutions have been proclaimed and defended, our industries developed, our culture enriched, our history made national, our arts and sciences improved and advanced.

In all of the many wars of America, two stand preeminent in our nations history, the American Civil War and World War II. The American Civil War was the first mass war of the era of modern warfare. It also made the great democratic experiment called the United States of America a nation. Less than eighty years later, World War II would see the nation emerge as a world power.

That war had its origin in the terrible European conflict originally known as "The Great War" though the only thing great about it was the vast amount of blood that had been spilt. The Treaty of Versailles, supposed to end end World War I, was a treaty made in a spirit of vengeance. It rewrote the map of Europe. Old nations vanished, new nations were born, and in the case of Poland, reborn. Its harsh and unjust terms, the war guilt clause, the demand for reprations, and the anexing Alsace and Lorraine by France as well as the "neutralization" of the Saar and the Rhineland, created resentment in Germany. When the Depression struck, the chaos it inspired added the final nail to the platform that the Nazi party leader Adolf Hitler need to become Chancellor, and very quickly, Fürher of Germany.

With bombast and bluff, history's maddest Pied Piper began to fulfill his promises to the German people to restore their lost prestige, prosperity, and property. In defiance of the Versailles treaty and against weak protests from England and France, Germany began to rearm and to take back what Hitler claimed to be "stolen" from Germany. German troops goosed-stepped into the Rhineland

and the Saar and received only a diplomatic slap on the wrist. Hitler then demanded the Sudentenland of Czechoslovakia with its German minority, and its invaluable Skoda war factories. With the Munich Pact negotiated with England and France who pursued a policy of appeasement, Hitler got what he wanted.

But when he demanded the return of territory given to Poland, England and France finally awoke to the danger. No longer would the attempt to appease the madman ruling Germany. If Hitler attempted to seize Poland, England and France would fight. Gambling that England and France would back down as they had before, On September 1, 1939, Hitler's troops invaded Poland. This time the gambler overplayed his hand. England and France honored their promises to Poland. Once again, Europe was at war.

On December 7, 1941, so, too, was America.

Withe the great Dreadnaughts of America's Pacific battle fleet resting at the bottom of Pearl Harbor, Japan moved quickly to seize the colonies of the Allies. Within eight months the banner of the Rising Sun flew over the Dutch East Indies, it surmounted the French tri-color in blotting out the Union Jack in Singapore where the soldiers double-timed through the streets. Burma, Malaya, and Thailand were also Japanese. India's hundreds of millions were imperiled, great china was all but isolated from the world, Austraila looked fearfully north to the Japanese bases being built on New Guinea, toward the long double chain of the Solomon Islands drawn like a knife across its lifeline to America. With the capture of Wake, Guam, and the Philippines, Japan had constructed a vast island shield to protect it from attack.

When he assumed power, Hitler had proclaimed the beginning of a Thousand-Year Reich. Japan believed its Co-Prosperity Sphere would secure its imperial ambitions. In 1945, because of America, both mad dreams were destroyed.

From the ruins of World War II America emerged as the leader of the Free World. With its Marshall Plan, in Winston Churchill's words "the most unsordid act in history," America rebuilt Western Europe. With a series of similar economic programs under the guidance of military governor General Douglas MacArthur, Japan, too, was rebuilt.

There have been many wars, both declared and otherwise, since then, of course. As we begin the second millennium, the future of mankind still seems uncertain, but to a much lesser degree than before. The solution to the problem of war , of course, is to develop the good society. But as Thomas More wrote nearly five centuries ago at the conclusion of his *Utopia*, society will be good only when men are good—and that, he thought, would not be for some time.

Robert Leckie
February, 2001

Editors' Forward

The telling of the story of World War II began long before the last shot was fired. Since then the interest in the world's greatest conflict has grown and if anything, shows no sign of abating. Almost sixty years after the surrender ceremony on the battleship Missouri, it would seem impossible for anything new to be told about World War II and its many battles. The World War II reader reveals in the following essays is that for all we know about the war, there is still much that remains to be discovered.

The Editors

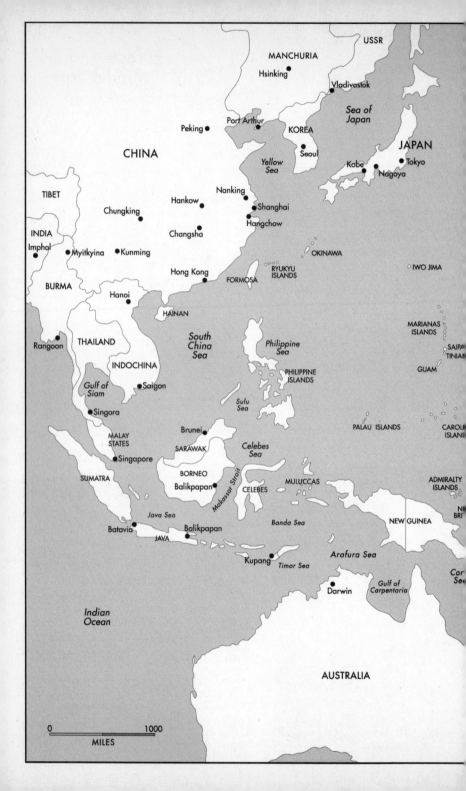

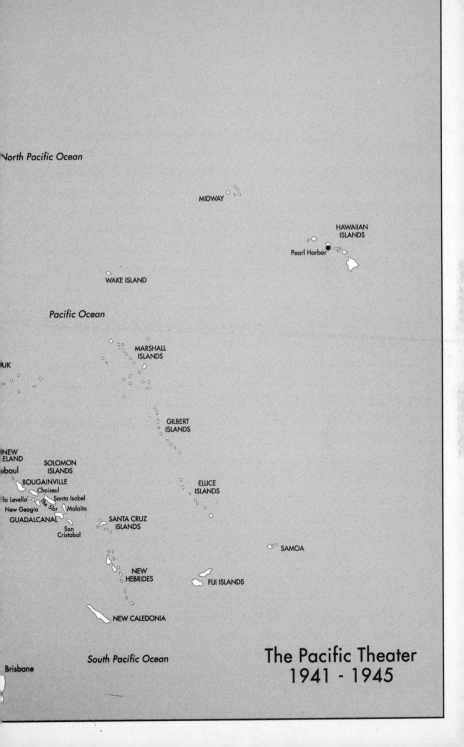

North Pacific Ocean

MIDWAY

HAWAIIAN
ISLANDS

Pearl Harbor

WAKE ISLAND

Pacific Ocean

MARSHALL
ISLANDS

UK

GILBERT
ISLANDS

NEW
ELAND

SOLOMON
ISLANDS

abaul

BOUGAINVILLE
Choiseul
la Levella
Santa Isabel
New Geogia
Malaita
GUADALCANAL

ELLICE
ISLANDS

SANTA CRUZ
ISLANDS

San
Cristobal

SAMOA

NEW
HEBRIDES

FIJI ISLANDS

NEW CALEDONIA

South Pacific Ocean

The Pacific Theater
1941 - 1945

Brisbane

1939

Hitler's Uncontained Revolution

By Williamson Murray

Fifty years ago the Second World War began. Today, long after its end, the conflict still determines the shape of our world, and historians continue to debate its causes. What strategic, diplomatic, and political factors brought the European powers into the second catastrophic conflict to occur within a generation?

The Second World War was an ideological war, a war fought to contain a revolution. That may explain why its savagery and cost surpassed anything the world had ever seen, even in the wars of religion. What made Germany's new bid for hegemony so terrifying was the fact that Adolf Hitler imbued his nation and military with a messianic sense of racial and cultural superiority. Under the cloak of ideological truth the Germans committed crimes surpassing even those committed by Joseph Stalin in his crusade for class purity. Hitler, too, led a revolutionary crusade, and our failure, from the beginning, to recognize it as such brought us the catastrophe that was World War II.

The First World War had not been a war about ideology, no matter what propagandists on both sides might pretend. Its most tragic result, beyond its ghastly slaughter, was that it settled

3

nothing. The supposed victors, Britain and France, lay exhausted and bankrupt by the struggle; the United States almost immediately disappeared into the self-indulgence of strategic and economic isolationism. The vanquished were in worse shape: The Austro-Hungarian Empire had entirely dissolved; Russia had collapsed into a paroxysm of revolution and civil war; and Germany, starved out by the Allied blockade, racked by revolution, its armies on the brink of devastating defeat, had to sue for peace.

Yet the German defeat was anything but complete. The commander of the American Expeditionary Force, General John Pershing, had argued during the prearmistice negotiations that only a peace dictated in Berlin would force the Germans to recognize their defeat, but the Allies allowed the Germans to sign an armistice in the field. The German army, while surrendering much of its heavy weaponry, marched back to the Reich and were greeted, even by the Social Democratic president of the new republic, as "unbeaten in the field." The "stab in the back" legend—that the army had lost the war not on the battlefield but because of Jewish and communist treason on the home front—became a cornerstone of German politics. But the strategic realities of 1919 forced the republic to sign the Treaty of Versailles.

The irony of the German reaction to the Treaty of Versailles is that the war's outcome had enormously strengthened that nation's strategic position. In 1914 Germany bordered on three of Europe's major powers. Now, in 1919, Austria-Hungary collapsed into a number of conflicting, weak states. To the east Poland and Lithuania had gained their independence, largely at Russia's expense (although Germany had also lost some territory), and now provided a buffer between Germany and the Soviet Union. Only in the west did Germany front on a major power, France, but that nation was exhausted by the war's bloodletting. Germany found herself in a position to establish a semihegemony over Central Europe.

Unfortunately, German dissatisfaction with the Treaty of Versailles, and Germany's continuing national arrogance, made a renewal of the 1914–18 conflict inevitable. As Marshal Ferdinand Foch despairingly noted in 1919, the Allies had granted the Reich a "twenty-year truce." He was correct to the year. Further exacerbating the situation, the German government carried out a massive disinformation campaign to mask Germany's responsibility for the war's outbreak. The German Foreign Office published carefully doctored documents that left out crucial pieces of evidence entirely or distorted their meaning. It provided subsidies and fellowships to foreign scholars favorable to the German point of view and allowed access to its carefully culled files only to Germans and foreigners willing to tell the German story. The Germans deliberately politicized and propagandized the history of World War I. They misled a whole generation of British and American scholars, and, even more disastrous, misled themselves. By the early 1930s most educated Englishmen—the political leadership in particular—believed that Germany bore no more war guilt than any other nation.

The nature of a future European conflict took a sinister turn when Adolf Hitler came to power in Germany in January 1933. Hitler made his intentions plain from the start. He had not been chancellor a week when he announced to his generals that if France had any true statesmen, they would soon pick a fight with Germany; if not, then it would be Germany that would determine the time and place of the inevitable conflict. Not content to fight merely to regain those little pieces of territory lost in 1919, he aimed to wage a great war that would completely destroy the European balance of power. In Hitler's vision, Germany would dominate Europe from the Urals to Spain and establish a great Aryan empire. She would settle accounts with the Jews—whom he blamed for defeat in the Great War—put the French in their place, destroy wretched little states such as Belgium that had blocked German designs in 1914, and finally dispossess the Slavic peoples of their land and lives. Those Russians, Ukrainians, and Poles whom he allowed to survive would lead a helotlike existence.

Marx had placed class at the center of his ideology; Hitler placed race at the center of his political *Weltanschauung* ("world view"). In every sense the Nazi movement was as revolutionary as Marxism in its most extreme forms. Both ideologies brought death to millions, and indeed came close to destroying European civilization.

Unfortunately, few of Germany's future opponents recognized either the danger of Hitler's ideology or its essential nature. The British, convinced by the early 1930s that victory in the Great War had been no better than defeat, concluded that anything was better than war. Their leaders were confident that in a world peopled by reasonable human beings, all international disputes could be settled by negotiation, and no national leader could possibly consider war an instrument of national policy. Appeasement found its justification in such an attitude. The French fully distrusted the new Germany, but French losses in World War I had created political paralysis.

Of all the European nations, the Soviet Union followed the most irresponsible course. Marx had excluded the possibility of revolutionary movements coming from the political right, and Stalin explained the rise of Hitler and the Nazi party in the early 1930s as merely a front for "monopoly capitalism." It was a movement, therefore, of little significance and one that, even if it came to power, would collapse before the political logic of communism. Stalin's obedient thugs in the German Communist party attacked the mildly left-leaning Social Democrats as "social fascists" and, in effect, cooperated with the Nazis in bringing down the Weimar Republic—a task made easier by the turmoil of worldwide depression.

When Hitler's dictatorship consolidated its power after 1933, Stalin made belated but halfhearted efforts elsewhere in Europe to form popular fronts against the "internal fascist enemy." The fact that beginning in May 1937 he had virtually all of his officer corps shot or imprisoned suggest his underestimation of Germany's growing military and strategic power. (See "White Queen in the Kremlin," by David Clay Large, on page 68.) Stalin's attention throughout the 1930s remained centered on his paranoid desire to cleanse the Soviet Union of those who in any way represented a threat to his personal power.

Not only did Hitler's natural opponents refuse to recognize the Nazi threat, but the Italian invasion of Ethiopia in 1935 and the ferocious civil war in Spain served to distract the European powers from the growth of German military power. These conflicts were not, as has been widely claimed, stepping-stones to the Second World War: They had no strategic importance outside of themselves. In the meantime, Hitler had given the German generals and admirals a blank check to create the world's strongest army, air force, and navy for the Reich. They were hampered by the fact that German industry had been hard hit by depression, and armament factories had become run-down in the 1920s. Nevertheless, Hitler demanded as rapid a buildup as possible.

From his first moments in power, Hitler moved relentlessly and ruthlessly toward his goal of a Europe *"Juden-frei"* and under German domination. For the short run, establishing Nazi control of Germany remained imperative, but rearmament topped his list of priorities—so much so that by 1937 Germany teetered on the brink of bankruptcy and collapse. Heedless of the warnings of German economists, Hitler drove onward; only the risky foreign-policy triumphs of 1938 kept the Reich afloat. But the success of Hitler's approach depended on risk, and only two options existed: Either *Weltmacht* ("world power") or *Niedergang* ("defeat"). To the führer, *Niedergang* meant not just defeat but complete destruction. The economic situation of Nazi Germany may have been at times desperate, but never did economic considerations sway Hitler from his fundamental policies or check his ideological drives.

Along with the armaments buildup came a series of diplomatic moves designed to strengthen Germany's strategic position: The Nazis withdrew from the League of Nations in 1933, signed a nonaggression pact with Poland in 1934, announced conscription and established the Luftwaffe in 1935, and in 1936 sent troops into the Rhineland—demilitarized since Versailles. The Western Powers failed to take any substantive action in reply. In effect, Hitler, with virtually no show of military power, reestablished Germany's position in Europe.

It is conceivable that Hitler would have waited longer if the costs of massive rearmament had not threatened to bankrupt the German state by the end of 1937. In November 1937 he gathered his military and diplomatic advisers to discuss Germany's strategic and economic position. He proposed an aggressive foreign policy to solve the Reich's current difficulties, but met substantial opposition. He responded in February 1938 by carrying out a purge of the senior German leadership, forcing out the defense minister, the commander in chief of the army, and the foreign minister. Hitler found himself in late winter 1938 facing not only economic difficulties but also considerable disaffection within the officer corps over his shabby treatment of the army's commander in chief, whom he had falsely branded a homosexual.

Hitler turned this impasse into an enormous foreign-policy success by manufacturing a crisis with Austria. First brow-beating the Austrian chancellor and then threatening the Austrians with outright invasion, Hitler overthrew the Austrian regime, replaced it with a Nazi one, and marched his troops in to occupy the tiny nation. Then while Europe looked on, he successfully incorporated Austria directly into the Third Reich—the Anschluss, or annexation, that the Allied powers, France especially, had long feared.

The British temporized by saying that the Nazis were only

"moving into their backyard," and Prime Minister Neville Chamberlain saw no reason his policy of appeasement should not continue. The French simply ran away from their responsibilities. The French Cabinet collapsed, and the Chamber of Deputies could not put together another government until the dust settled over Austria's grave. Hitler gained enormously: Annexing Austria raised his popularity at home to new heights. The officer corps, distracted by success and the problems of incorporating the Austrian army into the Wehrmacht, forgot about the February purge of the high command; the Third Reich gained considerable economic assets in Austria's underemployed work force and Austria's foreign exchange; and finally, the Germans gained a firm foothold in the Balkans and now hemmed Czechoslovakia in from three sides.

The Anschluss led directly to the Czechoslovakian crisis of summer 1938—one of the great might-have-beens of the 1930s. For months Hitler had been lamenting the plight of the ethnic Germans in the Sudetenland, which happened to be the fortified western frontier zone of Czechoslovakia. At the end of May 1938, Hitler determined to crush Czechoslovakia in a short war. The Germans mobilized over the summer and the Czechs prepared to resist. Meanwhile Hitler attempted to isolate Czechoslovakia diplomatically. Some senior German generals balked at the prospect of attacking the Czech republic. They could not conceive that the British, French, and Soviets would stand aside. The German economy possessed virtually no reserves of raw materials, or foreign exchange, as the stockpiles of the Austrian windfall quickly vanished. The Luftwaffe was undergoing teething problems as it moved to a new generation of aircraft. (It was still formidable enough to awe Charles A. Lindbergh a few months later—see "They Can't Realize the Change Aviation Has Made," by Richard M. Ketchum, on page 46.) And the army confronted major deficiencies that appeared during the occupation of Austria: German tanks broke down in large numbers, incidents of indiscipline occurred, and the mobilization of regular units faltered. Moreover, outside of the Landwehr, which consisted entirely of World War I veterans, no reserve forces existed.

Still, Hitler pushed the crisis to the brink of war. In mid-September, after flying to Berchtesgaden to meet with Hitler, Chamberlain forced the Czechs to agree to surrender their frontier districts and fortifications. But even that was not enough for Hitler; at a second meeting with Chamberlain at Godesberg, the führer made such outrageous demands that negotiations almost came to a halt. Hitler continued his maniacal drive for war. However, at the last moment, he changed his mind. Perhaps mobilization of the British fleet, perhaps the influence of the Italian dictator Mussolini, perhaps the complaints of his own generals and admirals—or all of these factors together—persuaded him to accept the surrender of the Sudetenland.

At the Munich Conference at the end of September 1938, Chamberlain and the French premier, Edouard Daladier, agreed to meet Germany's demands in full. Chamberlain returned to Britain to announce that he had achieved "peace for our time" and "peace with honor." Daladier, returning home by plane, showed more wisdom: Spotting large crowds on the ground, he had his aircraft circle Le Bourget airfield. He feared that they had come to lynch him; unfortunately they were there to cheer him.

The might-have-beens loom. Hitler probably would have achieved a relatively quick victory over the Czechs, but it would have been far more costly than his romp over Poland a year later. Such a campaign would have destroyed most of the Czech matériel and possibly damaged its arms industry, both of which the Germans received intact six months later. The Nazi regime would have embarked on a world war with an unprepared military and a precarious economic situation. The longer the Allies delayed in confronting Hitler, the worse the war would be for all involved.

In early October 1938, before a thoroughly hostile House of Commons, Winston Churchill caught the real significance of what the democracies had surrendered at Munich:

> All is over. Silent, mournful, abandoned, broken Czechoslovakia recedes into the darkness. . . . Every position has been successively undermined and abandoned on specious and plausible excuses. . . .
>
> [W]e have sustained a defeat without a war, the consequences of which will travel far with us along our road; . . . we have passed an awful milestone in our history, when the whole equilibrium of Europe has been deranged and . . . the terrible words have for the time being been pronounced against the Western democracies: "Thou art weighed in the Balance and found wanting." And do not suppose this is the end. This is only the beginning of the reckoning. This is only the first sip, the first foretaste of a bitter cup.

Incredible as it may seem, Hitler felt great displeasure over the Munich conference. Yet he had achieved one of the great diplomatic triumphs of the twentieth century. The Sudetenland, with its formidable defenses, had fallen into his hands without a shot being fired. Barely was the ink dry on the agreement when Hitler ordered the chief of the OKW (Oberkommando des Wehrmachts—the armed forces high command) to draw up plans to occupy the rest of Czechoslovakia.

Munich did not give Germany control of the famous Skoda Works, among the most modern complexes of armament factories in the world. Moreover, fall and winter 1938–39 were trying times for the führer; the Germans had displayed little enthusiasm at the prospect of war, and the economic outlook had once again turned bleak. In early October 1938 the Reich Defense Committee reported that Wehrmacht demands (due to occupation of the Sudetenland) and unlimited construction on the Westwall along the French border had created such severe shortages of coal, supplies for industries, and food that "continuing the tension past October 10" would make "catastrophe inevitable."

When the committee met in November, Hermann Göring acknowledged the severity of the economic strain: No additional manpower was available, factories already operated at full capacity, and the drain on foreign exchange had exhausted all reserves. In December the OKW reduced allocations of steel and raw materials to armament industries, and in January 1939 the economic situation forced Hitler to reduce steel allocations to the Wehrmacht by 30 percent, copper by 20 percent, aluminum by 47 percent, and rubber by 14 percent.

Not surprisingly, the Germans moved quickly against the remainder of Czechoslovakia. The rump Czech state still had considerable foreign-exchange reserves, in addition to the Skoda Works and the great arms dumps of the Czech army. From Hitler's viewpoint, especially given his contempt for Western leaders, it was difficult to see why the British or French might object to Germany's completing what Munich had started—the dismemberment of the Czech state. As he told his generals the following summer, he had seen his enemies at Munich, and they were worms.

So in mid-March 1939 the Germans created a political crisis with Czechoslovakia and then rolled over the frontier to occupy their next victim. They gained an enormous quantity of booty: Three of the ten panzer divisions that invaded France in May 1940 had Czech tanks; the Skoda Works continued manufacturing military equipment into May 1945; Czech foreign exchange let the Germans increase raw-material deliveries from abroad so their armament factories could resume full production; and they traded Czech arms throughout eastern Europe for more raw materials. Documents support Hitler's claims that by April the

Wehrmacht had gained 1,502 aircraft, 469 tanks, 500 antiaircraft guns, 43,000 machine guns, a million rifles, a billion rounds of ammunition, and 3 million rounds of artillery ammunition by occupying Czechoslovakia.

While the Germans totaled their gains, their move created shock waves throughout the rest of Europe. But the popular apprehension was hardly reflected in the behavior of the Allied governments, Britain's in particular. Chamberlain tried to placate the British, announcing that "it is natural . . . that I should bitterly regret what has now occurred. But do not let us on that account be deflected from our course." However, popular outrage that by now even reached Conservative Members of Parliament forced Chamberlain to reconsider. Within the week he was asking in pained disappointment whether the German move into Czechoslovakia was a "step in the direction of an attempt to dominate the world by force."

It was clear that Poland was next on Hitler's agenda. In a crisis atmosphere exacerbated not only by foreign rumors but also by internal political pressure, the British government acted without seriously thinking through its options. At the end of March, Chamberlain announced that

> in the event of any action that clearly threatened Polish independence, and which the Polish government accordingly considered vital to resist with their national forces, His Majesty's government would feel themselves bound at once to lend the Polish government all the support in their power.

The British guarantee to Poland surprised and infuriated Hitler. One of his entourage heard him exclaim that he would cook the British a stew on which they would choke. He broke off fitful negotiations with the Poles over realignment of the border, denounced their nonaggression pact, and ordered his staff to draw up plans for a massive attack on Poland. These plans set a terminal date for completion of preparations: September 1, 1939.

The führer's foreign policy further aimed to achieve what it had attempted the previous summer: To isolate the victim and deter British and French intervention. Hitler hoped to reach his goal by a mixture of propaganda, intimidation, and occasional promises of good behavior in the future ("the last German territorial demands on Europe"—a slogan that even the British were tiring of). But as for the Poles, Hitler was set on war, and this time, he told his advisers, no *"Schweinehund"* would dissuade him from using the Wehrmacht.

Hitler's determination on war seems to have rested on two disparate factors. The first was a sense that at age fifty his time was limited; he must act quickly to achieve his racial goals while his health (and Mussolini's) remained good. The second was Hitler's contempt for Western leadership, which misled him into believing he could get away with making war on Poland without risking a general European conflagration.

The British continued to turn a deaf ear to Hitler's expansionist demands, as if a messianic revolutionary could be treated as a normal politician. On the one hand they tried to fence the Germans in with diplomatic initiatives (the British and French passed out diplomatic guaranties to virtually every nation in eastern Europe). On the other they continued to approach Berlin, suggesting that the Germans could gain more by behaving peacefully. In late July, Sir Horace Wilson, one of Chamberlain's closest advisers, and Sir Joseph Ball, head of the Conservative party, met with a senior German official. They promised that if Germany agreed to a peaceful settlement of the German-Polish differences and to arms limitations, Britain would not only consider wide-scale economic cooperation but also secure financial aid for German industry. Such approaches only reinforced Hitler's contempt and his belief that the Western Powers would not dare intervene in a German-Polish conflict.

Since Western policy aimed at diplomatic deterrence, the British were little interested in creating an effective coalition that could fight and win a war. They were particularly dilatory in approaches to the Soviet Union. In retrospect, it is doubtful that the Soviets would have joined an anti-German coalition almost sure to involve them very shortly in a war. From Stalin's ideological point of view, it made more sense to encourage war among the capitalist powers and then sit on the sidelines while the two sides fought to exhaustion, as in the last year of World War I. Once certain that Britain and France had committed themselves to the defense of Poland, the Soviets held the diplomatic cards. Stalin could dicker with the Germans for territory in eastern Europe, and if no satisfactory deal was forthcoming, he could always turn to the Western Powers.

Chamberlain and his advisers viewed an agreement between the Soviets and the Germans as impossible because of their ideological differences. Even after the announcement of the Nazi-Soviet Nonaggression Pact, Lord Halifax, the British foreign secretary, discounted the agreement as having little strategic importance. (He did, however, admit to the Cabinet that its moral effect would be enormous.)

Given the fact that the Germans were about to launch themselves against Poland, Hitler was surprisingly reluctant to accept Stalin's overtures. But once the führer sensed that the Soviets would deal and that the British and French might stand with the Poles, he jumped at the opportunity. In early August the German leadership boiled with excitement at the prospect of a nonaggression pact. Now it was the Soviets who were standoffish—undoubtedly to increase their price—but when the Germans demanded a definite response, the Soviets moved. Stalin received immense booty: The Germans consigned Latvia, Estonia, Finland, eastern Poland, and the Rumanian province of Bessarabia to the Soviets. (Lithuania would be included in the Soviet sphere of influence later.) In addition, Hitler promised the Soviets the one thing that the Western Powers could not, namely peace.

Stalin's toast at a dinner honoring Nazi foreign minister Joachim von Ribbentrop suggests the moral parameters of the Nazi-Soviet Nonaggression Pact. Stalin raised his glass "to Heinrich Himmler, the man who has brought order to Germany." After another meeting with the Soviets in late September to tie up loose ends left by the August agreement, Ribbentrop gushed to Hitler that his reception by Soviet leaders reminded him of a gathering of old Nazi Party comrades.

The Nazi-Soviet pact had a number of long- and short-term advantages for the Germans. It eliminated the possibility of a two-front war, isolated Poland entirely, and promised the Germans substantial economic benefits—including grain, oil, hard-to-get ores such as manganese and nickel, and rubber from the Far East, which came via the trans-Siberian railroad. In fact, Soviet economic aid provided considerable support for the 1940 Western campaign and was an essential component in preparations for the invasion of the Soviet Union in 1941. With justice, Foreign Minister Vyacheslav Molotov would plaintively ask the German ambassador on the morning of June 22, 1941, "What have we done to deserve this?"

Of all the world powers, the Soviets seemingly gained the most from the fashion in which World War II began. In the long run, however, they may have lost the most. The Soviet Union looked on as the capitalist powers destroyed themselves in western Europe. But when Germany won a devastatingly complete and sudden victory in the West at minimal cost, the Soviets found themselves alone on the European continent with Adolf Hitler and his terrifying regime. Until June 1944 the Soviets would bleat about the need for the "second front," although Stalin's policies had played a major role in allowing the Germans to concentrate their forces on the western front in 1940 without fear of attack from the Soviets.

Hitler had now isolated the Poles even more completely than the Czechs the previous year. At the end of August, however, a desperate set of maneuverings took place. Hitler planned to begin the invasion of Poland on the morning of August 26, but news from Italy that Mussolini would not join the conflict momentarily disconcerted him. The army received orders to stop the invasion; in some cases frontline units failed to receive notification until they were actually on Polish territory. The Poles viewed these early incursions only as German efforts at intimidation, but Hitler was delaying in the hope that he could persuade Britain and France to stand aside; he had every intention of launching the invasion. As he told the chief of the general staff, General Franz Halder, September 2 was the last acceptable date for the attack. It was a rendezvous he would not miss.

On September 1, 1939, the Wehrmacht began sustained military operations to destroy the Polish state, and completed them less than a month later. (See "Poland 1939," by Caleb Carr, on page 56.)

What had been going on meanwhile in western Europe? Not much. During initial discussions in the British Cabinet after the German attack on Poland, one minister suggested that Britain should avoid a declaration of war. Chamberlain failed to ask for one that day. On September 2 he gave a long, whining speech to the House of Commons about the need to continue discussions. "If the German government should agree to withdraw their forces, then His Majesty's government would be willing to regard the position as being the same as it was before the German forces crossed the Polish frontier." Leo Amery, a member of Parliament, describes the result:

> The House was aghast. For two whole days the wretched Poles had been bombed and massacred, and we were still

considering within what time limit Hitler should be invited to tell us whether he felt like relinquishing his prey! And then these sheer irrelevancies about the terms of a hypothetical agreement between Germany and Poland. . . . Was all this havering the prelude to another Munich?

Amery, infuriated like most of the other members, shouted to Arthur Greenwood, who rose to give the Labour party's reply: *"Speak for England!"* The fury in the House reached such a pitch that Chamberlain asked for a declaration of war the following morning.

But that declaration did not lead to any significant action by the Western Powers. We might note here the strengths and weaknesses of Germany's strategic position, in order to judge the Anglo-French response. Across the board, that strategic position had improved in comparison to 1938. The Wehrmacht, while concentrating overwhelming military power on Poland, could now also protect Germany's western frontiers with a significant body of troops. Although in 1938 there had been only ten divisions (five of them regular) available for the defense of the French border, the Germans deployed over thirty divisions (ten of them active-duty) a year later. The number of panzer divisions had doubled from three to six, while the Luftwaffe had largely completed reequipping with a new generation of aircraft. In this light, the might-have-beens of the Czechoslovakian crisis stand out even more starkly.

But if Germany's military posture had improved since September 1938, it still had serious weaknesses. The German economy remained vulnerable to the Allied blockades. The tonnage and value of German imports and exports dropped by three-quarters between August and late fall of 1939. Nowhere did German vulnerabilities in raw materials show more clearly than in petroleum. At the beginning of the war, German reserves were 2.4 million tons; by May 1940 they had sunk by 33 percent to 1.6 million tons, although the Germans had done virtually no fighting. Gasoline stockpiles sank from 300,000 to 110,000 tons, while diesel fuel dropped from 220,000 to 73,000 tons. No wonder Hitler pushed so strongly for a fall 1939 offensive against the Western Powers.

The army, however, resisted Hitler's demands for a fall offensive, because it felt that battlefield performance, even by regular units, had not reached the expected standards. A massive training effort was needed. Considering the extent of the German triumph over the Polish armed forces, this suggests how high the Germans had set their sights in terms of military effectiveness. It also underlines their persisting military weaknesses, a result of the frantic pace of rearmament.

The British and French leadership proved incapable of taking advantage of these weaknesses. Though there were few prospects for success against Germany in 1939, a number of areas where the Allies might have exerted serious pressure did exist. But the British had discounted one of those areas—Italy—even before the war began. In June 1939 Chamberlain suggested that the Allies take a strong stand against the Italians by blockading their imports if a war occurred. Such a stand would have propelled the Italians into the war in early September. But that in fact would have been to the advantage of the Allies. Italy's presence in the war at that time would have allowed the Western Powers to destroy the Italian position in the Mediterranean (especially their Libyan stronghold), would have forced the Germans to help their ally with much-needed troops and matériel, and would have closed off a major chink in the blockade of Axis Europe. But the French proved uninterested; even the British Chiefs of Staff threw cold water on Chamberlain's suggestion. The Joint Planning Committee went so far as to suggest that Italy might "be in a position to hit us more effectively at the outset than we can hit her. . . ."

Another potential area of pressure was the Franco-German border. The Germans had considerably strengthened their position in the West since 1938, and the French "offensive" against the Westwall in mid-September did not even reach the German outposts. In fact, the French failed to undertake any serious military operations. In reply to desperate Polish appeals, General Maurice Gamelin, commander of the French army, said that half his regular divisions were in contact with the Wehrmacht, but the French army faced a well-prepared enemy that the French artillery could not move. Gamelin also claimed that the French air force kept most of the Luftwaffe bottled up in the west (a particularly disingenuous claim given what was happening in the skies over Poland). He concluded, according to an official British report, that he had "therefore already fulfilled his promise to undertake the first French offensive within fifteen days of mobilization. It is impossible to do more." At the same time, the British reported that Gamelin told them "he does not envisage casualties on a large scale. The object underlying the operation now in progress is to help Poland by distracting the attention of Germany. His offensive is confined to activities in 'no-man's-land' and he has no intention of throwing his army against the German defenses."

While the French could not have broken into the Rhineland, one of the most important industrial regions of Germany, the Saar, lay on the Franco-German frontier. Not only was the Saar a significant center of heavy industry, but nearly 8 percent of Germany's coal came from its mines. Even if the French had failed to seize the province, a major offensive here would have shut down German industry in the region.

The final area where the Allies might have exerted pressure on the Germans lay in the north. Every winter the crucially needed iron ore that the Germans imported from Sweden passed through the Norwegian port of Narvik and down its Atlantic coast. (The Baltic sea lanes were frozen in the winter.) Winston Churchill, reappointed first lord of the admiralty on September 3, 1939, urged the government to let the Royal Navy mine the Norwegian leads, thus ending iron-ore movement during the winter. Unfortunately, he ran into substantial bureaucratic and military caviling that once again saw danger in every action and produced endless excuses as to why safety lay in inactivity. Since Churchill did not yet have the authority to override such bureaucratic obstructionism, the Royal Navy did not mine Norwegian territorial waters until April 1940. By then the German invasion of Norway was already under way.

The pause between the end of the Polish campaign and the opening of the German offensive in May 1940 was *the* crucial factor in the overwhelming victory of the Wehrmacht that month. A particularly perceptive Allied study of April 1940 pointed out that "the Reich appears to have suffered relatively little wear and tear during the first six months of war, and that mainly as a result of the Allied blockade. Meanwhile it has profited from the interval to perfect the degree of equipment of its land and air forces, to increase the officer strength and complete the training of its troops, and to add further divisions to those already in the field." The result would contribute decisively to the defeat of Allied forces in spring 1940.

In conclusion we might examine two questions: What pushed Hitler into making the decision for war? And what was the nature of the war that he unleashed? In effect, war was inevitable from the moment Hitler came to power: not some small European war to adjust territorial boundaries but a major war, one in which Germany would either gain *"Weltmacht"* or suffer *"Niedergang."* From the beginning, this war was an ideological crusade, and all that the word implies.

By early 1939 the Germans had destroyed the restraints

imposed on her by the Versailles Treaty and was well on the way to full rearmament; she had seized Austria and the Sudetenland; and in the west a great defensive wall neared completion. With a minimum of military power, Hitler's diplomatic and strategic triumphs achieved a level of German dominance over Central Europe more far-reaching than Bismarck's successes in the 1871–90 period.

But it was not enough. The revolutionary dynamics of National Socialism demanded greater and greater risks; the rearmament program alone had achieved a momentum that soon would have compelled the German government to choose between bankruptcy and war. There is an air of complete unreality about Nazi armament plans in 1939, which can be explained only by the dominance of ideology. The change that March in British foreign policy so angered Hitler that he ordered Admiral Erich Raeder, the navy's commander in chief, to create a fleet as large as the Royal Navy. When one considers that the Luftwaffe planned to expand its strength fivefold (into a force whose gasoline requirements alone would have equaled 85 percent of the world's yearly production), while the army was expanding into one of the largest ground forces in Europe, it is difficult to see any connection in the Third Reich between means and ends.

Hitler was pushed by his own myth, his belief that fate had ordained him to create the "Thousand-Year Reich." That, too, was part of the nature of the war. By 1939 he was becoming more determined to force events into channels that he determined, rather than take advantage of the world as it was. Consequently, when the Poles withstood German pressure and Britain supported Poland, Hitler decided that the time had come for Germany to destroy the Warsaw regime.

Hitler's crusade for racial purity also involved a desire to settle matters with the Jews for all time. In January 1939 he explicitly warned "international Jewry" that if a general European war occurred, regardless of the outcome, the Jews of Europe would not survive. From the first days of the German invasion of Poland, wild excesses and atrocities against the Jewish and Polish population took place. While the "final solution" did not fully begin until Operation Barbarossa in 1941, the wide-scale annihilation of European Jews was implicit in German actions from the very start of hostilities.

On the western side, Anglo-French policy aimed to deter Germany from starting a war, not to win the sequel to World War I. That policy inevitably failed. But strategic opportunities that might have mitigated the disaster of May 1940 went by the boards. By refusing to take any action against the Germans from September 1938 to May 1940, the Western Powers magnified their danger. They failed to recognize the nature of Hitler's revolution, and by the time they finally sought to contain his crusade, it was almost too late. Yet one must have some sympathy for men whose fundamental desire was for peace. Churchill's moving tribute to Chamberlain after the latter's death in the fall of 1940 sets out the dilemma that statesmen in a democracy confront:

Whatever history may say or may not say about these terrible, tremendous years, we can be sure that Neville Chamberlain acted with perfect sincerity according to his lights and strove to the utmost of his capacity and authority, which were powerful, to save the world from the awful, devastating struggle in which we are now engaged. . . . Herr Hitler protests with frantic words and gestures that he has only desired peace. What do these ravings and outpourings count before the silence of Neville Chamberlain's tomb?

Poland 1939

By Caleb Carr

In the last days of August 1939, the German Seventh Armored Reconnaissance Regiment was moving east, along with the rest of the Wehrmacht. "Officially," recalled one officer in the Seventh A.R., "we were to take part in 'grand maneuvers under combat conditions.' Although live ammunition was being carried, we were issued only blanks. . . . Local people greeted us everywhere with flowers and drinks. 'Are you going to Poland?' we were asked. 'Of course not,' we replied. 'We're going on maneuvers.' "

On August 26 the Seventh A.R. reached the Polish border with Czechoslovakia, a nation recently occupied by German forces and now offering an excellent launching point for an attack into Poland. "Suddenly," the same officer went on, "the blank cartridges were exchanged for live ammunition. Now there was no longer any doubt: We were going to invade."

The attack was launched on September 1. The German navy shelled the contested port city of Danzig (Gdańsk) in the north while the German army embarked on a huge pincer movement from north and south, aimed at the Polish capital, Warsaw.

Although Polish resistance at the outset was disorganized—or nonexistent—the Germans soon found themselves fighting hard. Another German veteran wrote, "We admired our opponents for their national pride and commitment. They demanded our respect."

This is not the impression of the Polish campaign that has been generally fostered in the years since 1939. The German army's humiliation of France in 1940 and its early successes against the Soviet Union so stunned the world that the brief war the Wehrmacht waged against Poland is often seen as a mere dress rehearsal for those more momentous events. In hindsight, it seems impossible that little Poland with its obsolete army and antiquated military tradition could have stood even a remote chance against the world's most advanced military juggernaut. From this point of view, it is remarkable not that Germany defeated her eastern neighbor but that the campaign took as long as it did: seventeen days to decide the issue in the field, twenty-seven days to force the capitulation of Warsaw.

This assessment of the Polish campaign, while common, does little justice to either antagonist. In both the quality of their fighting and their occasional displays of tactical (if not strategic) ability, the Poles proved themselves a fighting force of far greater merit than, say, the French army that was sent reeling eight months later. And the German army in 1939 had not yet been transformed into the amazing war machine it would become in later years. That metamorphosis would actually begin during the heat of the Polish campaign, and constitutes a testament to the skill and innovative acumen of the German officer corps.

Perhaps the most erroneous impression created by many commentators (including Nazi propagandists during the war) concerning events in 1939 is that Germany's military leaders were eager to involve themselves in a war with Poland. To most

German generals, such a conflict—Hitler's statements notwith-standing—meant war with Poland's allies, England and France. Virtually no senior German officer faced that prospect with any certainty of ultimate success. The führer's ambitions were viewed with cultivated skepticism.

This attitude was not purely military in origin. During the previous year the German army had seen its three top officers removed by Nazi intrigues. The commander of the combined forces, General Werner von Blomberg, had been replaced after his wife was falsely accused of once having been a prostitute. General Ludwig Beck, chief of the general staff, was removed after repeatedly voicing his belief that Hitler was taking Germany down a road toward world war and ruin. Most ludicrous of all, the commander in chief of the army, Colonel General Werner Freiherr von Fritsch, was falsely accused of homosexual activities by the SS. Tried and exonerated, Fritsch was nonetheless demoted. (He volunteered for hazardous duty in Poland soon afterward, and was quickly killed.)

In the wake of this stunning attempt by Hitler to gain tighter control over the regular army (always a hotbed of anti-Nazi sen-timent), sixteen more German generals left the army and forty-four were given new assignments. In nearly every case these reassignments were made on the basis of political sympathies. For example, General Beck's deputy chief of the general staff, General Erich von Manstein—the German army's most gifted strategic planner but a man with little use for the Nazi party—was transferred to a divisional command.

Hitler apparently believed he could bring the army under his control through such tactics, but he was soon proved wrong. For while the new commander in chief, General Walther von Brau-chitsch, was slow to press his complaints against Nazi policies, he did eventually begin to press them; and the new chief of the gen-eral staff, General Franz Halder, proved troublesome to Hitler from the beginning. Halder's bristly hair and mustache, pince-nez, and perpetual frown seemed to accentuate the contempt he felt for Germany's new leaders—contempt that, by the end of the Second World War, would evolve into open opposition and imprisonment at Dachau.

In this atmosphere of distance and disinterest at best, and distrust and hostility at worst, the German army received orders in the spring of 1939 to begin preparing operational plans for "Case White"—war with Poland. General Halder assumed that to gain concessions from Poland, Hitler once again intended to use the army as an instrument of blackmail. This had been the führer's tactic in dealing with the nations of Europe to date, and it had succeeded. Determined to undo the terms of the 1919 Treaty of Versailles, Hitler had already reoccupied the Rhineland, achieved Anschluss with Austria, taken the Sudetenland, and occupied the rest of Czechoslovakia—all without firing a shot.

But Poland's attitude seemed to indicate a less propitious outcome to Hitler's latest round of brinkmanship. Following the First World War, Poland had been remade in a form that would have pleased her ancient warrior kings: Included within her borders were not only traditionally Polish territories but also healthy slices of German, Ukrainian, Russian, and Lithuanian lands. Hardest for the Germans to accept had been the creation of the "Polish Corridor," a wide swath of territory that ran north from Poland, severed East Prussia from the rest of Germany, and made an "international city" out of the port of Danzig. This region was largely inhabited by Germans, who after 1919 became Polish subjects. A good number of these people were military families, and more than a few German army leaders looked forward to the day when this humiliation would be reversed.

Nevertheless, nearly every senior German officer felt that if such reversal required war, Germany would have to wait to fight it. From its prescribed post-Versailles size of 100,000 men, the

German army had recently expanded to well over a million, and would eventually grow to 4 million; but the expansion had come too fast, and the new soldiers lacked thorough training. The appearance of organized and armed SS military units—the force that would become the Waffen SS—was also of deep concern to Germany's regular army officers. How would these new soldiers, so thoroughly indoctrinated with Nazi dogma, so ferociously loyal to the party elite—and most important, so openly scornful of the regular army—behave in the field?

Even more crucial was the question of incorporating Germany's new military arms—the Luftwaffe and the panzer (armored) divisions—into the operations of the German army as a whole. In Germany as elsewhere, the debate over mobile armored warfare had raged ever since British tanks had made their presence felt in World War I. In England, Captain Basil Liddell Hart and Major J. F. C. Fuller had spent the decade of the twenties calling loudly but in vain for a new kind of army, in which masses of tanks would shatter linear fronts, race to the enemy's rear, and disrupt military and political control. It was warfare wholly unlike what had been the rule from 1914 to 1918. Fast and fluid, limiting destruction through mobility and seeking decision rather than devastation, mobile armored warfare represented a quantum leap in military thinking.

The idea was at variance with Britain's military tradition, as well as with that of the other victorious Allied powers, and was slow to take root. But in Germany it found fertile soil, for it must be remembered that the protracted attrition that was World War I was an anomaly in German (and especially Prussian) military history. Because of her geographic position—in a word, surrounded—Prussia's military goal since the days of Frederick the Great had consistently been quick, decisive campaigns that would allow her forces to turn speedily from one enemy to the next. Multiple-front wars were anathema to Prussian soldiers; protracted wars equally so.

The philosophy of mobility and quick decisions developed steadily in eighteenth- and nineteenth-century Prussia, and was given its fullest embodiment by Helmuth von Moltke during his stunningly swift victories over Austria in 1866 and France in 1870–71. Thus the new armored tactics did not represent a departure from the German emphasis on quick decisions and mobility; on the contrary, they simply sped those processes up, to a point where—to older, more conservative minds—they were scarcely recognizable. But the link between blitzkrieg and Prussian campaigns of the past was real and evident, even if senior commanders could not see it.

Of course, the partisan attitude of many armored and air enthusiasts during the interwar years was not altogether helpful in easing the German army's old school into the new era of blitzkrieg. This was particularly true of the father of Germany's panzer tactics and divisions, General Heinz Guderian. Building on the theories of Fuller and Liddell Hart, Guderian envisaged a new style of warfare in which tanks were supported by motorized infantry, mobile artillery, and air power—an integrated force that could achieve decisive results at the *strategic* as well as the tactical level. Whole nations, he believed, could be brought to capitulation within a matter of days through the use of such a force.

Guderian was not a member of the Prussian military aristocracy. He was plainspoken to the point of bluntness—even, on occasion, rudeness—and his opinions of junior and senior officers alike were ill-shrouded. For example, General Beck, the much-admired chief of the general staff who had been dismissed by Hitler, had been to Guderian "a procrastinator," a "paralyzing element wherever he appeared," "a disciple of Moltke . . . [with] no understanding of modern technical matters." Recalled another armored commander, General Ritter von Thoma, following the Second World War, "It was commonly said in the German army that Guderian was always seeing red, and was too inclined to charge like a bull."

The fact that Adolf Hitler was one of Guderian's earliest converts to mobile-armored tactics did not help to win the panzer leader friends in the army high command. Attending one of Guderian's first panzer maneuvers, Hitler stated emphatically, "That's what I need. That's what I want to have." The issue was as yet a bit more complicated than that, and the development of first-class German tanks took much longer than Guderian would have liked. But the führer's support was both of immense value to the development of armor and an irritant to many of Guderian's superiors.

Such was the state of the senior German officer corps that was assigned, in April 1939, the task of preparing for the invasion of Poland: reluctant, politically disdainful (and because of that, distanced from the overwhelming majority of the German people), and finally divided on the future development of weapons and tactics. Fortunately for the Germans, the actual job of planning Case White fell to a small group of officers whose insight allowed them to make use of all the resources and talented men at their disposal—whether "old school" or new—in preparing a plan that was at once quintessentially Prussian and daringly advanced.

Overall responsibility for design and coordination of the attack was left, as was customary, to the commander in chief of the army, General Brauchitsch, and to the director of operations of the general staff, General Halder. Their design of the assault could well have come out of the pages of nineteenth-century Prussian history. Accepting the risks involved in stripping their western border of trained combat troops, Brauchitsch and Halder concentrated forty-two divisions into two army groups along the lengthy border around Poland and Slovakia to Pomerania. Army Group North was to cut the Polish Corridor and then advance southeast; Army Group South would engage the main Polish forces—hopefully before they could retreat behind the Vistula River—and then move to link up with Army Group North. This massive pincer thrust from north and south was centered on Warsaw. To achieve it, the Germans accepted the further risk of leaving their own center exposed to possible counterattack.

In the Moltke tradition, General Halder did not exclude field commanders and their staffs from contributing to Case White. Suggestions for the actual deployment and composition of armies were accepted (some willingly, others less so) from army group, army, and corps headquarters.

Command of Army Group South was given to General Gerd von Rundstedt, one of Germany's best-loved soldiers. Already in his mid-sixties, Rundstedt was a true aristocrat but even in appearance had a penchant for idiosyncrasy. In the words of his chief of operations, General Günther von Blumentritt, he "did not wear a general's or a field marshal's uniform, but preferred the simple jacket of the commander of an infantry regiment, with a marshal's shoulder badges and the regimental number 18. It often happened that young officers thus mistook him for a colonel and did not know that it was the Field-Marshal who was standing before them, which Rundstedt always accepted good-humoredly." Rundstedt was primarily interested in the movement of troops in actual battle. Peacetime staff planning and details held little fascination for him. Such an attitude placed immense responsibility on both his chief of staff and his chief of operations.

These posts had been secured by two of the most intellectually gifted officers in the Wehrmacht. Rundstedt's chief of staff was Erich von Manstein. The son of a Prussian artillery general, Manstein had been adopted in his infancy by his aunt and uncle— the latter a Prussian infantry general of noble lineage. Thus by blood and upbringing, Manstein was steeped in the Prussian military code. Behind his thin, penetrating eyes and beaklike nose worked a prodigious mind, one that would later spawn the remarkable German plan for the invasion of France and contribute significantly to Germany's early successes in Russia.

Manstein had many talents that made these successes possible, but one stood out above the rest: an unmatched capacity to fuse traditional Prussian strategy with the new armored tactics. He had broken step with many of his fellow military aristocrats by recognizing that General Guderian's new panzer divisions must not be slowed or hampered by the actions of infantry and artillery. (In fact, one of Manstein's most significant interwar achievements had been the development of mobile and self-propelled support artillery, which freed more tanks for the job of penetration and exploitation.) Faced with the task of planning the movements of Army Group South in the Polish campaign, Manstein quickly decided to concentrate most of the available armor in one of the group's three armies—the Tenth, under General Walther von Reichenau—in order to achieve a decisive breakthrough and the earliest possible encirclement of Polish forces west of the Vistula. The other two armies—the Fourteenth on the right flank, commanded by General Wilhelm List; and the Eighth, forming the group's left wing and commanded by General Johannes Blaskowitz—would play roles in this hoped-for envelopment, but the spearhead assignment went to Reichenau's panzers.

In this effort to blend the Prussian strategy of envelopment with modern armored tactics, Manstein was assisted by Army Group South's chief of operations, Colonel Günther von Blumentritt. The two men shared the same intellectual style, and during the months before the invasion they put in many extra hours attending to every detail of the operation. Manstein later recalled: "As often as not, the things that attract us to another person are quite trivial, and what always delighted me about Blumentritt was his fanatical attachment to the telephone. The speed at which he worked was in any case incredibly high, but whenever he had a receiver in his hand he could deal with whole avalanches of queries, always with the same imperturbable good humor."

Army Group North was given to General Fedor von Bock, a forceful and sometimes difficult commander, and comprised the Third and Fourth armies. The Third Army troops were transported to their launching area in East Prussia by sea, under the guise of participating in a huge celebration of the German victory over the Russians at Tannenberg in August 1914. The Fourth Army, under General Günther von Kluge, was positioned in east Pomerania, opposite the Corridor.

General Guderian's Nineteenth Panzer Corps—the first unit that came close to embodying the panzer leader's ideas concerning armored operations—was placed under von Kluge. There was initially some resistance to the idea of including such a heavy armored force in the Fourth Army's operations, but Guderian's careful cultivation of Hitler soon told, and the führer personally intervened to secure Guderian's role as the spearhead of the forces that would cut the Polish Corridor.

By August 20 the German army was ready. Yet despite the immense effort they had devoted to marshaling their forces, the German generals remained unenthusiastic. Throughout the summer, Chief of Staff Halder had secretly contacted the governments of both France and Great Britain, trying to relay the message that the army high command was powerless to stop Nazi designs because of Hitler's immense popularity with the German people. Only firm commitment on the part of the Western Allies, Halder said, could take the wind out of Hitler's sails. Halder's urgings fell on deaf ears.

On August 22 Hitler called his senior commanders to Obersalzberg for a "conference," which, as was often the case, degenerated into a long diatribe by the führer. The tone was set by

Hermann Göring, who arrived wearing a comical jerkin, shorts, and long silk socks. "Up till now," Manstein later wrote, "I had assumed that we were here for a serious purpose, but Göring appeared to have taken it for a masked ball. . . . I could not resist whispering to my neighbor, General von Salmuth: 'I suppose the Fat Boy's here as a strong-arm man?'"

Informing the generals of secret negotiations with the Soviets that had produced a nonaggression pact (but not of the treaty's secret clause providing for the partition of Poland), Hitler spoke about his determination to redress by force the last remaining German grievance against the Versailles peace: the dismemberment of East Prussia and the subjugation of millions of Germans to Polish rule as well as, according to propaganda chief Joseph Goebbels, Polish abuse of them. Hitler claimed to have made proposals in good faith to the Polish government—all of them rejected. War with Poland was now a certainty. Hitler announced that he would probably order the attack for August 26:

> The destruction of Poland has priority. . . . I shall provide a propaganda reason for starting the war—never mind whether it is plausible or not. The victor will not be asked afterward whether or not he told the truth. In starting and waging war it is not right that matters but victory. Close your hearts to pity! Act brutally!

The generals listened in depressed silence. One fell asleep.

The preparations of the Polish army during this time of very real crisis revealed that while Polish commanders took the danger of invasion seriously, they lacked the skill and the character to meet the challenge. The Poles had a peacetime army of some twenty-three infantry divisions (which would grow to thirty on the eve of the invasion) and eleven cavalry brigades, plus two armored brigades; the latter were equipped with only small numbers of up-to-date tanks and many obsolete models. Still, the overall quality of this army was not to be dismissed: As Blumentritt wrote after the war, "The Polish officer corps was competent and courageous, and was highly regarded by the Wehrmacht."

But it was the cavalry that embodied the most outstanding features of Poland's military style, both good and bad. For hundreds of years, Polish horsemen had been among the world's finest, famous for their daring shock tactics and particularly for their terrifying night attacks. Napoleon had incorporated Polish lancers as an elite unit of his own Grande Armée. Yet pride in their success had made many of Poland's senior officers complacent. For example, the commander in chief of the Polish army, Marshal Edward Rydz-Smigly, had had his portrait painted against a background of charging Polish cavalry while his opposite numbers to the west were wrangling with the problems of mobile armored warfare.

Excessive pride also marred the Polish army's preparations for war with Germany. Geographically, Poland was in an almost hopeless situation. By seizing Czechoslovakia, Hitler had given his army three possible avenues of assault into Polish territory. The Poles' only real hope was to pull their defenses in form the very start—perhaps even as far back as the barrier of the Vistula— and fight a defensive war while waiting for France and England to force the Germans to disengage and attend to their western border.

From the start, however, such ideas were rejected by the Polish high command—in fact, they were rarely put forth for fear of the reception they would get. Some of Poland's most valuable industrial regions lay to the west of the Vistula, and the Corridor had become a symbol of the reborn and resurgent Poland. Few generals dared suggest that these regions be abandoned before even an attempt was made to defend them.

One who did have the courage to raise the issue was a General Kutzreba, director of the Polish Military Academy and commander of the Poznań army during the battle for Poland. While even Kutzreba's ideas were probably not radical enough to have prevented eventual disaster, his suggestion that the Polish army abandon not only the Corridor but the western section of the province of Poznań (bordering on Germany) might have given the Poles a better chance of concentrating their forces and successfully holding out until the pressure was relieved by their allies.

Instead, the Polish army spread its forces out along the entire border with Germany, from the Carpathian Mountains in the south, up past the Silesian border, on into the Corridor, and then east to the frontiers of East Prussia. Some seven frontline armies were formed out of the slender Polish resources in an attempt to hold the line everywhere. It was a prescription for disaster. Yet apparently not content with this gross error in judgment, the Polish high command next failed to pursue a rigorous program of fast mobilization, and spent their more imaginative moments planning for an eventual counterattack into Germany.

As he had said he would, Hitler ordered the German army to attack on August 26, and on the 25th German troops began to move toward the Polish frontier. But within hours an emergency message arrived at the headquarters of both army groups: The attack was canceled, and the troops were to be pulled back. Whether Hitler still had one or two eleventh-hour diplomatic tricks to try or simply balked when the moment of decision came is unclear—but despite the immensely difficult job of recalling five advancing armies, the German commanders were not displeased. As even Guderian said, "We did not go lightheartedly to war and there was not one general who would not have advocated peace." The mood at Army Group South headquarters was positively jubilant. Blumentritt recalled that "Rundstedt had some bottles of Tokay fetched from the town of Neisse to celebrate . . . this happy release."

The celebration was short-lived. On August 31 a terse new order was received by both army groups: "D = 1.9; H = 0445." And at 4:45 on the morning of September 1, 1939, the Wehrmacht swarmed over the borders of Poland.

In most areas, initial resistance was slight or nonexistent, owing to the slow Polish mobilization and to the fact that the Luftwaffe quickly destroyed Poland's air units. Whether the Polish planes were destroyed on the ground or managed at least to get into the air has been debated. The fact remains that within days the Germans had mastery of the skies. The German pilots, most tasting combat for the first time, went on to smash bridges and rail lines leading to the fronts. General List's Fourteenth Army in the south met the stiffest Polish resistance in the first days, but soon the Poles had collected their wits and were fighting bravely everywhere.

While many historical accounts of the campaign portray the participation of the Polish cavalry brigades as ludicrous, the German soldiers did not find it so. Blumentritt recalled, "In the course of the campaign [the Polish cavalry] gave several German divisions something serious to think about and distinguished itself by its great bravery." The horsemen "appeared like phantom hosts to surprise us in the night."

The Germans were also plagued by the greenness of their own troops. Many units were stunned or broken by the steadily stiffening Polish resistance, and were pulled together only by the determination and loyalty of their officers. As a result of the bravery shown by all ranks of the officer corps, German casualties during the campaign were inordinately weighted toward that group.

Army Group North quickly discovered just how unprepared

for war many German soldiers were. Guderian remembered that when his panzers crossed into the Corridor, the "Polish antitank gunners scored many direct hits." Only by taking charge himself at the front was he able to restore order. His account of the first day's action went on revealingly:

> Shortly after midnight the 2nd (Motorized) Division informed me that they were being compelled to withdraw by Polish cavalry. I was speechless for a moment; when I regained the use of my voice I asked the divisional commander if he had ever heard of Pomeranian grenadiers being broken by hostile cavalry. He replied that he had not and now assured me that he could hold his positions.

By the second day of the campaign, the Nineteenth Panzer Corps had crossed its first obstacle, the Brahe River inside the Corridor, and its lead units had reached the Vistula. Guderian's tireless peacetime promulgation of mobile armored warfare was beginning to bear fruit in the field.

Then, on September 3, occurred perhaps the most famous incident of the entire Polish campaign. As Guderian's tanks—mostly fast training rigs armed only with light artillery and machine guns, but including some heavier models—raced to close the Corridor, the renowned Polish Pomorska Cavalry Brigade appeared west of the town of Graudenz. The Polish horsemen, Guderian recalled, "in ignorance of the nature of our tanks ... charged them with swords and lances." Polish losses were predictably heavy—"tremendous," in Guderian's estimation—yet the Germans did not sneer at the attack. Rather, it was taken as further evidence of the enemy's immense courage and determination.

On September 4 the Polish Corridor was closed when Guderian's forward units made solid contact with the Third Army's Third Panzer Division, which was moving west out of East Prussia. Between two and three Polish infantry divisions and one cavalry brigade had been shattered in three days by the Nineteenth Panzer Corps, which had operated mostly on its own. Guderian's theories were triumphantly vindicated.

Hitler, in the meantime, had taken to rushing about the Polish front in the heavily armored train *Amerika,* seemingly oblivious to the dangers of battle. On the train the oppressive atmosphere that characterized all of the führer's headquarters dominated. "We have been living in the train for ten days now," wrote Hitler's secretary. "It's location is constantly being changed, but since we never get out the monotony is dreadful. The heat is unbearable . . . [and] to top it all, there is hardly anything worthwhile to do. . . . Obviously it gives the soldiers' morale a boost to see the führer in the thick of the danger with them, but I still think it's too risky."

On September 5, Hitler visited Guderian's corps and, impressed by the wreckage left in its wake—the smashed bridges and artillery—asked: "Our dive bombers did that?"

"No," Guderian answered, "our panzers!"

The former infantryman was, in Guderian's words, "plainly astonished." By September 6 the Nineteenth Panzer Corps was across the Vistula, moving faster than planned. While his superiors tried to decide what to do with an armored corps that had completed its primary assignment in just five days, Guderian spent the night contentedly in a castle chamber once used by Napoleon.

At Army Group South, meanwhile, armor was also providing the key to preventing the courageous but slow-moving Poles from organizing a coherent defense. As the Fourteenth Army began to smash its way through stubborn Polish resistance in the region of the Carpathians, the Poles in western Galicia made a surprisingly apt decision to fall back toward the Vistula before they were encircled. The main fear of both Rundstedt and Manstein was that such a move would lead to a generalized Polish retreat that would frustrate their aim of engaging the main Polish forces west of the Vistula.

This possibility was eliminated by the quick movements of the Twenty-second Panzer Corps under General Ewald von Kleist. Kleist—considered by Hitler to be one of the army's most "incorrigible" enemies of the Nazi party—broke through the western Carpathians with the Second Panzer and Fourth Light divisions and raced toward the juncture of the Vistula and the San. Within days this speedy advance, along with Guderian's movements in the north, was to prove decisive in destroying any Polish hope of establishing a river defense.

Meanwhile, northwest of the Fourteenth Army, the Eighth and Tenth armies were advancing against heavy Polish troop concentrations in the Lódź-Radom region. The Tenth Army's job was to force an engagement with these troops as soon as possible; the Eighth was to cover the Tenth's left flank and prevent the Poles around Lódź and Radom from joining forces with the Poznań Army to the north.

Army Group South's ability to realize its goal of forcing the Poles to fight west of the Vistula was decided, according to Manstein, by "two factors which had appeared for the very first time in this campaign": the panzer divisions and the Lufwaffe. Reichenau's tanks tore open the Polish front line and, rather than assaulting the Poles from the front, were soon actually a good distance behind them. All attempts by the Poles to organize a systematic defense in the meantime were consistently prevented by the screaming Stuka dive bombers that continued to smash transport and communication lines without opposition.

During the first week of fighting, the Poles drew together in the vicinity of Random. At this point, Rundstedt and Manstein decided to move quickly to encircle this pocket of enemy resistance instead of first gaining control of the Vistula and advancing on Warsaw, as originally planned. The accelerated pace offered by armored and motorized infantry movement meant that such an encirclement might be achieved without any significant alteration in the larger pincer concept of Case White. By September 9 the Random pocket was closed, and though the Poles tried for three more days to break out, their fate was unavoidable. Seven divisions were lost, and the southern approach to Warsaw was suddenly wide open.

In the north, meanwhile, General Bock was giving thought to attaching Guderian's Nineteenth Panzer Corps to the Third Army, which was moving toward Warsaw. But Guderian protested that the Third Army was made up almost entirely of infantry—the usefulness of his panzers would be severely limited. The panzer leader formulated his own plan, which was to put the corps under direct army-group control and release it to the east, where, he claimed, it could quickly cross the Narev River and drive on to Brest Litovsk and the river Bug, the next significant barrier east of the Vistula. Such a move would invalidate the east bank of the Vistula as a Polish sanctuary; any Polish forces that were stationed there or managed to reach it would already be encircled. The German plan for Case White had cast a wide net—and Guderian's tactics offered them a chance to cast that net dramatically wider.

Von Bock approved the idea, and Guderian's Nineteenth Panzer Corps thus became, effectively, the world's first armored army: autonomous and freed from the constraints of coordinating its movements with the infantry. At the Narev, Guderian's troops encountered stubborn Polish resistance and once more displayed confusion, which their gregarious but tough commander again cleared up with numerous frontline appearances. Moving from unit to unit in a half-track rigged with a wireless radio, he organized a powerful assault, and by September 12 the Tenth

Panzer Division had gotten across the Narev and was in a position to surround the Polish defenders. This freed the Third Panzer Division to race for the citadel of Brest Litovsk, and by the 13th the lead elements of the division had reached the city.

Still, there were surprises in store for the Germans—Army Group South had already learned this the hard way. Despite the fact that the first nine days of fighting had gone well, Manstein later recalled, he "still had a vague feeling that something was brewing on the northern flank of the army group." That "something" turned out to be the Polish Poznań Army. Though Manstein continually told the Eighth Army's chief of staff to be alert to the possibility of attack from the north, that army's attention remained focused on driving to the east. When the Poznań Army struck with surprising strength along the Bzura River on September 10, the Eighth Army was unprepared, and quickly called for reinforcements.

But Rundstedt and Manstein were, as Manstein later said, "by no means disposed to see the situation of Eighth Army restored by a reinforcement of its front." The Poles were displaying tactical daring and were enjoying some success—but they were only destroying their own strategic situation by attacking south rather than retreating toward their capital and the Vistula. Manstein went on to say: "Even if a local crisis—and possibly a serious one at that—were to arise here, it would have not the least bearing on the operations as a whole. On the contrary, it actually offered us the chance of winning a big victory."

Rundstedt and Manstein issued orders to the Tenth Army to move into position to cut the Poznań Army's lines of retreat eastward. They then flew to the headquarters of General Blaskowitz, the Eighth Army's commander, and directed the Battle of the Bzura from there. The Polish situation—again because of strategic ineptitude—was hopeless. The German Tenth and Eighth armies moved into position for another pocket encirclement, and the last nail was driven into the Poznan Army's coffin when Army Group North's Third Corps was detached to play a role in this encirclement.

One more shock, however, awaited the German army. On September 17, news that Soviet troops had entered Poland shot through the ranks of the Wehrmacht. Many a German soldier, junior and senior, wanted to know whom the Soviets had come to fight. But when word of the Russo-German agreement to partition Poland was received, as well as news that Russian troops were engaging Poles and quickly occupying Polish territory, the German soldiers returned to the task at hand. (One Polish officer fought the Germans in the morning and the Soviets in the afternoon, and escaped from both.) There was irony in the fact that many of these same German troops would have to fight in the not-too-distant future to conquer the areas of Poland taken by the Soviets; but such irony was unforeseeable.

At this point the situation for the Poles became hopeless. As the battle raged on the Bzura, Guderian's troops to the east prepared an assault on the citadel of Brest Litovsk. Kleist's panzers, meanwhile, had linked up with other advancing elements of Army Group North above the juncture of the Vistula and San rivers. The Poles were faced with a double envelopment. On September 16, confident that the Twentieth Motorized and Tenth Panzer divisions could take Brest Litovsk, Guderian ordered his remaining forces to move farther south and link up with advancing elements of the Fourteenth Army.

On September 16 the Poznań Army capitulated, and the German Tenth Army reported the taking of 80,000 prisoners. The Eighth Army had taken 90,000. Although not as large as later German armored envelopments in France and Russia, the Battle of the Bzura set the pattern for those subsequent dramatic conquests. Of more immediate importance, it sounded the death knell for Polish resistance.

Already there had been ominous signs of what German occupation held in store for the Poles. Regular German army units were being followed into Poland by SS formations, whose job it was to root out members of the Polish nobility and government, as well as the intelligentsia and all Jews. As one Polish prisoner of war recalled, these Germans "began to select Jews 'by sight.' They avoided officers, but concentrated on privates and noncommissioned ranks, pulling out soldiers with 'Semitic' features and leading them away, to the accompaniment of shouts and face-slapping."

As to the British and the French, on whose efforts the fate of Poland ultimately rested, they had declared war on Germany soon after the invasion, as they were treaty-bound to do. But neither ally had been able to offer anything more substantial by way of support. For if the German generals were somewhat startled by the speed with which they were able, through creative use of their panzer and air forces, to bring the Polish campaign to a climax, the British and French governments were even more so. There were no Allied provisions for launching a western relief attack within the two and a half weeks between the German invasion of Poland and the capitulation of the Poznań Army—thus the Poles were left to face their fate alone.

While the German troops east of the Vistula began to wrangle with the problem of pulling back to that river—everything east of it having been promised to Stalin by Hitler—the main body of Army Group South and the remainder of Army Group North prepared for the last task left to them: the taking of Warsaw. Under the civilian leadership of its determined mayor, Stefan Starzynski, the capital had been turned into a maze of barricaded streets. Such obstructions, however, would prove to be of as little value to the city as the influx of exhausted survivors of the Battle of the Bzura.

For the Germans had no intention of engaging in brutal street fighting. Assembling their artillery in a ring around the capital, they opened fire first on Warsaw's outer forts and defenses.

Leaflets were dropped, calling for surrender and threatening the
bombardment of the city proper. When no response came, the
guns opened fire. By September 25, life in Warsaw had been
brought to a standstill. As one German recalled:

> The mortars spoke incessantly, one battery after another,
> showering a hot rain of metal over Poland's capital,
> bursting in windows and tearing out window frames and
> doors. Watching by night we saw curves of colored fire
> flashing gracefully toward Warsaw. The earth quivered
> and our eardrums seemed about to split. . . . In all direc-
> tions long smoky tongues of fire spurted up every sec-
> ond. In the heavens the clouds were as red as blood.

On September 27 the Poles offered to give in, and the shelling
was immediately halted. On the following day the capitulation
was signed, the Polish general in command of Warsaw telling the
German conquerors, "A wheel always turns."

Pockets of Polish resistance remained to be cleared up, and the
job of conceding conquered territory in eastern Poland to Soviet
troops proved complicated in spots. But by October 5 the German
army had put Hitler in a position to parade victoriously through
the streets of Warsaw. The Germans had taken hundreds of thousands of prisoners; Army Group South alone took more than half
a million, at a cost of just over 6,500 officers and men killed.

The German synthesis of traditional Prussian strategy and
advanced armored doctrines had brought about a stunning success. That synthesis was best embodied in the person of Erich von
Manstein, and it is therefore appropriate to record his final
thoughts concerning the Polish campaign:

> In the German Wehrmacht it had been found possible [in
> Poland], with the help of the new means of warfare, to

reacquire the true art of leadership in mobile operations. Individual leadership was fostered on a scale unrivaled in any other army, right down to the most junior NCO or infantryman, and in this lay the secret of our success. So far, the troops had had a purely military battle to fight, and for that reason it had still been possible to fight chivalrously.

That sense of chivalry soon became an irritant to Hitler and his Nazi henchmen, and caused the battle that the senior German officer corps was forced to wage to become more than "purely military." Following the Polish capitulation, General Blaskowitz, commander of the Eighth Army, became military governor-general of the conquered territories. A soldier of the old school, Blaskowitz had been appalled by the behavior of SS units in Poland. As governor-general he set up military tribunals that sentenced SS soldiers—including members of the Leibstandarte Adolf Hitler, the führer's pet unit—to death for the crimes of murder, arson, and rape. This policy soon changed when Austrian Nazi party officials arrived to take over the civilian administration of Poland.

But Blaskowitz had not been the only general to have runnins with the SS and other party organizations. Drawing on the experiences of his colleagues as well as his own, Blaskowitz submitted a lengthy report to the commander of the German army, General Brauchitsch, on Nazi behavior during the Polish campaign. Hitler heard of the report but did not read it, choosing instead to lecture Brauchitsch about the German officer corps's "outmoded conception of chivalry."

Despite the inner tension between regular army officers and SS leaders, the German Wehrmacht emerged from the Polish campaign transformed, battle-tested, and ready. The crucial theories of air and armored power had been applied and vindicated; officers of all ranks had learned how to lead men under fire; and an army whose quality had worried its own commanders (because of the rapid expansion before the war) had proved itself a remarkable battlefield force. The German officer corps had known that war with Poland meant war with the world. Following the Polish campaign, some of those men might still have been reluctant to face such an eventuality— but their reluctance was now based not on doubts about the units under their command but on doubts about the sanity of their superiors. In France, Russia, and Africa, the methods honed in Poland would be expanded in scale and perfected in technique. And even during the closing months of the war, those methods would delay Allied victory to an extent deemed impossible by Allied commanders.

1940

"Another Bloody Country Gone West"

By William Manchester

At dawn on Friday, May 10, 1940, Adolf Hitler plunged his bloody fists into the Low Countries and headed for France; at 5:00 P.M. that same evening, Winston Churchill became prime minister of Great Britain. The new P.M. felt confident of victory then, but the French high command had made a grave miscalculation. Believing that the enemy would be coming through Belgium, as in 1914, the sixty-seven-year-old generalissimo Maurice Gamelin had sent the flower of the French troops and the entire British army—the British Expeditionary Force, or BEF—into Flanders. Instead, Nazi tanks struck through the Ardennes Forest and crossed the Meuse. When the French defenders panicked, the panzers rolled up the entire Allied line all the way to the sea, trapping the Allies' force.

On the fifth day of the enemy offensive, the extent of the disaster began to emerge. Paul Reynaud, the French premier, wired Churchill: "The German army has broken through our fortified lines south of Sedan." He then asked for ten more Royal Air Force squadrons "immediately." The prime minister sent four squadrons, then decided it was "imperative to go to Paris." At 3:00 P.M. on

May 16, he took off in an unarmed Flamingo, a civilian passenger plane, accompanied by Generals Hastings Ismay and Sir John Dill and an inspector from Scotland Yard, his bodyguard.

Over the French coast Churchill peered down, and the inspector saw his face go gray. He was looking, for the first time, at the war's refugees. There were seven million of them fleeing from the Germans, swarming down the highways, shuffling, exhausted, aching from the strain of heavy loads on their backs. Barns, sheds, and garages had vomited into roads an extraordinary collection of vehicles: tumbrels, trucks, horse-drawn carts, and ancient automobiles with sagging loads of mattresses, kitchen utensils, family treasures, and bric-a-brac. Churchill later wrote: "Not having had access to official information for so many years, I did not comprehend the revolution effected since the last war by the incursion of a mass of fast-moving heavy armour." This German drive would not have to pause for supplies. As Charles de Gaulle had foreseen, the panzers would be filling their tanks at the filling stations of northern France.

The prime minister's Flamingo landed at Le Bourget airport, and as they alighted Ismay felt "an unmistakable atmosphere of depression." Events were moving swiftly in Paris. The panic had reached the French capital. Suddenly Parisians realized that there were an extraordinary number of automobiles with Belgian license plates on the streets—"Just passing through," the drivers told them; "the Boche is right behind us." Suddenly everyone seemed to know that Gamelin had told the highest officials of the republic: *"Je ne réponds plus de rien"*—"I am no longer responsible for anything."

At the Quai d'Orsay, the foreign ministry, Reynaud; Edouard Daladier, former premier and now the defense minister; and Gamelin awaited the British in a large room looking out on a garden, "which," Ismay wrote, "had appeared so lovely and well-kept on my last visit, but which was now disfigured with clusters of bonfires." The French were burning their papers. This was Churchill's first meeting as a member of the Conseil Supérieur de la Guerre. He asked for a briefing. Gamelin gave it. Stepping up to a map on an easel, he talked for five minutes, describing the German breakthrough. At the end Churchill asked him where his mass of maneuver was: *"Où est la masse de manoeuvre?"* Gamelin shook his head and replied: *"Aucune."* He had none.

There was a long pause while Churchill, speechless, stared absently at the elderly men carrying wheelbarrows of documents to the fires. It had never occurred to him that commanders defending 500 miles of engaged front would have left themselves without reserves; no one could defend with certainty so wide a front. When the enemy broke the line, the defenders should have a mass of divisions ready to counterattack.

This, the P.M. said, was a time to "hold fast." The records of the French quote him as telling them, "I refuse to see in this spectacular raid of the German tanks a real invasion. . . ."

Of course, that is precisely what it was, and Reynaud silenced him by pointing out that all the field commanders, including Lord Gort, the commander of the British army in Belgium, believed they should fall back.

Of all the French leaders, Reynaud was the most impressive, and he remained so until events collapsed about him. He had made his Paris reputation as a brilliant lawyer. Like Churchill, he had established himself as the first of his countrymen to see through Hitler. Disdaining political maneuvering, he didn't even belong to a party. His admirers applauded this show of independence, but some said it was carrying idealism too far. So it proved to be in the crisis now imminent.

Churchill rightly asked Gamelin when and where he proposed to attack the flanks of the German bulge. Yet the generalissimo's dismaying opinion was that he saw only one hope of salvation:

the commitment of six more RAF squadrons to the battle. It was, he said, the only way to stop the panzers.

Churchill vigorously replied that tanks should be the target of artillery, not fighter planes; fighters should "cleanse the skies" ("*nett* [sic] *le ciel*") over the battle. He had just sent four more squadrons, sixty-four planes, and it was vital that Britain's metropolitan air force command the air over Britain. He did not think another six squadrons would "make the difference" here.

Daladier said, "The French believe the contrary." The discussion became acrimonious.

Gamelin had touched a vital nerve. Both sides were, to a degree, disingenuous. What the French really believed was that the British should throw everything they had into the struggle for France, and that if the Allied cause were to lose, both countries should go down together. The British believed that if France went down—and they were beginning to contemplate that possibility— England should go on alone.

At the British embassy that evening, the prime minister wired the war cabinet that they should give this "last chance to the French Army to rally its bravery and strength." They reluctantly agreed to the French request for more planes, provided the Hurricanes returned to English bases each night.

Because of this generosity in sending RAF fighters to France, Churchill very nearly lost the subsequent, and crucial, Battle of Britain. After the French surrender, his fighter command was even weaker than most historians recognize, owing to an extraordinary misunderstanding on his part.

In his memoirs of the war he would later write that on May 16, Air Chief Marshal Sir Hugh Dowding, at the head of the metropolitan fighter command, "had declared to me that with twenty-five squadrons of fighters he could defend the island against the whole might of the German Air Force, but that with less he would be overpowered."

This is a remarkable error. What Dowding had actually told the prime minister and the war cabinet on May 16 was that fifty-two squadrons were needed to stave off the Luftwaffe, and that he was already down to thirty-six. At the present rate of destruction, he had warned them, within two weeks "we shall not have a single Hurricane left in France *or in this country*."

Although he had laid these figures before Churchill and put them in an official letter to the air ministry, during the days that followed, the prime minister, promising the French that he would "cut England's defenses to the bone," had given them ten more squadrons. Then, in the skies over Dunkirk, Dowding lost another 106 planes and 75 pilots, reducing Fighter Command to fewer than twenty-six squadrons, half the strength that he had regarded as a dangerous minimum.

Back in London, Churchill tried again and again to reach Reynaud by telephone. It was impossible. All lines between Paris and London had been cut. Desperate for information, the prime minister—against the advice of the chiefs of staff—decided to fly to Paris the following morning, Wednesday, May 22.

The Flamingo landed at Le Bourget shortly before noon; the P.M. and his party went straight to the generalissimo's GHQ in the Château de Vincennes, an old *Beau Geste* fort guarded by spahis in white cloaks bearing long, curved swords. Reynaud had sacked Gamelin three days earlier. His successor was seventy-three-year-old Gen. Maxime Weygand, a short, spruce, fox-faced officer who, as one Englishman said in describing him, resembled an "aged jockey." Weygand had never before commanded troops in battle; he had made his reputation as a staff officer. He was a political general—a monarchist, a hero of the militantly conservative Croix de Feu—and an an-glophobe. Despite his age he was exceptionally vigorous, but he had arrived in Paris exhausted, recalled from Syria, where he commanded French forces in the

Levant. Weygand, greeting them, "was brisk, buoyant, and incisive," Churchill wrote. "He made an excellent impression on us all." Telling them that the panzers "must not be allowed to keep the initiative, he gave them a detailed description of what instantly became known as the Weygand Plan.

Specifically, the plan provided for an attack southward "at the earliest moment, certainly tomorrow," by eight divisions of the BEF and the French 1st Army. Simultaneously, a new French army group would "strike northward and join hands with the British divisions." The more Churchill thought about it, the better he liked it. That evening, the chief of the Imperial General Staff, Gen. Sir Edmund Ironside, noted, "Winston came back from Paris about 6:30 P.M. and we had a Cabinet [meeting] at 7:30 P.M. He was almost in buoyant spirits, having been impressed by Weygand."

In fact, the plan was impossible—all of it. The Allied forces in the north could not drive southward; all were heavily engaged with the enemy. And Weygand's own orders to his divisions in the south merely directed them to recapture local objectives.

Weygand had actually believed from the beginning that the Allied cause was doomed. His only hope, he had told one of his generals on May 20, was *"sauver l'honneur des armées françaises"*— to "save the honor of the French armies," whatever that meant. His distrust of England and Englishmen was profound, though not unusual among Frenchmen with his convictions. Reviewing his deception, Jock Colville, one of the P.M.'s assistant private secretaries, later concluded that "Weygand was determined . . . that we should go under if he did."

Capturing Paris was every German's dream, and the panzers could have turned that way. Instead they had wheeled northward and were driving toward the Channel ports, historically England's front line. On the Sunday before Churchill's flight to Vincennes, Ironside had warned the prime minister that the BEF might soon be cut off from the French. The German armored columns seemed irresistible; on Wednesday, while Churchill was being introduced to Weygand, evacuation of Allied troops had begun on the Channel coast. In his diary Ironside wrote: "4 P.M. Boulogne was definitely gone. . . . So go all the people in Boulogne, including our two Guards battalions. A rotten ending indeed." He added: "[Field Marshal Lord John] Gort is very nearly surrounded. . . . I don't see that we have much hope of getting the B.E.F. out." But the following evening he noted: "The German mobile columns have definitely been halted for some reason or other."

Although no one realized it at the time, this "Halt Order" was one of the turning points in the war. Two days of downpours had made the Flanders swamps virtually impassable for armored vehicles—Gen. Heinz Guderian, the panzer leader, who had first opposed the halt, conceded that "a tank attack is pointless in the marshy country which has been completely soaked by the rain."

With each passing hour Gort realized that he would have to do something, and soon. His army—the only army Britain had—was in mortal danger, nearly encircled, trapped in a pocket seventy miles in depth from the sea and only fifteen to twenty-five miles across. His lines of communications had been cut. His only allies were the Belgians and the remnants of the French 1st Army.

During the afternoon of Saturday, May 25, Gort decided to cut through to the sea at Dunkirk and attempt a mass evacuation. His telegram was delayed, but in London, Churchill independently reached the same conclusion.

Tuesday afternoon King Leopold of Belgium, without informing his allies or consulting his advisers—a violation of the nation's constitution—surrendered the entire 274,000-man Belgian army, opening a twenty-mile gap between Gen. Sir Alan Brooke's corps and the coast near Nieuport. In his diary, Brooke wrote: "Nothing but a miracle can save the B.E.F. now, and the end cannot be far off."

Suddenly all England was told that the Nazis were 140 miles *behind* the Allied lines in Belgium—and heading for the Channel ports. The crisis brought the war effort some unlikely converts. Bertrand Russell wrote a friend that he had renounced pacifism, declaring that if he were young enough to fight, he would enlist. On that desperate Tuesday when the Belgian king surrendered, George Orwell wrote in his diary: "Horrible as it is, I hope the B.E.F. is cut to pieces rather than capitulate."

Even as the evacuation at Dunkirk was taking place, Churchill decided to convene another meeting of the Conseil Supérieur de la Guerre in Paris on May 31. The French were demanding more British divisions, but Churchill's real fear was that they would seek a separate peace. He was determined to keep France in the war. With him he would take Clement Attlee, one of the Labour members of his war cabinet, Ismay, and Dill. Gen. E. L. Spears, Churchill's personal representative, would meet them at the airport.

Flying over France had become more hazardous since Churchill's last flight. Although the Flamingo was escorted by nine Spitfires, the sky was swarming with Nazi fighters north of Paris. Churchill's plane detoured and arrived late.

The *conseil* met at 2:00 P.M. in a large first-floor room, giving out on a garden, in the ministry of war in the rue St. Dominique. Those present sat at an immense, green, baize-covered oval table, the visitors on one side and, facing them, their hosts: Reynaud; Adm. Jean Darlan, the commander of the navy; Paul Baudouin, the secretary of the war cabinet; Weygand—booted and spurred, the cast of his wizened face somehow more oriental than before—and, finally, a newcomer to the war council, eighty-four-year-old Maréchal Henri-Philippe Pétain, in mufti.

Reynaud was Churchill's strongest ally in Paris, but he was deeply handicapped by his mistress, *la peu boulotte mademoiselle* ("the slightly plump mademoiselle") la comtesse de Portes, an appeaser, a defeatist, an Anglophobe, and an admirer of fascism who ruthlessly exploited Reynaud's love for her. The comtesse was already responsible for a disastrous new appointment, that of Baudouin, a fellow defeatist, as a principal adviser to the premier. And now, at her insistence, her lover had named Pétain his deputy premier. The premier seems to have been unable to say no to her. He told her everything. At one critical meeting of the *conseil*, proceedings were delayed for forty-five minutes while aides searched for a paper classified "Most Secret." It was finally found in her bed—actually, in her panties.

Churchill told them that the Dunkirk operation was succeeding beyond all expectations: The latest dispatch reported that 165,000 men had been taken off, including 10,000 wounded. It was then that Weygand sounded the first dissonant note. In an aggressive, querulous voice he interrupted to ask: "But how many French? The French are being left behind?" (*"Les Français sont laissés en arrière?"*)

The Englishmen expected a Churchillian outburst. All the signs were there. The light had died out of his face, he was drumming his fingers on the table, and his lower lip jutted out like the prow of a dreadnought. Clearly he was angry, and with reason. Weygand had known of the Dunkirk order for six days but had issued no orders authorizing French participation in the evacuations. However, the P.M. controlled himself; his expression became sad; he said quietly, "We are companions in misfortune. There is nothing to be gained from recrimination over our common miseries."

Spears felt that "a stillness fell over the room." At that point the French translator, misunderstanding the P.M., said it was understood that British soldiers at Dunkirk would embark before the poilus. Churchill interrupted him; waving his arms, he roared in his extraordinary accent: *"Non! Partage—bras dessus, bras dessous!"*—the soldiers from both countries would leave together, arm in arm.

The French wanted still more RAF squadrons. Churchill pointed out that His Majesty's Government had already given ten additional squadrons needed for the defense of Great Britain. If they lost the rest, the Luftwaffe could, with impunity, attack "the most dangerous targets of all, the factories producing new aircraft." It was, he said, "impossible to run further risks" with British aircraft.

It is odd that in these several colloquies during the fall of France, none of the Englishmen confronted their Gallic allies with the question of the French air force. France had one, commanded by Gen. Joseph Vuillemin, a daring pilot in the last war but now obese and incompetent. Vuillemin had angered the British by commenting that RAF support in the opening days of the German offensive had arrived "tardily and in insufficient numbers." In fact, Britain had sent 100 bombers, all the RAF had at the time, to bomb the Meuse bridges; it had lost forty-five of them. On May 28, Vuillemin had also said the RAF had 300 planes in England and had sent only thirty to France—this, at a time when eight to ten front-line British squadrons were in action every day supporting the poilus.

During the fall of France, the British lost at least 1,000 aircraft and nearly 300 pilots. Indeed, in 1980 the French official account, *Histoire de l'aviation militaire,* put the British sacrifice even higher: "The losses suffered by the RAF in France are enough in themselves to demonstrate its effective participation in the battle of May—June 1940. Over 1,500 fliers were killed, wounded, or missing, and over 1,500 planes of all types were destroyed." The French themselves lost about half that number of planes, 235 of them destroyed on the ground before they could take off. The performance of their air force was baffling, even to its leaders and even after the war. At the outset, French warplanes had outnumbered the Luftwaffe nearly three to two. Yet only a third of French aircraft saw action. Furthermore, between May 10 and June 12, French factories delivered more than 1,000 new machines. Indeed, when France dropped out of the war, the French found that they actually had more first-line aircraft than they did when the great Nazi offensive began.

"What is this mystery about our planes?" Gamelin asked, testifying later. "Why, out of 2,000 fighters on hand at the beginning of May 1940, were fewer than 500 used on the northeast front? I humbly confess to you that I do not know." Commenting on the confusing figures, he said: "We have a right to be astonished." Certainly the historian has a right to express astonishment at the generalissimo's astonishment.

Churchill wanted the *conseil* to know that England meant to crush Nazi Germany, whatever the cost. "I am absolutely convinced," he said, his voice rolling with oratorical cadences, "that we have only to fight on to conquer. If Germany defeats either ally or both, she will give no mercy. We should be reduced to the status of slaves forever. Even if one of us is struck down, the other must not abandon the struggle. Should one comrade fall in battle, the other must not put down his arms until his wounded friend is on his feet again."

Attlee endorsed every word the prime minister had said. Spears thought that Baudouin had been swept away by Churchill's fire. Not so; in his diary the Frenchman wrote that he had been "deeply troubled" by the prime minister's vow and asked, "Does he consider that France must continue the struggle, cost what it may, even if it is useless? We must clear that up."

Beaming, Churchill said merrily: *"Fini l'agenda."*

But he himself was not finished. As they rose from the table, gathering in groups to discuss this or that, Churchill headed for Pétain, followed by Spears. One Frenchman said that if events continued on their present course, France might have to reappraise its foreign policy, including ties to Britain, and "modify its position." Pétain nodded. Spears said in his perfect French: "I suppose you understand, *Monsieur le Maréchal,* that that would mean blockade—not only mean blockade but bombardment of all French ports in German hands." Afterward Churchill wrote, "I was glad to have this said."

No one had mentioned the Anglo-French Accord signed by both governments only nine weeks earlier, and at the insistence of the French. The two allies had solemnly agreed, in writing, to "neither negotiate nor conclude an armistice or treaty of peace except by mutual agreement." It was a sleeping issue now, but as Churchill prepared to return to England, it was on everyone's mind.

On June 4, when the evacuation had come to an end, Churchill told the House of Commons the story of Dunkirk. He said the British would fight on, "if necessary alone," and added:

> Even though large tracts of Europe and many old and famous states have fallen or may fall into the grip of the Gestapo and all the odious apparatus of Nazi rule, we shall not flag nor fail.
> We shall go on to the end.
> We shall fight in France.
> We shall fight on the seas and oceans.
> We shall fight with growing confidence and growing strength in the air.
> We shall defend our island, whatever the cost may be.
> We shall fight on the beaches, we shall fight on the landing grounds.
> We shall fight in the fields and in the streets, we shall fight in the hills; we shall never surrender.

This speech, which was rather well received elsewhere, was the source of considerable consternation at the French embassy, which asked precisely what it meant—especially the phrase "if necessary alone." Whitehall replied that it meant exactly what it said.

On June 7, panzers led by Gen. Erwin Rommel broke through toward Rouen, and on June 10, Italy declared war on Britain and France. That night, as the enemy armies advanced toward Paris, the prime minister decided to fly there once more, hoping to persuade the French to defend their capital. Then a message arrived telling him the government was leaving it, "What the hell," he growled, fuming until a second telegram told him they could meet at Briare, on the Loire, eighty miles south of Paris. Tuesday afternoon, June 11, he took off with Ismay, Anthony Eden, then the secretary of state for war, and Spears, escorted by twelve Hawker Hurricanes. He wanted to fly over the battlefields, but the pilot told him that the flight plan made that impossible.

Briare airfield was deserted. Churchill, massive in black, leaning on his stick, looked around beaming, as though this airstrip were the place he had sought all his life and finally found. Several cars drove up, the first driven by a sullen colonel. The ambience was distinctly unpleasant when they arrived at the red-brick Château de Muguet. Spears felt that "our presence was not really desired."

They were shown into a large dining room. There the Frenchmen—with one exception, Col. Charles de Gaulle, whom Reynaud had just made a brigadier general to serve as his undersecretary of state for defense and war—sat with hung heads, staring at the table, like prisoners awaiting sentencing. To Ismay, Pétain seemed "more woebegone than ever."

Weygand said that the army's plight was hopeless. "There is nothing to prevent the enemy reaching Paris. We are fighting on our last line, and it has been breached. I am helpless. *C'est la dislocation.*" It was the breakup of the army. He blamed the French politicians for entering the war with no conception of Nazi power.

Churchill refused to believe that France was in extremis. His mouth was working; he sought the words, found them, and spoke warmly and deeply. He wished, he said, to express his admiration for the gallant resistance of the French. But Winston was determined to set the French afire with the flame of Britain's defiance. His words, Spears wrote, "came in torrents, French and English phrases tumbling over each other like waves rushing for the shore when driven by a storm. No matter what happened, he told them, England would fight "on and on and on, *toujours*, all the time, everywhere, *partout, pas de grâce,* no mercy. *Puis la victoire!*" He wanted Weygand's army to fight in Paris, telling the French how a great city, if valiantly defended, could absorb immense enemy armies. He suggested that the French government retreat to North Africa. If all else failed, he proposed guerrilla warfare.

The French were hostile: Weygand, scornful; and Pétain, who had sat silent until now, incredulous, mocking, and, finally, angry. The old maréchal dismissed the prime minister's vow that the British would fight on alone as absurd: To make Paris "a city of ruins," he said, would not affect the issue. As for guerrillas, he said: "That would mean the destruction of the country: *"Cela veut dire la destruction du pays."*

The most protracted discussion arose from the French demand that every plane left in the RAF be committed to the battle now raging. "Here," said Weygand, "is the decisive point. Now is the decisive moment. The British ought not to keep a single fighter in England. They should all be sent to France."

After a long pause Churchill said very slowly: "This is not the decisive point. This is not the decisive moment. The decisive moment will come when Hitler hurls his Luftwaffe against Britain. If we can keep command of the air over our own island—that is all I ask—we will win it all back for you." Reynaud, according to Ismay, was "obviously moved."

At 10:00 P.M., the conferees dined. Weygand invited de Gaulle, until recently the commander of an armored division, to sit beside him and flushed when the new general chose the chair beside Churchill instead. Already there was an unspoken bond between Churchill and Reynaud's protégé. The formation of that bond was probably the only accomplishment of the Briare meeting.

For Churchill the last straw came at bedtime. Before retiring, the prime minister and the premier had coffee and brandy together. Reynaud said Weygand had told him: "In three weeks Britain will have her neck wrung like a chicken." Then Reynaud revealed that Pétain had told him that "it will be necessary to seek an armistice." Churchill, appalled, thought Pétain should have been ashamed to have supported "Weygand's demand for our last twenty-five squadrons of fighters when he has made up his mind that all is lost and that France should give in."

After Churchill had exacted a promise from Admiral Darlan never to surrender the French fleet—it was to prove worthless—the British party left at midmorning. Near-tragedy brushed them on the way home. Unescorted by Hurricanes—an overcast had grounded them—they were flying over Le Havre when the sky cleared and the pilot saw two Heinkels below, firing at fishing boats. The unarmed Flamingo dove to 100 feet above the sea and raced for home. One of the Nazi fighters fired a burst at them, but then they were gone, and the prime minister landed safely at Hendon.

After midnight, when Churchill was donning his sleeping smock, Reynaud phoned. The connection was bad. Eventually an aide got through to one of the premier's aides. The message was grim: The premier and his advisers had moved from Briare to Tours; he wanted Churchill to meet him at the *préfecture* there that same afternoon. This would be the prime minister's fifth flight to France in less than four weeks. At 11:00 A.M. on June 13, he and his party gathered at Hendon. Escorted by eight Spitfires, the Flamingo detoured around the Channel Islands and entered French air space over St. Malo.

Lashed by a thunderstorm, they landed on an airstrip pitted with bomb craters. The field was deserted. No one was there to meet them. They taxied around the craters, looking for someone, and found a group of French airmen lounging outside a hangar. The prime minister disembarked and told them, in his appalling French, that his name was Churchill, that he was the prime minister of Great Britain, and that he would be grateful if they could provided him with "*une voiture*" to carry him and his small staff to the town's *préfecture*. The airmen loaned them a small touring car. No one at the *préfecture* knew who they were or had time for them. In a small restaurant they lunched on cold chicken and Vouvray wine.

It was there that they were found by Paul Baudouin. In what Churchill called "his soft, silky manner," Baudouin lectured them on the hopelessness of further resistance. At length the premier arrived, followed by spears and the British ambassador. The meeting—destined to be the last of the Conseil Supérieur de la Guerre—was to be held in the *préfet*'s study, a small, shabby room looking out on an unkept garden. The study was furnished with a desk, behind which Reynaud presided, and assorted, unmatched chairs.

Churchill took a leather chair and eyed his French hosts warily. He was confronting France's split personality. Reynaud still stood for a death-before-dishonor last stand against Nazi barbarism. Baudouin, Churchill knew, represented the defeatists. But even now Churchill had not grasped how eager for peace such men were. The American ambassador, William Bullitt, no admirer of the British, told Washington that "to have as many companions in misery as possible, [the French] hoped England would be rapidly and completely defeated by Germany. As for their own country," Bullitt reported, they hoped France would become "Hitler's favorite province."

Reynaud told them that Weygand had declared Paris an open city. He himself wanted to "retreat and carry on, but France would cease to exist." Therefore he asked what the British position would be "should the worst come" and raised the issue of the pledge—made at France's insistence and signed by him—that neither ally would make a separate peace. The French wanted to be left off the hook. Would Britain face the hard facts now confronting France?

It was quietly pointed out to him that capitulation was not the only alternative to war. Norway had not surrendered; neither had Holland. Meantime Churchill scowled, weighing his words. The reason for the present crisis, he replied at last, was not a lack of fighter planes. It was the French GHQ's decision to ignore the Ardennes threat and send the best Allied troops into Belgium.

The British had not "felt the German lash" but knew its force, the prime minister rasped. "England will fight on. She has not and will not alter her resolve: no terms, no surrender." He hoped France would carry on, fighting south of Paris and, if it came to that, in North Africa. Although Britain would not "waste time in reproaches and recriminations," that was "a very different thing from becoming a consenting party to a peace made in contravention of the agreement so recently concluded." Then he reported that the Royal Navy was fast approaching a tight blockade of the Continent, which could lead to famine, from which an occupied France could not be spared. The French could not withdraw from the war and remain on good terms with the British. Reynaud, disturbed, darkly remarked: "This might result in a new and very grave situation in Europe."

They had reached an impasse. Spears scribbled a note to Churchill suggesting a pause, and Winston told Reynaud he must confer with his colleagues *dans le jardin.* The eight Englishmen withdrew to pace around the garden, "a hideous rectangle," in Spears's words, surrounded by a muddy path. After twenty minutes Churchill's friend and adviser, Lord Beaverbrook, spoke up: "There is nothing to do but repeat what you have said, Winston. . . . We are doing no good here." Then he added, "Let's get along home."

What Baudouin did then is unforgivable. From time to time in the *préfet*'s study, when Reynaud was speaking, Churchill had nodded or said, *"Je comprends,"* indicating his comprehension of words before they were translated. After Churchill's car had left, de Gaulle called Spears aside to tell him that Baudouin was "putting it about, to all and sundry, notably to the journalists," that Churchill had shown "complete understanding of the French situation and would understand if France concluded an armistice and a separate peace." De Gaulle asked, "Did Churchill really say that?" If he had, it would sway those not prepared to break France's pledge and permit defeatists to argue that there was no point in fighting on when even the English didn't expect it.

Spears replied that Churchill had said no such thing, and decided to race to the bomb-pitted runway before the Flamingo would take off. He arrived in time and confirmed Churchill's reaction. The prime minister told him, "When I said *'je comprends,'* that meant I understood. *Comprendre* means understand in French, doesn't it? Well, when for once I use the right word in their own language, it is going rather far to assume that I intended it to mean something quite different. Tell them my French is not so bad as that." Spears did, but few listened, perhaps because Baudouin was telling them what they wanted to hear.

All France seemed disintegrating, and one of the tragic victims of this national *défaillance* was the premier's anglophobic *fornicatrix*, Mme la comtesse de Portes. Like thousands of other couples, Paul and Hélène were fleeing southward in a hastily packed car. He was driving, she was in the passenger's seat, and the back was crammed with untethered luggage. Suddenly the truck in front of them stopped. The premier braked swiftly, and the luggage shifted forward, instantly breaking her neck.

De Gaulle, who had been commuting between London and France as a liaison officer, now proposed a measure of desperation. On June 16, lunching at the Carleton Club with Churchill and the French ambassador, he argued that "some dramatic move" was essential to keep France in the war. He advanced the idea of a joint Allied declaration. The British and French governments would declare the formation of an Anglo-French Union, the two nations uniting as one. Churchill liked it; so did the war cabinet. But when de Gaulle immediately took off for Bordeaux and submitted the proposal; it was rejected.

Meantime Churchill was preparing to cross the Channel once again, but a "ministerial crisis" in Bordeaux made the meeting impossible. Churchill abandoned his plans "with a heavy heart," as he later wrote. He knew what was coming next, and Jock Colville, his aide, set it down: "Reynaud has resigned, unable to stand the pressure . . . Pétain has formed a Government of Quislings . . . and France will now certainly ask for an armistice in spite of her pledge to us." Churchill growled, "another bloody country gone west."

In Bordeaux, as Spears entered his hotel's huge, darkened lobby around midnight on June 16, he noticed a tall figure standing bolt upright behind one of the columns, "shrouded," as he recalled afterward, "by shadow." it was de Gaulle, who whispered, "I have very good reason to believe Weygand intends arresting me."

De Gaulle explained a plan to encourage a French *résistance* movement, using London as his base. Spears approved; he phoned Churchill, who agreed. Spears had a plane at the Bordeaux airport. It was decided that de Gaulle would behave as though he had come to see Spears off early the next morning. In Spears's words, "We had begun to move when with hooked hands

I hoisted de Gaulle on board." De Gaulle was at Number 10 Downing Street for lunch. Pétain, upon learning what had happened, convened a military court. The expatriated general was found guilty of treason and sentenced to death in absentia. Churchill, of course, took another view. He wrote that de Gaulle had "carried with him, in this small aeroplane, the honour of France."

The Battle of Britain:
How Did "The Few" Win?

By Williamson Murray

O n June 18, 1940, a little more than two weeks after the last British ship left Dunkirk, a tired but defiant Prime Minister Winston Churchill announced to the House of Commons:

What General Weygand called the Battle of France is over. I expect that the Battle of Britain is about to begin. Upon this battle depends the survival of Christian civilisation. Upon it depends our own British life, and the long continuity of our institutions and our Empire. The whole fury and might of the enemy must very soon be turned on us. Hitler knows that he will have to break us in this island or lose the war. . . . Let us therefore brace ourselves to our duties, and so bear ourselves that, if the British Empire and the Commonwealth last for a thousand years, men will still say, "This was their finest hour."

These words, today familiar to every student of World War II, reflect a national determination among the British people to make a desperate stand on their island. While the British braced themselves in June 1940 for the Battle of Britain, the Germans had little sense that they confronted a serious opponent. After it was all over, in the shambles of the Luftwaffe's defeat, Adolf Hitler and his chief henchman, Hermann Göring, stood out as the villains of the piece. What has not been so clear in the historical record, however, is the degree to which the German high command deserves a major share of the blame for the Wehrmacht's first defeat in World War II.

In the glow of victory, the Germans concluded that anything was possible for Hitler's Third Reich. The French army—the very same army that had fought the Reich to a standstill over four long years in World War I—had this time collapsed in barely a month. Hitler himself concluded that the war was over. After playing to Joseph Goebbel's film crew at the signing of the armistice at Compiègne, on June 22, the führer went on vacation. Accompanied by his court, he arrived in Paris for an early-morning visit, then took a picnic tour up and down the Rhine and visited World War I battlefields with his closest associates. He maintained only the loosest contact with his military staff, and that state of affairs resulted in the removal of the chief driving force behind the Nazi war machine. By its very nature, the German high command that Hitler had created was incapable of making critical strategic and planning decisions on its own.

Göring, self-styled Renaissance prince of the Third Reich, had even less interest in pushing the German war machine toward its next confrontation. It was a time to bask in the glories of victory, to add to his collection of Flemish masterpieces, and to dream of medals and other new honors—certainly not a time to worry about the nasty business of digging the British out of their island refuge. Britain could be bluffed and bullied into accepting German peace terms. The attitudes of the rest of the German military leadership reflected those of the führer and his paladin. General

Alfred Jodl, chief of operations of the Armed Forces High Command (the OKW—Hitler's military staff), noted on June 30 that "the final victory of Germany over England is only a question of time."

Yet had the German leadership looked at the strategic situation, they would have realized that the difficulties involved in finishing Britain off before autumn were daunting. The German navy had managed to get its only two battle cruisers, the *Scharnhorst* and the *Gneisenau,* badly damaged in operations off Norway's North Cape in June. These operations served no strategic purpose—in fact the German navy's war diary admitted that the purpose of the June battle-cruiser raid was to influence the postwar debates over service budgets. As a result of the Norwegian campaign, the German navy was left with only one heavy cruiser and four destroyers at the beginning of summer 1940. The army, meanwhile, had done no thinking about the complexities of a massive amphibious operation such as crossing the English Channel and landing on the British coast. As an overconfident Field Marshal Wilhelm Keitel, chief of the OKW, commented in June, such an operation represented nothing more than an enlarged river crossing.

As a result, the responsibility for removing Britain from the war fell to the Luftwaffe—fully in accordance with Göring's view of himself and *his* air force. But the Luftwaffe now faced strategic problems and issues that had never before existed in history: in sum, how to fight and win a great aerial campaign independent of ground and naval forces. There had been much theorizing about such a "strategic" bombing campaign before the war (including the writings of Trenchard, Douhet, Mitchell, and the Air Corps Tactical School in the United States, all of whom had argued that the proper role of bombers was to attack population centers or industry, certainly not to support armies or navies). But there was no actual experience from which one could draw lessons. How easy would it be to find and identify targets? What kinds of targets should one attack? How would national will and morale stand up to bombing? How tenacious would enemy air defenses be? Could an air defense interfere with or even thwart "strategic" bombing attacks?

Besides having few lessons from past wars to plot out a campaign strategy, the Luftwaffe confronted the coming campaign with a force that had lost heavily in the Battle of France. Between May 10 and the fall of France, the Luftwaffe had lost nearly 30 percent of its bombers, 30 percent of its twin-engine fighters, and 15 percent of its single-engine fighters. The fighting had been concentrated almost entirely within a three-week period, straining German pilots and aircraft to the limit.

The Luftwaffe of summer 1940 reflected the traditional strengths and weaknesses of German military institutions. Contrary to the postwar myth that the Germans had neglected their "strategic" bombing force, they in fact had the only air force in the world that was technologically and operationally prepared for such a campaign. Although their twin-engine bombers lacked the range and payload capabilities of the four-engine bombers that came later in the war, the Germans felt that their air force was capable of destroying nearby targets such as Prague, Warsaw, and even London. Meanwhile, like the British, they were working hard to design and build a four-engine bomber. Fortunately, the Heinkel He 177 prototype turned out to be a technological disaster.

Two other factors are also notable in comparing the Luftwaffe to the Royal Air Force and, later, the U.S. Army Air Force. The Germans took the protection of their bombers seriously, and therefore possessed not only a short-range fighter, the Messerschmitt Me 109, but a long-range escort fighter, the Me 110. Moreover, of all the world's air forces, the Luftwaffe was the only one that had done substantial development work on a blind bombing and navigation system—code-named "Knickebein" ("dog leg")—in which radio impulses would guide a plane to its target. Fortunately for Britain, the Luftwaffe's long-range fighter, the Me 110, proved inferior to both the Spitfire and the Hurricane, and British intelligence learned about Knickebein in time to develop countermeasures, such as listening posts and jamming apparatus, before the Battle of Britain.

The Luftwaffe faced the challenge of the unknown with remarkable blitheness. Throughout the war, the Germans gave intelligence a low priority; thus the Luftwaffe's estimate of British defenses was thoroughly inadequate. General Josef ("Beppo") Schmidt, Göring's chief of intelligence, wrote the basic appreciation, entitled "Study in Blue," that the Luftwaffe issued on July 16. This document arrogantly overestimated German capabilities and British weaknesses.

Schmidt did get some of the numbers right—calculating that with 50 fighter squadrons the British possessed approximately 900 fighters, 675 in commission (in fact, the RAF had 871 fighters, 650 operationally ready in 59 squadrons)—but from there his estimates fell off the table. He characterized both the Hurricane and Spitfire as inferior to the Me 109 in combat, and said that only a "skillfully handled" Spitfire was superior to the Me 110. He calculated that British industry produced 180 to 300 fighter aircraft per month (actual production reached 496 in July, 457 in August, and 660 in September) and said British production would soon drop due to German air attacks and British raw-material shortages.

Schmidt's greatest error, however, was his evaluation of Fighter Command's defense system. According to him, the British at the highest levels were

> inflexible in [their] organization and strategy. As [fighter] formations are rigidly attached to their home bases, com-

mand at medium level suffers mainly from being controlled in most cases by officers no longer accustomed to
flying. . . . Command at low level is generally energetic
but lacks tactical skill.

Reflecting the Luftwaffe's lack of technical intelligence,
Schmidt's report made no mention of the British radar system
and its implications for the attacking German forces. His report
ended with the confident assertion that

the Luftwaffe is clearly superior to the RAF as regards
strength, equipment, training, command, and location of
bases. In the event of an intensification of air warfare,
the Luftwaffe, unlike the RAF, will be in a position in
every respect to achieve a decisive effect this year if the
time for the start of large-scale operations is set early
enough to allow advantage to be taken of the months
with relatively favorable weather conditions [July to the
beginning of October].

While the Luftwaffe was gathering its forces for its aerial
assault on Britain, the German high command began planning an
amphibious assault on the coasts of Britain. Of all the unrealized
campaigns and battles of World War II, this was one of the most
unlikely. Even the German services seem not to have taken Operation "Sealion" seriously: The army planned for a landing on
nearly ninety miles of beaches, far in excess of what the British
and Americans, with their vast resources, would achieve in June
1944. This would have made it virtually impossible to break out
of the initial beach lodgment. It is well worth noting that the
Allies had two years of massive preparation behind them before
they landed at Normandy. A reasonable explanation would seem
to be that the German army commanders, knowing the German

navy had virtually no surface force left after Norway, had no expectations of making such a landing.

Overall German strategy can be reduced to a formula: the Luftwaffe would break the back of the RAF early in the battle; after two months of air attacks on British industrial and population centers, British morale would crack; then, in the confusion of civil strife and governmental paralysis, "Sealion" would deal the death blow to British participation in the war.

If the Luftwaffe had achieved such a level of success, "Sealion" might have had a chance. But as a combined-arms operation against any kind of resistance, it had no chance at all. The Germans had no navy, the army had no experience in combined operations, and the lift for the invading troops and their equipment consisted largely of Rhine River barges. Considering that the Royal Navy had thirty-plus destroyers stationed at each end of the Channel, "Sealion" would have represented a desperate risk with small chance of success. It is clear that Hitler had serious doubts about the operation from the beginning. Indeed in July 1940 he was more interested in terminating the Soviet Union in the coming year. Thus, Germany's effort to drive Britain from the war had to come from the air.

There, the Germans confronted a more dangerous opponent than the one pictured in their intelligence documents. In addition to its up-to-date fighters, the RAF's command and control system for the air defense of Britain was the most modern in the world—thanks largely to the foresight, drive, and imagination of Air Chief Marshal Hugh Dowding, one of the great commanders of World War II. In the early 1930s Dowding, as Air Council member for supply and research (later, research and development), was responsible for the development of radar and the advanced fighters with which the RAF reequipped its squadrons in 1938 and 1939. In 1936 Dowding became the commander in chief of Fighter Command, where he oversaw the introduction of radar,

Spitfires, and Hurricanes into the air defense of Britain. At the same time he also oversaw creation of a command and control system that tied fighter, ground controller, and radar together in an effective air defense system.

Dowding's first contacts with Winston Churchill during the French debacle were not auspicious. The prime minister, desperate over the plight of France (a plight he fully recognized as having resulted from the strategic policies of previous British governments), argued forcefully for a massive diversion of England's fighter strength to the Continent. Dowding argued with equal vehemence against any further reductions in the strength of his command, a portion of it having already been committed to the battle on the Continent. Dowding won. Legend has it that Churchill browbeat his senior military leadership into a number of foolhardy schemes and punished those who disagreed with his policies. It is clear that Churchill did not suffer fools, but those who disagreed with his policies received a fair, if tough-minded, hearing. In early July 1940 the minister for air, Sir Archibald Sinclair, reflecting a cabal within the Air Ministry, reported to the prime minister that he was considering relieving Dowding of his position. (It is not clear why the ministry had it in for Dowding—perhaps simply because he was not a bomber boy; perhaps because his success was showing British prewar bombing theories to be false.) Churchill's reply to Sinclair was brief and to the point:

> Personally, I think he is one of the very best men you have got, and I say this after having been in contact with him for about two years. I have greatly admired the whole of his work in the Fighter Command, and especially in resisting . . . the immense pressure to dissipate the Fighter strength during the great French battle. In fact he has my full confidence.

Churchill's confidence in Dowding was to prove justified.

The burden of defending Britain from the Luftwaffe fell chiefly on Dowding's subordinate, Air Commodore Keith Park, commander of 11 Group in the southeastern corner of the British Isles. Backing up Park's forces was 12 Group in the Midlands, which could support 11 Group in defending London. Separate fighter groups defended western England, as well as Scotland and northern Ireland. Fighter Command thus covered the entire British Isles—a fact that German intelligence had missed entirely. This coverage allowed Dowding to replace fought-out squadrons in the south with fresh squadrons from the north.

In all, Fighter Command's strategic position was not so dangerous as it appeared in the summer of 1940. The British air industry had already overtaken German fighter production; by late summer, under the demanding pressure of the minister for aircraft production, Lord Beaverbrook, the ratio favored the British by a two-to-one margin. In France, the Luftwaffe deployed two Luftflotten (equivalent to air forces in U.S. terms): Luftflotten Two and Three. Together, on July 20, those Luftflotten controlled 1,131 bombers (769 in commission), 316 dive bombers (248 in commission), 809 single-engine fighters (656 in commission), and 246 twin-engine fighters (168 in commission). In addition, the Germans deployed 129 bombers and 34 twin-engine fighters with Luftflotte Five in Norway to launch flank attacks on northern Britain. On the basis of their intelligence estimates, the Germans believed there was no fighter defense for the northern portion of Britain.

In microcosm, the strategic problem the Luftwaffe faced was similar to the one the United States confronted in its daylight bomber offensive against Germany in 1943. For maximum effect, bomber raids had to be carried out by day—when the risk to bombers was greatest. Due to the Me 109's limited range, escorted German bombers could strike targets only in southern England (although at night, when they had less need of fighter escort, the bombers could reach farther north); any raids beyond the range of Me 109s would drive bomber losses up to unacceptable levels. This allowed the RAF to use a sizable portion of the British Isles as a sanctuary. Free from the threat of air attack there, the RAF could establish and control its reserves, and protect much of Britain's industrial production, particularly in the Midlands.

By mid-July the Germans were deep into operational planning. In a speech to senior air force commanders, Reichsmarschall Göring enunciated the Luftwaffe's task in the coming battle. He emphasized that the RAF and Britain's aircraft industry would be the critical targets for winning air superiority over Britain. In contrast to the position he took later in the battle, when he demanded that fighters accompany bombers closely, he argued that Luftwaffe fighters should possess maximum operational latitude in protecting bomber formations. Bomber raids would bring up Spitfires and Hurricanes, and the Me 109s would destroy them. The initiative would thus remain with the German fighters, since they would not be tied exclusively to the protection of the bombers.

Unfortunately for the Germans, by summer 1940 Göring was neither consistent nor firm in his command of the Luftwaffe, and Luftwaffe subordinate headquarters had aims other than gaining air superiority. Fliegerkorps I placed support for an invasion, attacks on ports and merchant shipping, and terror raids against major cities on an equal footing with air superiority. The explanation undoubtedly lies in German overconfidence about the coming battle as well as in Göring's loose control. Luftwaffe estimates were that just four days of air attacks over southern England would break Fighter Command; and four more weeks would suffice to eliminate the remainder of the RAF and destroy aircraft factories on which an RAF recovery would depend. Then, completely vulnerable, the British would see the wisdom of accommodation with Nazi Germany; after removing Churchill, they would surrender and accept a subservient position within Europe's new order.

The Battle of Britain was supposed to open with a massive aerial assault. The date, code-named "Eagle Day," was first postponed from August 10 to August 13, and then at the last moment the Germans again delayed—both times due to weather—but they were unable to recall their bombers already in the air. Initial attacks thus crossed the Channel without fighter cover. Already by mid-July, however, the Luftwaffe had embarked on heavy air operations to drive the RAF from the English Channel and to shut down the coastal convoys in the south. This the Germans managed to do by early August without unbearable losses, but their success was offset by the experience that Fighter Command picked up in managing the early air battles. The British worked the technological weaknesses out of their radar system, and the slow buildup in the size of Luftwaffe operations gave radar operators considerable practice in estimating the size and course of approaching raids. There were some significant errors at first: For example, on July 11 Fighter Command controllers scrambled six Hurricanes to meet a lone raider making for Lynne Bay; to their shock, the Hurricanes ran into a major raid of fifteen dive bombers escorted by thirty to forty twin-engine fighters. But such unpleasant surprises became less frequent.

Dowding and Fighter Command gained two other important advantages from these early battles. First of all, Fighter Command began discarding outmoded, interwar tactics; British fighters adapted to the nasty world of the dogfight. (They had forgotten the lessons of World War I, assuming that airplanes were simply too fast for traditional dogfighting.) Second—and perhaps most important—Dowding had time to reorganize and refashion Fighter Command after the heavy losses of the French campaign. The units that had suffered most in France during May and early June were now recovering in Scotland and the Midlands, while Dowding's freshest units lay in southern England with a substantial number of experienced aircrews. By the end of July, Fighter Command was better off than it had been at the end of June.

The Germans, on the other hand, not only made few inroads against the British defenses but, as an early August intelligence summary suggests, had failed to learn much about the enemy they had been fighting for nearly a month:

> As the British fighters are controlled from the ground by radio-telephones, their forces are tied to their respective ground stations and are thereby restricted in mobility, even taking into consideration the probability that the ground stations are partly mobile. Consequently, the assembly of strong fighter forces at determined points and at short notice is not to be expected. A massed German attack on a target area can therefore count on the same conditions of light fighter opposition as in attacks on widely scattered targets. It can, indeed, be assumed that considerable confusion in the defensive networks will be unavoidable during mass attacks, and that the effectiveness of the defenses may thereby be reduced.

That the Luftwaffe incorrectly estimated what was going on behind the Straits of Dover was more than a mere intelligence failure. Conceptually the Germans were considerably behind the RAF in developing an air defense system. While they possessed radar, they had not yet developed a real air defense system and thus were unable to recognize the effectiveness of their opponent's system. In fact they failed even to recognize that their own radar might prove useful in estimating how the British were reacting to their attacks. Had the Jafüs, the officers responsible for fighter operations, possessed radar plots of air operations over Britain, they might have played a more significant role in the battle. Instead, with little active or passive intelligence, they spent a dismal summer trying to make some sense of pilot reports.

By early August, Keith Park and Dowding had a fair picture of the parameters within which they would have to conduct the air battle. On the strategic level, Fighter Command had only to hold out until autumn brought bad weather. On an operational level, RAF fighter squadrons in the south would have to meet enemy bomber attacks with sufficient strength to impose a heavy rate of attrition on the attackers and to tie the Me 109s closely to the defense of vulnerable bomber formations. Meanwhile, beyond the Me 109's limited range, Fighter Command's reserves would rest and refit. They would be in position to savage whatever German bomber formations moved beyond Me 109 range.

In some respects, August 13, the official "Eagle Day," came as an anticlimax. On August 11 the British lost nearly thirty fighter pilots—7 percent of 11 Group's total. On August 12, German bombs severed power to the radar stations at Dover and Rye; it took the British almost all day to get them back in working condition—though the latticework towers themselves withstood the pounding. But it was not until the afternoon of the 13th that the Germans attacked the RAF and its support structure. Raids on airfields, sector stations, and aircraft factories began in earnest. Almost inexplicably, German intelligence misidentified the parent factory for Spitfire production in Southampton as a bomber factory, and not until much later did German bombers attack it. These raids hit the British hard. Fighter Command suffered severe attrition of fighter pilots—losses that put in question how long the RAF could sustain the battle for air superiority.

While the pressure on Fighter Command was intense, Luftwaffe units also took a beating. The effectiveness of British resistance came as a nasty shock—especially on August 15, a day that Luftwaffe aircrews (the surviving ones) refer to as "Black Thursday." Luftflotte Five's first appearance in the battle resulted in catastrophic losses that prevented it from launching another daylight raid on northern England: so much for intelligence estimates that the RAF had no fighter defenses in the north. In the south, German raids failed to destroy Fighter Command's radar network. While a number of RAF airfields were badly damaged, most were soon back in working condition. By mid-August the Luftwaffe had lost nearly 300 aircraft (including 105 Me 109s), while the British had lost 148 fighter aircraft. Compounding the attrition of German strength was the fact that aircrews shot down over the British Isles, even if they survived, were lost for the remainder of the war—in the words of one fighter pilot, felled in October 1940, "We were one-way fliers." Many British fighter pilots returned immediately to active duty.

It didn't take long for Göring to become discouraged by the heavy losses. On August 15 he called his senior air force commanders to his Berlin estate, Karinhall, to discuss the failure of the initial air attacks on Britain. Göring berated his generals for everything from faulty target selection to weak leadership. But he provided precious little advice and few solutions to their problems. He also made a serious error: On the basis of inadequate damage estimates, he removed British radar stations from Luftwaffe target lists.

Within the week, Göring further handicapped the Luftwaffe's ability to break Fighter Command. On August 19 the operations staff stated that Dowding's fighters were the primary objective of the German air campaign and urged that the ground support structure, the aircraft industry, and aluminum-production facilities therefore be the major targets of German attacks. At the same time, however, Göring ordered the Me 109s to guard bomber formations closely and no longer to seek out Fighter Command in free-chase missions. He thus robbed his fighters of the advantages of surprise and flexibility. As a result the British generally dictated the tempo of fighter operations, and the Me 109s found it even harder to protect the German bombers while they themselves were at greater disadvantage in air-to-air combat.

By late August the RAF's tenacious resistance and the resulting German losses had reduced Göring to slandering the courage of his fighter crews. The fighter ace Adolf Galland recalled after the war a conference with the Reichsmarschall:

[Göring] had nothing but reproach for the [German] fighter force, and he expressed his dissatisfaction in the hardest of terms. The theme of fighter protection was chewed over again and again. Göring clearly represented the point of view of the bombers and demanded close and rigid protection. The bomber, he said, was more important than record bag figures. . . . We received many more harsh words. Finally as his time ran short he grew more amiable. He asked what were the requirements for our squadrons. [Werner] Mölders asked for a series of [Me] 109s with more powerful engines. The request was granted. "And you?" Göring turned to me. I did not hesitate long. "I should like an outfit of Spitfires for my squadron."

In fact, Dowding's Fighter Command was under serious pressure. German bomber formations had devastated its front-line airfields and severely stressed its command and control system and maintenance structure. Churchill, in his memoirs, recalled the British difficulties:

Extensive damage had been done to five of the group's forward airfields, and also to the six sector station.

Manston and Lympere on the Kentish coast were on several occasions and for days unfit for operating fighter aircraft. Biggin Hill Sector Station, to the south of London, was so severely damaged that for a week only one fighter squadron could operate from it. If the enemy had persisted in heavy attacks against the adjacent sectors and damaged their operations rooms or telephone communications, the whole intricate organization of Fighter Command might have broken down.

Dowding was almost out of fresh squadrons in the north, and the new pilots coming into Fighter Command had virtually no experience in flying operational fighter aircraft. In August, Fighter Command had lost one-quarter of its pilot strength; it was clear to Dowding that it could not afford losses much longer. The question of the hour was which of the two adversaries could last out the battle of attrition.

In early September the Germans made their final mistake. Discouraged by Luftwaffe failures to break RAF resistance, Hitler and Göring switched the air campaign's emphasis from an air-superiority strategy to a "strategic" bombing offensive against the British capital. The change was prompted by two factors. First, the Nazi leadership was outraged by Britain's temerity in bombing German cities, particularly Berlin. Second, the führer was undoubtedly eager to see whether he could break the "soft" British plutocracy. Interestingly, Field Marshal Albert Kesselring, often regarded by Anglo-American historians as one of the more effective German military leaders, enthusiastically supported the shift to terror attacks. "Smiling Albert" argued that Fighter Command was toppling, that major air attacks on London would finish the job and also break the will of the British people to continue the struggle. His counterpart, Field Marshal Hugo Sperrle, disagreed, but it was an argument he could not win.

The shift in Luftwaffe strategy came with startling suddenness after Berlin was first bombed. On September 7 the pressure on Dowding's forces relaxed. That afternoon Kesselring launched nearly 1,000 bombers and fighters against London. The move caught 11 Group so much by surprise that the British almost entirely missed the raid. They responded as if the massive attack were aimed at 11 Group's defensive structure. Consequently, British fighter attacks hit the German formations, if at all, after they had dropped their bombs on London. The East End docks suffered catastrophic damage, and the great fires there served as beacons for further nighttime attacks. The damage was terrible, but the population did not break.

The easing of pressure on Fighter Command came as a great relief to the hard-pressed fighter pilots and to the strained support structure of Fighter Command itself. And barely one week later the British showed how valuable that respite was. Luftwaffe intelligence, adding to its dismal record, suggested that the RAF was through. But when Kesselring's forces returned for a repeat performance on September 15, their bomber and fighter formations met a resolute and prepared fighter defense. A massive, swirling dogfight covered southern England from the coast to London and resulted in roughly equivalent fighter losses: The British lost twenty fighter pilots, the Germans seventeen. But Fighter Command also savaged the German bombers: Besides Me 109 losses, the Germans lost forty-one other aircraft in the day's fighting.

Pushed to the limit, Dowding's forces bent but did not break. Winston Churchill spent the day at 11 Group's command center at Uxbridge. His memoirs, often so eloquent, fully capture the strain of the day:

Below us was the large-scale map-table, around which perhaps twenty highly trained young men and women, with their telephone assistants, were assembled: Opposite to us, covering the entire wall ... was a gigantic blackboard divided into six columns with electric bulbs, for the six fighter stations. ... Presently the red bulbs showed that the majority of our squadrons were engaged. A subdued hum rose from the floor, where the busy plotters pushed their discs to and fro. ... In a little while all our squadrons were fighting, and some had already begun to return for fuel. All were in the air. There was not one squadron left in reserve. At this moment Park spoke to Dowding ... asking for the three squadrons from Number 12 Group. ... Hitherto I had watched in silence. I now asked, "What other reserves have we?" "There are none," said Air Vice Marshal Park. ... Afterwards, he said that at this I "looked grave." Well I might. ... The odds were great; our margins small; the stakes infinite.

As we now know, British fighters did not come close to their claims for German aircraft. Instead of 183, Fighter Command shot down only 60 German aircraft on September 15. The numbers, however, are irrelevant. On September 15, Luftwaffe morale cracked. Faced with serious opposition, a significant number of German bombers dumped their bomb loads over southern England and fled for France. Why this happened is not difficult to understand in light of two factors. First, the Luftwaffe had been engaged in major, sustained air operations since early May, a five-month period. Equally important, there came a point where smooth assurances by Luftwaffe intelligence that Fighter Command was almost through lost credibility in the minds of those who flew, especially since the opposite was so palpably the case.

The postbattle period held considerable irony. Dowding, so instrumental in the victory, was almost immediately retired.

Despite Churchill's effort to employ him again, the RAF resolutely refused to give him an important assignment. Even more astonishing was the fact that the British failed to award Dowding any significant honors. Keith Park's treatment was not much better. Despite his contribution to the victory, he found himself shuffled off to a subsidiary, nonoperational command. On the losing side, interestingly, those responsible for the defeat suffered no repercussions: "Beppo" Schmidt continued as Luftwaffe intelligence chief and soon received a major operational assignment. Göring and Kesselring, of course, remained as senior military leaders to the end of the war. But then, they continued to provide the führer with the optimistic reports he so loved to hear.

Not only was there little correlation between battle performance and reward, but the two combatant air forces learned little from their clash. Luftwaffe chief of staff General Hans Jeschonnek summed up the German response when he remarked shortly before the invasion of Russia the following spring, "At last a proper war!"

For the British, the Battle of Britain confirmed what they had learned over the Heligoland Bight the previous December, when German fighters had savaged a raid of Wellington bombers: that daylight operations in the face of enemy fighters would involve prohibitive losses. But the RAF largely ignored the lesson suggested by the solidity of British morale in the face of the German air assault when it began the area-bombing campaign on Germany.

The U.S. Army Air Force, a major observer of the activities in summer 1940, also misread virtually all of the combat lessons. Its observers in Britain attributed high Luftwaffe losses to inadequate defensive armament, small bomber size, and bad formation discipline. By summer 1941 U.S. air planners were predicting that "by employing large numbers of aircraft with high speed, good defensive power, and high altitude," U.S. bombers without fighter escorts could penetrate deep into Germany without suffering serious losses. The U.S. Army Air Force's lack of interest in a long-range escort fighter is, in the words of the official historians, "difficult to account for." In light of the Battle of Britain, indeed it is.

In one respect, however, British and U.S. airmen did draw an essential, war-winning lesson: Both air forces, unlike the Germans, concluded that numbers would play the crucial role in winning the air war over the Continent. The resulting great aircraft-production programs drawn up in 1940–41 by both nations eventually won control of the air in 1944.

The Battle of Britain was one of the most uplifting victories in human history. "The few" had triumphed, but they had triumphed because of outstanding leadership in the RAF and sloppy, careless execution on the German side. The major reason for the Luftwaffe's failure was overconfidence. Its task admittedly presented operational problems wholly beyond those that had confronted military commanders before. But a cavalierly incompetent intelligence service understated the difficulties, causing the Luftwaffe to dally in July while its opponent, inspired by his desperate situation, rallied his forces. By engaging in irrelevant operations over the Channel in July and early August, the Luftwaffe built up Fighter Command's confidence and expertise.

The muddled execution of "Eagle Day" was a fitting anticlimax to a bad beginning. With its commander in chief and senior commanders far removed in their comfortable mansions, the Luftwaffe moved from one operational concept to another with no clear overall strategy. Ignorant of the importance of the radar system, misguided as to the locations of British factories supporting fighter production, the Luftwaffe nevertheless managed to inflict excruciating pain on Fighter Command. But that pain, without the discipline of a strategic concept (in the classic sense), could not be turned into a decisive victory.

When all is said and done, Winston Churchill's elegant tribute to Fighter Command underlined the fact that even in the "modern" and "civilized" twentieth century, such virtues as courage and sacrifice are essential to the maintenance of civilization: "Never in the field of human conflict was so much owed by so many to so few."

There is considerable irony in the Battle of Britain. Throughout the interwar period, airmen had argued that air power would allow nations wise enough to invest in air forces to escape the horror of the trench battles of World War I. Moreover, they argued that the past lessons of war and military history were irrelevant to the future employment of air power. They were wrong. The conduct of air operations in the Second World War resembled the strategy of the previous conflict except that the attrition was now in terms of aircraft and aircrews rather than mud-stained infantry. In a larger sense the traditional factors and lessons of war governed the conduct of air operations throughout the war. To quote one of the premier air historians, Anthony Verrier:

> Thus we are left with one clear reminder of a painful truth: The laws of war applied as much to the strategic air offensive waged over Europe's skies through five-and-a-half bitter years as they did to the sailors and soldiers on the distant seas or in the mud or the sand below. Occasionally the airman may have felt himself living or fighting in a new dimension, just as the air commander may have sometimes felt he employed a freedom of maneuver denied to admirals and generals. But the airman died, and the air force commander was defeated and stalemated

unless the laws were kept. When they were kept, success came; until they could be kept, hope was kept alive by courage alone.

For all the newness of the arena in which it was fought, the Battle of Britain reflected war in the modern world, and the air war for the next five years would follow the path so clearly marked out in the summer of 1940.

1941

Pearl Harbor Survivor's Story

by Stephen A. Kallis

At about 5 p.m. (as it was still referred to before the war started for us) on November 27, the alert siren at Fort Kamehameha, which abutted the U.S. naval facility at Pearl Harbor, sounded. The men boiled out of the barracks, while I went directly to post headquarters, slinging on my field belt and gas mask as I went. Reporting to Major Venn (commanding officer of the 41st), I was informed that what had been called was an anti-sabotage alert. I was to take my anti-sabotage position, protecting the Pearl Harbor Groupment headquarters and the telephone exchange at Battery Hasbrouck.

We proceeded to Battery Hasbrouck, setting up our two .50-caliber M-1 machine guns on the parapet and our two .30-caliber machine guns to cover the ground approaches to the battery. Strong patrols covered the adjoining lumberyard, while a guard of six posts was organized. The war reserve of small-arms ammunition was drawn from ordnance and placed in one of the magazines at Hasbrouck.

In the next week, the alert was relaxed to the point of reducing the guard to six men and returning the machine guns to their normal storage place, about a mile away from Hasbrouck. We were scheduled to do some target practice, firing the.50-caliber guns at balloons. For this, eighteen hundred rounds of belted ammunition were drawn from ordnance and stored with the guns. However, before we could do so, the remainder of the battery and both officers were assigned to the dust control project on December 1, so the ammunition was not fired and thus was immediately available on the seventh.

December 7 dawned, as usual, a clear, beautiful day. Lieutenant Macauley and I had attended a dinner dance at the Pearl Harbor Navy Club on Saturday night and, with one thing and another, had returned late. The usual percentage of enlisted men were on overnight pass, and since there was no Sunday reveille, the majority of the remainder slept late.

I was awakened by a noise like a crash at about 0755. Several more explosions sounded, and I tried to figure out why anyone should be firing artillery on a Sunday. Suddenly, I heard machine-gun fire interspersed with the loud explosions and noticed that the house was shaking terribly with each explosion. I slid hastily into my uniform and stepped out to the lanai.

As I stepped out the door, I saw a plane, silver and blue, passing parallel to Officers' Row at about 500 feet altitude. The plane had wheel pants, and I could see the red ball of Japan on the fuselage, just behind the cockpit. I looked out to sea and saw what seemed to be dozens of planes coming in at extremely low altitudes. Another series of explosions sounded from the direction of Hickam Field.

I started immediately for the barracks on foot. The whole effect was nightmarish. The houses and trees of the post, long familiar to me, seemed strange. The atmosphere was like that which preceded a thunderstorm on the mainland, each feature of the view standing out with an almost menacing clarity. My feet fairly flew, but I felt as if I were traveling at a snail's pace.

As I ran down the street, I noticed sparks bouncing from the pavement near my feet. I glanced over my shoulder and saw a plane firing on me. At that point I jumped out of the road and traveled the next hundred yards among the hibiscus hedges and coconut trees. A car came along with Lieutenant Pomeroy at the wheel, and he slowed down to pick me up. He was an ordnance officer, and we exchanged perhaps a dozen words about supplies before he dropped me at the office.

It couldn't have been much after 0805 when I got to the office. The first sergeant was there, and he and I went to the supply room. Sergeant Duzyk was already issuing ammunition to a long line of half-dressed men. I decided to move the battery to Hasbrouck, since the greatest fear I had was that the Japanese would combine their bombing assault with a paratroop drop. Hasbrouck was the closest position to Hickam Field, a key point of the harbor defenses at Pearl and, incidentally, where the remainder of my small-arms ammunition was stored.

A two-ton truck reported in, and I detailed Sergeant Cowd and a couple of men to go down and secure the machine guns. Lieutenant Macauley, who had been caught by the blitz just outside Hickam Gate, appeared at this time, and I directed him to take the battery up to Hasbrouck. The first sergeant and I remained behind until the last man had cleared.

The battery moved out in extended order, and I was gratified to observe that there was no bunching up as the soldiers proceeded to the street, even though the strafing was continuous. The barracks had also been strafed while the ammunition was being issued, and the men formed up for the move; however, owing to the broad veranda, there was no direct vision from the air. Nearly all of the bullets struck in the squad rooms, which were already deserted.

The first sergeant and I waited for the men to leave and then started up the street. We got a lift from Lieutenant Harnett and arrived just after the first of the men had reached the battery.

There was a bunch of civilian workers, mostly Orientals, under the trees when we arrived. Lieutenant Macauley had sent a couple of men to watch them, fearing possible attempts at sabotage. We arrived just in time to see our men moving toward the workers with fixed bayonets. The workers started to move off, and one of the men said, in the coldest voice I'd ever heard, "Don't run! You're not going anywhere!"

The engineer officer in command took charge of the workers and volunteered their service wherever they could be used. He was told to stand by in case of fires.

As soon as I arrived at Hasbrouck, I climbed the old battery command station on top of the emplacement and looked over Hickam Field and the navy yard. It looked like any of the war movies that we'd always thought were pure Hollywood. The background was an immense pall of smoke from Pearl Harbor. It seemed to come from the oil tanks, but was actually the explosion and burning of Arizona. Hickam Barracks was also burning, and five or six planes along the warm-up apron were blazing fiercely, sending up huge clouds of pitch-black smoke. A large hangar ballooned up and exploded as I watched. The whole sky was dotted with black smoke puffs from the anti-aircraft fire, with an occasional yellow-gray burst among them.

Everywhere, Jap planes dived and zoomed, for all the world like gnats over a trout stream, sliding down to just above the barrage to release their bombs, then diving through or circling out over the sea to come in low for ground strafing. A B-17E bomber came in to land, then reared up like a horse and tore away, with two Japs after it, but unable to catch it.

The din was unimaginable. As I could see tracers whipping past me in my exposed position, I only stayed up long enough to see that there were no parachutists in sight. Then I slid down and reported to Colonel Rhein that all was clear. He had a teletype message in his hand. He instructed me to take all the battery down to the gun position, leaving only twenty men as a security guard, since the teletype message reported Jap transports only twenty miles off Barber's Point.

We started the men back down the road, picking up the .50s, which had just arrived, but leaving the .30s for the guard. The first sergeant and both of the officers rode down in the recon vehicle, a silly way of putting all the eggs in one basket, but though fired upon, we were not hit. We broke some speed regulations, however.

We arrived at the guns long before the first of the men got down and took cover in an old sandbag emplacement left over from the September maneuvers. The lack of buildings between us and Hickam Field offered a beautiful view of the damage being done, while the beach in front of our position was the turning point of the ground strafers, many of whom favored us with a burst as they came over.

We had time to observe the sight that gave us the biggest kick of the day, the destroyers leaving Pearl Harbor. It was heartening to see them roar out of the channel heading for what, according to the reports we had, might have been certain death at the hands of a large Japanese fleet. The Japanese planes could see the channel very clearly from the air, and they concentrated their bombs at the channel mouth. Destroyer after destroyer sped out of the harbor, all guns blazing, and disappeared into the waterspouts, lost to view as they made their turns in the midst of the bombs, and streaked back into sight, apparently unscathed, heading for the horizon and the reported enemy fleet.

As the first of our men appeared, we put them into trucks and sent them to the magazines to draw shells and powder. We spotted a small dump near each gun and manned the plotting car and the two guns for which we had personnel. A detachment of C-41 soldiers made this possible. The .50s were set up in the duckweed, and they were able to fire on a series of enemy planes, two of which they damaged badly. A fifty-pound bomb landed between the guns but luckily did not explode. Our machine guns chattered away, and many of the men cut loose with Springfields, probably doing little or no damage but giving vent to the anger that was our prime emotion.

In trying to recapture our mood during the attack, the main thing that stood out at all times was anger. Nearly everyone was scared; all were filled with self-disgust at the way we had been caught napping, but sheer rage was the thing that stood out. Men rejoined the battery after a wild ride from the city, and an even wilder ride through Hickam Field. Each had picked up stories, mainly false, about events downtown and about damage to military and naval installations.

Every succeeding tale made us more enraged. The water was reported by higher authorities as having been poisoned, and though there was a hydrant nearby, we thus could not drink from it. Being under fire makes a man extremely thirsty. I sent a truck up to the mess hall to get the milk out of the icebox. When they arrived, the kitchen blew up in their faces. No food, no drink, and a lot of battery fund property smashed to fragments. All of this fanned the flames of our fury.

I had been concerned, before the blitz, as to how we would perform under fire. None of us, with the exception of the first sergeant, had been under fire previously, and I had wondered how the men would react, especially in a situation where it was not a question of fighting but largely a matter of taking a pasting without being able to fight back. An officer has to watch over his men, and that responsibility helps steady his nerves. This is also true of the noncoms, especially the sergeants. But the privates had nothing to do but take cover in a place where there was no cover. I circulated among the men to calm them, if necessary, but it wasn't needed. Many had the same lump in their stomachs as I had in mine, a very unpleasant feeling that someone is tying knots in your intestines. Some were pale, as I imagine I was, but all were functioning at top efficiency.

Our reinforcements were taken away, and a detachment of our own men with them. Those of us who remained took cover and watched the bombing. We had a grandstand seat from where we were.

Two flights of level bombers came in at about fifteen thousand feet, and we could see them open up their bomb bays and lay their eggs. The sunlight glinted on the bombs as they fell, and they were visible all the way down. A series of explosions, merging one into another, marked their arrival on the hangar line. The effect was theatrical in the extreme, flash after flash, growing into a billow of dirty brown smoke, with girders and huge slabs of roofing spinning through the air. It looked as if there would be nothing left of Hickam Field, but when I looked at the damage on the 8th, I saw that most of the string of bombs had fallen neatly in a road, and much of the damage could be repaired by a bulldozer.

Some incredible escapes occurred. One of the men coming down to the gun park stopped for a moment to speak to another, and a 20mm shot struck the pavement close enough to tear his shoe but he sustained no injury. Two girls from the post exchange, passing through Hickam, were put under a truck for shelter until a lull came. Bullets sprayed around the truck without hitting it; when they got out from under it, they discovered it was a filled gasoline truck.

The raid quieted in the afternoon, and we were able to get a little food but no water. After dark, I took over the group from Major Venn, who went to Honolulu to arrange for moving the two batteries to field positions. He returned around 2100 and the creepiest experience I had that whole day was walking about a mile in the pitch-black night through invisible troops with very itchy trigger fingers.

The whole night was filled with shooting. Some gunner

would test his gun by firing a burst in the air, and every gun within earshot would do the same. The sight was awe-inspiring: Tracers seemed to float slowly up, and the field and the fort appeared to be full of Roman candles. This was especially noticeable during the last short raid at about 2230, when considerable lead went flying skyward. The sight was so beautiful that I stood out in the open watching the fireworks display until two tracer bullets went between my feet, reminding me that the display was lethal as well as beautiful. [There were no Japanese raids on Pearl Harbor the night of December 7. Tragically, the beautiful bursts of anti-aircraft fire described by Kallis downed four U.S. Navy aircraft that were attempting to land on Ford Island.]

With morning came more rumors, all cheering, and as false as the discouraging ones of the day before. We got orders to move our field position but had to wait for the other battery to move first, so we were not able to do more than make up the train on the 8th. The night of the 8th, my second sleepless night, was marked by being concerned with what turned out to be some imaginary gliders; these were tracked faithfully for an hour or two. They proved to be as false as the story of parachute troops on the north shore, and that of the transports off Barber's Point had been on Sunday.

We moved out Tuesday morning, in two trains: troops, equipment, and armament in one train; ammunition, with six Browning Automatic Rifle-armed guards, in the other. A little matter of some forty-six bridges and culverts to cross, combined with authentic reports of sniping, made me issue orders to shoot to kill anyone observed tampering with bridges, switches, or the like.

We cleaned the barracks of everything we could use in the field and took off. Our communications and observing sections had gone the day before so that we could be ready to fire as soon as we got into position. It is hard to recall it now, but at that time we expected the Japs to attack again any day, before we could draw on the mainland for reinforcements. As a result, we worked under terrific pressure and a fairly high degree of nervous tension, trying to be ready for "Nichi Nichi" when he came back.

I reported in to Colonel Anderson, a field artilleryman who commanded a composite groupment with coast artillery batteries from two regiments and three field artillery batteries. To make it more complicated, he had three naval officers from damaged ships attached for duty. I got a cordial reception, and was offered the use of fifty civilian laborers to help construct my position. I jumped at the chance, and we used them for the next two weeks.

I got back to the battery at dusk and saw how the emplacing of the two guns we could man had been progressing. Lieutenant Macauley and I oriented the guns with a compass and a flashlight. That sounds simple, but a railroad gun is quite a mass of metal, and it also rides on steel rails, both of which have a strong influence on a compass needle. Although it wasn't an easy task, we finally did it, posted our crews, and set out our guards. Then we went to a tent that had been set up for us, for our first sleep since the start of the war.

The Niihau Incident

By William Hallstead

By midmorning, December 7, 1941, 22-year-old Airman 1st Class Shigenori Nishikaichi knew his Mitsubishi A6M2 Zero fighter was in serious trouble. Flying escort for a flight of bombers from the Japanese aircraft carrier *Shokaku* during the attack on Pearl Harbor, Nishikaichi and seven other fighter pilots from the carrier *Hiryu* had attacked targets in southeastern Oahu. The fighters strafed the U.S. Naval Air Station on the Mokapu Peninsula and then hit Bellows Army Airfield, 10 miles to the south. In both attacks, bombing followed the strafing. The fighters then made another pass to hit additional targets of opportunity.

After the raids, the Zeros reassembled and began the return flight to the carriers. The plan was to rendezvous with returning bombers just north of Oahu's northern tip. The bombers would then lead the fighters—which had few navigation aids—back to the carriers waiting nearly 200 miles away. Before the Zeros neared the rendezvous point, however, a flight of nine American Curtiss P-36A fighters dived out of nowhere and a one-sided battle ensued. The lightly armed P-36As looked fierce, but they were already obsolete. The Zeros outclimbed, outturned and out-ran the slower, less maneuverable Curtisses. The American pilots went down one after the other, victims of the Zeros' superior maneuverability.

In the aerial melee Nishikaichi's fighter was hit, but at first the damage seemed superficial. As the Zeros regrouped, however, the pilot noticed an excessive rate of fuel consumption. In fact, one of the half-dozen hits on the plane had punctured its gas tank. The engine began to run rough, and Nishikaichi soon fell behind the others. By the time he reached the rendezvous area, he was alone. Then he spotted another Zero approaching, this one ominously trailing smoke.

During the morning briefing aboard *Hiryu*, the pilots had been told that crippled aircraft should attempt to make emergency landings on tiny Niihau, the westernmost of Hawaii's seven main islands. There, survivors were to wait along the coast for the arrival of an Imperial Navy I-class submarine assigned to rescue duty. There would be no problems with locals on the island they were assured, since Niihau was uninhabited.

Nishikaichi made a quick calculation based on his rate of fuel consumption and reduced airspeed caused by the now faltering engine. He decided that a try for Niihau, about 130 miles to the west, was more feasible than attempting to reach *Hiryu*, which probably would be steaming away from Hawaii and back toward Japan. With the other damaged Zero trailing behind, he turned due west.

Twenty minutes later the two limping Zeros passed to the south of Kauai's green slopes. After a few more minutes, Nishikaichi spotted dead ahead the lava cliffs on the east coast of 18-mile-long, 6-mile-wide Niihau. In tandem, the two faltering Japanese fighters circled the island. At that point Nishikaichi discovered that Japanese Intelligence had blown it. Contrary to the information he had received, the island was clearly inhabited. About a third of the way up the west coast was a large central building, along with several smaller structures. A mile or so beyond that was a small settlement, where he could see a cluster of people standing in front of what appeared to be a church. From his low altitude, Nishikaichi observed that the people appeared to be Polynesian natives.

In some confusion, Nishikaichi flew southwest, away from the island. The other plane followed. Then Nishikaichi faced the inevitable, realizing that he would have to either land on Niihau or crash at sea. He slipped back toward the other plane and signaled its pilot to head back to the island.

The pilot of the other stricken Zero, Airman 2nd Class Saburo Ishii, waved away that suggestion. He had just radioed his carrier, *Shokaku,* that he intended to return to Oahu and crash-dive into some worthwhile target. A few minutes later, Nishikaichi watched Ishii climb steeply, then inexplicably dive straight into the sea. The shaken Japanese pilot turned toward Niihau and began looking for a place to land.

Nishikaichi soon discovered that whoever lived on Niihau had better prepared that small island for a possible war than the military authorities had on Oahu. With admirable foresight, Niihau's manager had ordered potential landing sites to be heavily plowed or studded with rock piles.

With his fuel almost gone, Nishikaichi finally found a relatively level, uncluttered stretch of pasture near an isolated house. He eased the Zero into a shallow approach glide and braced himself for a hard landing.

The island Nishikaichi was about to land on was strictly *kapu,* or forbidden, to any outside member of the public. In 1864, King Kamehameha V had sold Niihau to the Robinson family, in whose hands it has since remained. The native Niihauans—and the Robinson family, for whom most of them work—were and still are a fiercely independent lot. In 1959, Niihau was the one out of Hawaii's 240 precincts to vote against statehood.

The predominantly native Hawaiian inhabitants herd sheep and cattle and gather honey, and they have made the island famous through the export of highly prized jewelry made of tiny shells collected on the island's beaches. Humpbacked little Niihau—known throughout Hawaii as the "forbidden island"—has a very dry climate since most rainfall is intercepted by the towering mountains of Kauai, 17 miles to the east across the Kaulakahi Channel.

As the Japanese pilot flared out for a landing in this benevolent private fiefdom, the Zero's wheels struck a wire fence, and the plane nosed in hard. Nishikaichi's safety harness tore loose, and he slammed against the instrument panel.

Watching the dramatic arrival of the sleek airplane with its red circle markings from his front yard was native Hawaiian Howard Kaleohano. Born and educated on the Big Island of Hawaii, he had been permitted by island manager Aylmer Robinson to visit his sister on Niihau in 1930. He had stayed on and married, becoming one of the few native Hawaiians on the island who was fluent in English.

Kaleohano rushed to the crashed Zero, hauled the groggy pilot out of the wreckage and took away his sidearm and what looked like official papers. Speaking in schoolboy English, Nishikaichi asked Kaleohano if he was Japanese. "I am Hawaiian," Kaleohano told him. He then took the pilot into his house, where his wife served the visitor breakfast.

When it became evident that Nishikaichi's limited English was of little use, Japanese-born Ishimatsu Shintani, a 60-year-old beekeeper, was summoned to help. When he arrived, the beekeeper was not at all happy about being asked to translate for the Japanese pilot. Shintani had lived in Hawaii for 41 years, and his children had been born there, so they were by birth American citizens. But Shintani himself was barred from U.S. citizenship by the law then applicable in the Territory of Hawaii. With his own background in mind, Shintani was nervous about becoming involved in this unusual situation. After he and Nishikaichi spoke briefly, Shintani was seen to turn pale, as though he had received a shock. The beekeeper then left the house without relaying much useful information to Kaleohano. Clearly, Kaleohano needed to find someone else to help him.

Next summoned to the scene were the Haradas, who spoke both Japanese and English. Yoshio Harada, 38, had been born to Japanese parents on Kauai in 1903. His birth in Hawaii made him an American citizen, but he had three brothers in Japan, and his wife, Irene, had been born to Japanese parents. Speaking Japanese, Nishikaichi told the Haradas of the attack on Oahu. He also demanded that his pistol and documents be returned. Because the Haradas knew the Niihauans regarded them as more Japanese than Hawaiian, they kept what Nishikaichi had said to themselves. That was the beginning of a sell-out that would cost them—as well as the nation—dearly.

Unaware that the United States was now at war with Japan, the Niihauans treated the pilot to a luau at a nearby house. Nishikaichi even sang a Japanese song at the gathering, accompanying himself on a borrowed guitar. He was probably wondering when the rescue submarine would arrive and send a shore party to escort him aboard. He was not going to be rescued by sub, however. A submarine had indeed been in the vicinity, but at 1:30 p.m. Hawaiian time its commander had been ordered to sail on toward Oahu and intercept any incoming American relief ships.

By nightfall, word of the attack on Pearl Harbor and the other Oahu military installations had reached Niihau by radio. The pilot was questioned anew, and Yoshio Harada realized he had better accurately report what Nishikaichi had told him.

Now the problem was what to do with the enemy pilot. Aylmer Robinson, Niihau's absentee landlord, lived on Kauai and made weekly visits to Niihau to look after family interests there. The island's former resident superintendent, John Rennie, had died in September, and Robinson had appointed Harada paymaster in Rennie's place. That had made Harada a man of stature on Niihau, and he was now torn between his American citizenship and his Japanese heritage. While the Niihauans debated what to do with the enemy interloper, Nishikaichi was lodged for the night at the home of John Kelly, the luau host. The Haradas stayed there with the pilot.

The next day Nishikaichi was taken by tractor to Kii Landing, near the northern tip of the island. Robinson's boat from Kauai docked at Kii when he made his inspection visits, and he was expected to arrive on December 8. Robinson did not appear, however. Unbeknown to the Niihauans, newly imposed wartime restrictions had precluded boat traffic across the 17-mile channel between the island and Kauai.

The time spent waiting at Kii was an opportunity for Nishikaichi and Harada to converse on the beach by themselves. The pilot apparently had sensed Harada's ambivalent loyalties, and he began to play on them. If the shaky defense of Oahu was a typical American response, he told the uncertain Harada, Japan was sure to win the war. Nishikaichi gradually won over Harada and, to some degree, Harada's wife Irene.

On Thursday, December 11, with the pilot still being treated as a guest, albeit not a very welcome one, Harada brought the beekeeper Shintani back into the picture. The three of them conferred privately at Harada's home, where Nishikaichi was then staying, and the following day Shintani appeared at Howard Kaleohano's house and demanded the papers he had taken from the plane. Kaleohano refused to give them up. Shintani muttered a threat, and Kaleohano threw him out.

At that point, Harada and the pilot realized they could not count on the old beekeeper, but they were determined to proceed with Nishikaichi's newly chosen plan for himself—death with honor. By now, the pilot was under casual guard by several Niihauans.

That same day Harada had stolen a shotgun and a pistol from the building near which the Zero had crashed—the Robinsons' ranch house, now unused and locked. Harada had been entrusted with a key. He loaded the firearms and took them to a warehouse used to store honey from the island's thriving beekeeping industry.

Returning home, Harada notified his wife and the pilot about the weapons he had secured. Only one of the four assigned guards was on duty at that point. When Nishikaichi asked to use the Haradas' outhouse, Harada accompanied him outside, followed by the guard. When the pilot emerged, Harada said he had something to attend to at the nearby honey warehouse. The unsuspecting guard accompanied them there. Thereupon Harada and Nishikaichi grabbed the hidden weapons and locked the guard in the warehouse.

Just then, the guard's wife appeared in a horse-drawn wagon. The two plotters commandeered the wagon and ordered the woman to drive them to Kaleohano's house, where they allowed the woman to flee on the horse. When they discovered that Kaleohano was not home, the pilot and Harada made a quick trip to the nearby downed plane, which was now guarded by a 16-year-old boy. Nishikaichi tried to work the radio, but to what purpose is uncertain. The two men then forced the young guard to go back to Kaleohano's house.

Now Kaleohano's apparent absence was explained when he suddenly rushed from his outhouse, where he had hidden in an effort to escape the armed duo. Harada leveled the shotgun and fired at him—but missed. Being shot at settled Kaleohano's politics, and he managed to get away from Harada and Nishikaichi. He rushed to the village and warned the residents, then borrowed a horse and headed for the northern tip of the island, intending to build a signal fire. First, however, Kaleohano stopped at his now deserted house and picked up the plane's papers, which he took to his mother-in-law's home.

The guard who had been locked in the warehouse was able to escape at that point and dashed to the village, where he corroborated Kaleohano's earlier story. As a result, nearly all of the villagers fled to remote areas of the island.

A bonfire had already been set on Mount Paniau, Niihau's highest point, by a group of alarmed men, but when Kaleohano arrived he decided that relying only on signals was too chancy. Shortly after midnight, he and five others set off in a lifeboat from Kii Landing to Waimea, on Kauai, a 10-hour pull against the wind.

Robinson, who had learned about the signal fire and was chaffing under the travel prohibition, was astounded when he received a phone call from Kaleohano in Waimea. For several days Robinson had been trying to get the commander of the Kauai Military District to send a boat to Niihau, but the Navy's ban on all boat traffic had frustrated his efforts. Now briefed by Kaleohano on the situation, Robinson finally received approval to organize a rescue mission.

In the meantime, Nishikaichi and Harada recaptured the escaped guard and forced him to walk through the deserted village, calling on any remaining inhabitants to come out of their houses. Only one man, Kaahakila Kalima, appeared, giving the renegades their second prisoner. They then returned to the plane, stripped off the Zero's machine guns and remaining ammunition and stowed them on a wagon. They also tried to burn the plane, but the fire they set in the cockpit did not spread. Harada sent Kalima to tell Irene that he would not be returning that night.

Then he and the pilot—apparently drunk with power—walked through the now silent village firing their weapons and yelling for Kaleohano to surrender.

Once away from his captors, Kalima made for the beach, where he found his wife along with Ben Kanahele and Ben's wife. Kanahele, 49, was a 6-foot native Hawaiian sheep rancher, noted for his prodigious strength. Kalima and Kanahele managed to avoid Nishikaichi and Harada and removed the machine-gun ammo from the wagon. But when they and their wives attempted to return to the village for food, they were captured.

After nightfall on December 12, Nishikaichi and Harada searched Kaleohano's house for the plane's papers, then burned it down in frustration. They then forced Ben Kanahele to search for Kaleohano. Kanahele, who knew that Kaleohano had left for Kauai, put on a show of calling for him.

Nishikaichi, now holding the shotgun and with the pistol stuck in his boot, told Kanahele that if he could not produce Kaleohano, he and all the others on the island would be shot. The placid Niihauans were normally slow to anger, but by this time the islanders had had enough. Speaking Hawaiian, Ben Kanahele demanded that Harada take away the pilot's pistol. Harada refused, but he indicated to Nishikaichi that he needed the shotgun.

As the pilot handed over the gun, Kanahele and his wife lunged at him. Nishikaichi was too quick for them. He yanked the pistol from his boot and shot Kanahele in the chest, hip and groin. Enraged, the big Hawaiian grabbed the pilot, hoisted him in the air and threw him against a nearby stone wall. Grabbing a rock, Kanahele's wife began to bash the fallen pilot's head. Kanahele then drew a knife and slit Nishikaichi's throat. Harada, no doubt realizing that he had abetted a disastrous chain of events, jammed the shotgun muzzle into his own gut and pulled the trigger.

When an Army rescue party from Kauai finally arrived the

following morning, it seemed that the remarkable episode was over. But that was not the end of the story.

Ben Kanahele recovered from his wounds. In August 1945 he was awarded two presidential citations, the Medal of Merit and the Purple Heart.

For his peripheral part in the Niihau incident, Ishimatsu Shintani was taken into custody and interned on the U.S. mainland throughout the war. He blamed Japan more than the United States for his actions. With the postwar repeal of racial barriers to immigration, he became a naturalized American citizen in 1960.

Irene Harada lost not only her husband but also her freedom. Thought to be a Japanese spy, she was jailed on Kauai on December 15, 1941. She was transferred to a military prison on Oahu, where she was reportedly questioned but held her silence. Irene was released in late 1944 and returned to Niihau, embittered for life.

The actions of Shintani and the Haradas, all Niihauans of Japanese ancestry, were noted in a January 1942 Navy report as indications of the "likelihood that Japanese residents previously believed loyal to the United States may aid Japan." With the nation in an uproar over the sneak attack on Pearl Harbor, there can be no doubt that the Niihau event influenced the administration of President Franklin D. Roosevelt to summarily remove more than 100,000 persons of Japanese ancestry from the West Coast and intern them in the U.S. interior.

In Hashihama, Japan, the hometown of young pilot Shigenori Nishikaichi, there is a stone column that was erected in his honor. Chiseled in granite is a version of his exploits over Oahu that claims he died "in battle." Also engraved there are the words: "His meritorious deed will live forever."

Why Hitler Declared War on the United States

By Gerhard L. Weinberg

When news of the Japanese attack on Pearl Harbor reached Germany, its leadership was absorbed by the crisis in its war with the Soviet Union. On December 1, 1941, after the serious defeat the Red Army administered to the German forces at the southern end of the Eastern Front, Adolf Hitler had relieved Field Marshal Gerd von Rundstedt, the commander in chief of the army group fighting there: the next day Hitler flew to the army group headquarters in the southern Ukraine. Late on December 3 he flew back to his headquarters in East Prussia, only to be greeted by more bad news: The German army group at the northern end of the Russian front was also being pushed back by Red Army counterattacks. Most ominous of all, the German offensive in the center, toward Moscow, not only had exhausted itself but was in danger of being overwhelmed by a Soviet counteroffensive. Not yet recognizing the extent of the defeat all along the front, Hitler and his generals saw their reverses merely as a temporary halt in German offensive operations.

The reality was just beginning to sink in when the German

leaders got news of Japan's attack on Pearl Harbor. On the evening of December 8, within hours of hearing about the previous day's attack, Hitler ordered that at any opportunity the German navy should sink American ships and those of Central and South American countries that had declared their solidarity with the United States. That evening, too, he left East Prussia by train for Berlin, but not before sending out a summons to the members of the German parliament, the Reichstag, to meet on December 11 and, in a formal session that would be broadcast to the whole country, declare war on the United States.

Why this eagerness to go to war with yet another great power, and at a time when Germany already faced a serious situation on the Eastern Front? Some have argued that it was an irrational reaction by Hitler to his failure to take Moscow; some have attributed the delay of a few days to reluctance on Hitler's part, when it had more to do with the fact that Japan's initiative had caught the Germans by surprise; still others imagine that Germany had finally reacted to America's policy of aiding Britain, even though in all his prior declarations of war Hitler had paid scant heed to the policies, for or against Germany, of the countries invaded. Ideological considerations and strategic priorities as Germany saw them were always more important. The most recent case was that of the Soviet Union, which had been providing critical supplies to Germany until minutes before the German attack of June 22, 1941.

The reality is that war with the United States had been included in Hitler's agenda for years, that he had deferred hostilities only because he wanted to begin them at a time, and under circumstances, of his own choosing, and that the Japanese attack fitted his requirements precisely. It had been an assumption of Hitler's since the 1920s that Germany would at some point fight the United States. Already in the summer of 1928 he had asserted in his second book (not published until I did it for him in 1961, as

Hitlers zweites Buch) that strengthening and preparing Germany for war with the United States was one of the tasks of the National Socialist movement. Because his aims for Germany's future entailed an unlimited expansion and because he thought the United States might at some time constitute a challenge to German domination of the globe, a war with the United States had long been a part of the future he envisioned. It would come either during his own rule or during that of his successors.

During the years of his chancellorship before 1939, German policies designed to implement the project of a war with the United States had been conditioned by two factors: belief in the truth of the stab-in-the-back legend on the one hand and the practical problems of engaging American military power on the other. The former, the widespread belief that Germany had lost the First World War because of the collapse at home rather than defeat at the front, automatically carried with it a converse of enormous significance, and one that has generally been ignored. The more credence one gave to the stab in the back, the more negligible the military role of the United States in that conflict seemed. To Hitler and to many others in Germany, the idea that American participation had enabled the Western powers to hold on in 1918 and then move toward victory was not a reasonable explanation of the events of that year but a legend instead.

Only those Germans who remained unenlightened by nationalist euphoria could believe that American forces had played any significant role in the past or would do so in the future. A solid German home front, which National Socialism would ensure, could preclude defeat next time. The problem of fighting the United States was not that the inherently weak and divided Americans could create, field, and support effective fighting forces. Rather it was that the intervening ocean could be blocked by a large American fleet.

Unlike the German navy of the pre-1914 era, in which discussions were really debates about the relative merits of landing on Cape Cod versus landing on Long Island, the German government of the 1930s took a more practical approach. In line with its emphasis on building up the air force, specifications were issued in 1937 and 1938 for what became the Me 264 and was soon referred to inside the government as the "America bomber" or the "New York bomber." The "America bomber" would be capable of carrying a five-ton load of bombs to New York or a smaller load to the Midwest, or of flying reconnaissance missions over the West Coast and then returning to Germany without refueling at intermediate bases. Several types and models were experimented with, the first prototype flying in December 1940, but none of them advanced beyond preliminary models.

Instead, Hitler and his advisers came to concentrate ever more on the concept of acquiring bases for the German air force on the coast of northwest Africa, as well as on the Spanish and Portuguese islands off the African coast, to shorten the distance to the Western Hemisphere. Hitler also held discussions with his naval advisers and with Japanese diplomats about bombing the United States from the Azores; but those consultations did not take place until 1940 and 1941. In the meantime, prewar planning had shifted its focus to naval matters.

Like the Japanese, the Germans in the 1930s faced the question of how to cope with the American navy in the furtherance of their expansionist ambitions; without the slightest consultation, and in complete and deliberate ignorance of each other's projects, the two governments came to exactly the same conclusion. In both countries the decision was to trump American quantity with quality, to build super-battleships, which by their vastly greater size could carry far heavier armament that could fire over greater distances and thus would be able to destroy the American battleships at ranges the enemy's guns could not match.

The Japanese began constructing four such super-battleships

in great secrecy. The Germans hoped to construct six super-battleships; their plans were worked out early in 1939 and the keels laid in April and May. These 56,200-ton monsters would outclass not only the new U.S. battleships of the North Carolina class then beginning to be built but even the successor Iowa class.

The precise details of how a war with the United States would actually be conducted was not a subject to which Hitler or his associates devoted a great deal of attention. When the time came, something could always be worked out; it was more important to prepare the prerequisites for success.

When World War II began in September 1939, work ceased on those portions of the blue-water navy not already near completion; that included the super-battleships. The immediate exigencies of the war took precedence over projects that could not be finished in the near future. Almost immediately, however, the German navy urged steps that would bring the United States into the war. Admiral Erich Raeder, the navy's commander in chief, could hardly wait to go to war with the United States. He hoped that the increase in sinkings of merchant shipping, including American, that would result from a completely unrestricted submarine campaign would have a major impact on Britain, whose surface navy Germany could not yet defeat. But Hitler held back. As he saw it, what was the point of marginally increasing U-boat sinkings when Germany had neither a major surface navy yet nor bases for it to operate from?

The spring of 1940 appeared to provide the opportunity to remedy both deficiencies. The conquest of Norway in April immediately produced two relevant decisions: First, Norway would be incorporated into the Third Reich, and second, a major permanent base for Germany's new navy would be built on the Norwegian—now German—coast at Trondheim. In addition, a large, entirely German city would be built there, with the whole complex to be connected directly to mainland Germany by special roads, bridges, and railways. Work on this colossal project continued until the spring of 1943.

The conquest of the Low Countries and France, soon after that of Norway, appeared to open further prospects. In the eyes of Hitler and his associates, the war in the West was over; they could turn to their next objectives. On land that meant an invasion of the Soviet Union, a simple task that Hitler originally hoped to complete in the fall of 1940. At sea, it meant that the problem of making war on the United States could be tackled.

On July 11, 1940, Hitler ordered the resumption of the naval construction program. The super-battleships, together with hundreds of other warships, could now be built. While that program went forward, the Germans not only would construct the naval base at Trondheim and take over the French naval bases on the Atlantic coast, but would push a land connection to the Strait of Gibraltar—if Germany could control Spain as it did France. It would then be easy to acquire and develop air and sea bases in French and Spanish northwest Africa, as well as on the Spanish and Portuguese islands in the Atlantic. In a war with the United States, they would be the perfect advance bases for the new fleet and for airplanes that did not yet meet the earlier extravagant specifications for long-range flight.

These rosy prospects did not work out. Whatever Francisco Franco's enthusiasm for joining the war on the side of Germany, and whatever his willingness to assist his friend in Berlin, the Spanish dictator was a nationalist who was not about to yield Spanish sovereignty to anyone else—neither in territory now held by Spain nor in French and British holdings that he expected to pick up as a reward for joining the Axis. The fact that the German leadership in 1940 was willing to sacrifice the participation of Spain as an equal fighting partner rather than give up on their hopes for German-controlled bases on and off the coast of northwest Africa is an excellent indication of the priority that they assigned to their concept of war with the United States. Franco's offer of the use of Spanish bases was not enough for them: German sovereignty was what they believed their schemes required. When the Spanish foreign minister went to Berlin in September 1940, and when Hitler and Franco met on the French-Spanish border in October, it was the sovereignty issue that caused a fundamental rift between the prospective partners in war.

But it was not only the bases that proved elusive. As the preparations for war with the Soviet Union made another reallocation of armament resources necessary in the late fall of 1940, the construction of the blue-water navy was again halted. Once more Hitler had to restrain the enthusiasm of the German navy for war with the United States. The navy believed that in World War II, as in World War I, the way to defeat Great Britain lay in unrestricted submarine warfare, even if that meant bringing the United States into the conflict. But Hitler was doubtful whether what had failed the last time would work now; he had other ideas for coping with Britain, such as bombing and possibly invading it. When it came to taking on the United States, he recognized that he could not do so without a large surface navy. It was at this point that Japan came into the picture.

Since the Germans had long regarded a war with the Western powers as the major and most difficult prerequisite for an easy conquest of the Soviet Union, and since it appeared to them that Japan's ambitions in East Asia clashed with British, French, and American interests, Berlin had tried for years to achieve Japanese participation in an alliance directed against the West. The authorities in Tokyo had been happy to work with Germany in general, but major elements in the Japanese government had been reluctant to fight Britain and France. Some preferred a war with the Soviet Union; others were worried about a war with the United States, which they saw as a likely result of war with Britain and

France; still others thought that it would be best to settle the war with China first; and some held a combination of these views.

In any case, all German efforts to rope Japan into an alliance actively opposing the West had failed. The German reaction to this failure—their signing of a nonaggression pact with the Soviet Union in 1939—had only served to alienate some of their best friends in a Japan that was then engaged in open hostilities with the Soviet Union on the border between their respective East Asian puppet states of Manchukuo and Mongolia.

In Tokyo's view, the defeat of the Netherlands and France the following year, and the need of the British to concentrate on defense of the home islands, appeared to open the colonial empires of Southeast Asia to easy conquest. From the perspective of Berlin, the same lovely prospects lay in front of the Japanese—but there was no reason to let them have all this without some military contribution to the common cause of maximum looting. That contribution would lie in pouncing on the British Empire in Southeast Asia, especially Singapore, before Britain had followed France and Holland into defeat, not after. It would, moreover, at one stroke solve the problem of how to deal with the United States.

In the short run, Japanese participation in the war would divert American attention and resources from the Atlantic to the Pacific. In the long run, and of even greater importance, the Axis would acquire a huge and effective navy. At a time when the United States had a navy barely adequate for one ocean, the Panama Canal made it possible to move that navy from the Pacific to the Atlantic, and back. This was the basic concern behind the American desire for a two-ocean navy, authorized by Congress in July 1940. Since it would be years before that two-ocean navy was completed, there would be a lengthy interval when any major American involvement in a Pacific conflict would make substantial support of Britain in the Atlantic impossible. Furthermore, it obviously made no difference in which ocean American warships were sunk.

For Germany in the meantime, the obvious alternative to building its own navy was to find an ally who already had one. The Germans believed that Japan's navy in 1940–41 was the strongest and best in the world (and it is quite possible that this assessment was correct). It is in this framework of expectations that one can perhaps more easily understand the curious, apparently self-contradictory policy toward the United States that the Germans followed in 1941.

On the one hand, Hitler repeatedly ordered restraint on the German navy to avoid incidents in the Atlantic that might prematurely bring the United States into the war against Germany. Whatever steps the Americans might take in their policy of aiding Great Britain, Hitler would not take these as a pretext to go to war with the United States until he thought the time proper: American lend-lease legislation no more affected his policy toward the United States than the simultaneous vast increase in Soviet assistance to Germany influenced his decision to go to war with that country.

On the other hand, he repeatedly promised the Japanese that if they believed war with the United States was an essential part of a war against Britain, Germany would join them in such a conflict. Hitler personally made this pledge to Foreign Minister Matsuoka Yosuke when the latter visited Germany early in April 1941; it was repeated on various occasions thereafter. The apparent contradiction is easily resolved if one keeps in mind what was central in the thinking of the German leader and soon became generally understood in the German government: As long as Germany had to face the United States by itself, it needed time to build its own blue-water navy; it therefore made sense to postpone hostilities with the Americans. If, however, Japan came into the war on Germany's side, that problem would be automatically solved.

This approach also makes it easier to understand why the Germans were not particular about the sequence: If Japan decided to go to war in the spring or summer of 1941, even before the German invasion of the Soviet Union, that would be fine, and Germany would immediately join in. When it appeared, however, that Japanese-American negotiations in the spring and summer might lead to some agreement, the Germans tried hard to torpedo those talks. One way was by drawing Japan into the war through the back door, as it were. At a time when the Germans were still certain that the eastern campaign was headed for a quick and victorious resolution, they attempted—unsuccessfully—to persuade the Japanese to attack the Soviet Union.

During the summer of 1941, while the Japanese seemed to the Germans to be hesitating, the German campaign in the Soviet Union appeared to be going perfectly. The first and most immediate German reaction was a return to its program of naval construction. In the weapons technology of the 1930s and 1940s, big warships were the system with the longest lead time from orders to completion. The German leaders were entirely aware of this and highly sensitive to its implications. Whenever the opportunity appeared to be there, they turned first to the naval construction program. Once again, however, in 1941 as in 1940, the prospect of prompt victory over the immediate foe faded from view, and once again work on the big warships had to be halted. (But the Germans, despite their much-vaunted organization, failed to cancel an engine contract; in June 1944 they were offered four useless battleship engines.) Stopping the battleship construction only accented the hope that Japan would move, as well as the enthusiasm with which such an action would be greeted.

Just as the Germans had not kept the Japanese informed of their plans to attack other countries, so the Japanese kept the Germans in the dark. When Tokyo was ready to move, it had only to check with the Germans (and Italians) to make sure that they remained as willing to go to war against the United States as they had repeatedly asserted they were. In late November and again at the beginning of December, the Germans reassured the Japanese that they had nothing to worry about. Germany, like Italy, was eager to go to war with the United States—provided Japan took the plunge.

There were two ways in which the German declaration of war on the United States would differ from her procedure in going to war with other countries: the timing and the absence of internal opposition. In all other cases, the timing of war had been essentially in Germany's own hands. Now the date would be selected by an ally that moved when it was ready and without previously notifying the Germans. When Hitler met with the Japanese foreign minister back in April, he had not known that Japan would dither for months; he also did not know, the last time Tokyo checked with him, that on this occasion the Japanese intended to move immediately.

As a result, Hitler was caught out of town at the time of Pearl Harbor and had to get back to Berlin and summon the Reichstag to declare war. His great worry, and that of his foreign minister, Joachim von Ribbentrop, was that the Americans might get their declaration of war in ahead of his own. As Ribbentrop explained it, "A great power does not allow itself to be declared war upon; it declares war on others."

Just to make sure that hostilities started immediately, however, Hitler had already issued orders to his navy, straining at the leash since October 1939, to begin sinking American ships forthwith, even before the formalities of a declaration. Now that Germany had a big navy on its side, there was no need to wait even an hour. The very fact that the Japanese had started hostilities the way Germany had begun its attack on Yugoslavia earlier that year, with a Sunday morning attack in peacetime, showed what a delightfully appropriate ally Japan would be. The American navy would now be smashed in the Pacific and thus incapable of aiding Britain, while American troops and supplies would be diverted to that theater as well.

The second way in which this German declaration of war differed from most that had preceded it was in the absence of opposition at home. For once the frenetic applause of the unanimous Reichstag, the German parliament last elected in 1938, reflected a unanimous government and military leadership. In World War I, it was agreed, Germany had not been defeated at the front but had succumbed to the collapse of a home front deluded by Woodrow Wilson's siren songs from across the Atlantic; now there was to be no danger of a new stab in the back. The opponents of the regime at home had been silenced. Its imagined Jewish enemies were already being slaughtered, with hundreds of thousands killed by the time of Hitler's speech of December 11, 1941. Now that Germany had a strong Japanese navy at its side, victory was considered certain.

From the perspective of half a century, one can see an additional unintended consequence of Pearl Harbor for the Germans. It not only meant that they would most certainly be defeated. It also meant that the active coalition against them would include the United States as well as Great Britain, its dominions, the Free French, various governments-in-exile, and the Soviet Union. And without U.S. participation, there could have been no massive invasion of northwest Europe; the Red Army eventually might have reached the English Channel and the Atlantic, overrunning all Germany in the process. If the Germans today enjoy both their freedom and their unity in a country aligned and allied with what their leaders of 1941 considered the degenerate Western democracies, they owe it in part to the disastrous cupidity and stupidity of the Japanese attack on Pearl Harbor.

1942

Japanese Amphibious Fiasco in the Philippines

By John W. Whitman

U nhappy with the pace of Japan's conquest of the Philippines, General Masaharu Homma ordered Lieutenant Colonel Nariyoshi Tsunehiro to lead his men on an amphibious operation that was intended to sweep the Americans from Bataan.

Although the vast majority of amphibious assaults during World War II succeeded, there were a few failures, the best known being the British raid on Dieppe, France, in August 1942. Less well known was an incredibly costly Japanese amphibious assault against American and Filipino beach defenders the same year.

When the Japanese invaded the Philippines in December 1941, they drove Lt. Gen. Douglas MacArthur's newly mobilized Philippine army onto the Bataan Peninsula. United States Army Forces in the Far East (USAFFE) now had the mission of holding the entrance to Manila Bay until reinforcements arrived. Once on Bataan, the Japanese ran into stiff resistance from the Filipinos and a small number of U.S. Army Regulars. Finding themselves behind schedule, the Japanese hoped to speed their conquest of Bataan by launching an amphibious landing on the left flank of the Filipino lines, along Bataan's west coast. Such a landing would outflank Maj. Gen. Jonathan M. Wainwright's I Philippine Corps and possibly collapse its defensive line.

Lieutenant General Masaharu Homma, commander of the Japanese Fourteenth Army, met on January 14, 1942, with Maj. Gen. Naoki Kimura, commander of the 16th Division's Infantry Group. Homma told Kimura that he was concerned about the slow progress that his men were making on the east coast, pointing out that the stalemate on the west coast opposite Wainwright's I Corps was equally unacceptable.

Homma noted that amphibious operations had proved successful against the British in Malaya. There, Lt. Gen. Tomoyuki Yamashita had cut behind British lines, avoided costly frontal attacks and forced the British to withdraw. Homma published an operations order late on the evening of January 15, putting Kimura in charge of the effort against Bataan's west coast and transferring all units there to him. Homma also ordered landing craft moved from Lingayen Gulf to the port of Olongapo, in Subic Bay. Planners established Caibobo Point as the operation's beachhead and the West Road as its objective, to be seized at all costs. The West Road was the only north-south road on the west side of Bataan. Capturing it would sever communications between the front-line units of the Philippine I Corps and cut off their supplies.

Kimura selected Lt. Col. Nariyoshi Tsunehiro's 2nd Battalion, 20th Infantry Regiment, to make the watery end run. Tsunehiro's men already had some amphibious experience under their belts, having stormed ashore along Luzon's east coast just three weeks earlier. At that time, they had been part of a division-size landing supported by the Japanese navy.

This time, Tsunehiro's infantry would be the sole assault force. The amphibious operation, however, was not to be a totally independent affair. When Homma made his decision to flank the

I Corps by sea, Japanese infantry had already penetrated Wainwright's main line. The amphibious operation would support Kimura's overland thrust after he defeated the I Corps and turned against the II Corps. If the Japanese succeeded and could reinforce their beachhead, they could destroy the I Corps by cutting off its line of retreat. With the I Corps gone, there would be little possibility of prolonged resistance from the II Corps, and the battle for Bataan would be over.

The amphibious attack would fall on the Bataan Service Command. In addition to the two infantry corps on the main line of resistance, a third corps area, the Service Command, administered and defended the southern third of the peninsula. The Service Command had at first been responsible for all coastal defense, but now it held only those beaches generally even with, and south of, Mariveles Mountain, roughly the lower third of the peninsula. Even with this reduced responsibility, it had to defend 40 miles of rugged terrain with scant resources.

Service Command had three major and several minor organizations with which to accomplish its mission. The 1st Philippine Constabulary Regiment (Filipino policemen turned into infantrymen) defended the west coast down to Mariveles, the 4th Constabulary guarded the coast between Mariveles and Cabcaben, and the 2nd Constabulary held the area from Cabcaben north to Limay. Those three regiments were part of the brand new 2nd Regular Division, whose designation was a serious misnomer, since its men were not Regulars and the poorly equipped outfit could hardly be classified as a real division.

Brigadier General Clyde A. Selleck had the mission of guarding the southwest sector of the Bataan coast. Selleck was the 71st Division commander, but he was missing the combat elements of his division, which had been detached to another unit. He retained only his division's headquarters, service troops and a reduced battalion of artillery. To compensate for his detached infantry regiments, he had a mixed bag of sailors, Marines, airmen, Constabulary and Philippine army troops. Some American airmen were serving as infantrymen after their planes had been destroyed. They had salvaged heavy machine guns from wrecked aircraft, fitted the weapons with improvised firing mechanisms and positioned them to overlook potential landing sites. Selleck's orders were to defend his sector against amphibious operations. If the Japanese established a foothold, he was to isolate them and drive them back into the sea.

Selleck had to construct obstacles, position his units along the beaches deemed most suitable for landings, maintain observation posts and ensure that a battalion-size reserve was ready to move by bus on 30 minutes' notice. As it developed, the men had two weeks to prepare themselves before the Japanese stepped ashore, and they put that time to good use. Selleck's men cut and improved trails to the more important peninsulas along the coast. The grounded American airmen were so intent on learning their duties and upgrading their positions that there was a marked strengthening in the defenses every day.

Selleck's men strung barbed wire, established a network of lookouts and connected their units by wire and radio. Four 6-inch naval guns became available, although Selleck had managed to mount only two of them before the Japanese landed. One gun was scheduled for Quinauan Point, where most of the Japanese would land, but the cement was still wet on the mounting platform when the enemy overran that position. Anti-aircraft artillerymen had selected locations for searchlights, but the lights arrived too late to be of use.

By January 22, after much effort, Selleck had on beach defense the 17th Pursuit Squadron; the 3rd Battalion, 1st Constabulary; the 34th Pursuit Squadron; the 2nd Battalion, 1st Constabulary; the 3rd Pursuit Squadron; and the Naval Battalion. In reserve were the 1st Battalion, 1st Constabulary, and the 20th and 21st Pursuit squadrons.

Luckily for Selleck, the Japanese were ill-prepared for the important venture they were about to embark upon. With time short, they omitted the detailed planning and preparations so necessary to amphibious operations. Although Japan had more than 2,600 years of amphibious operations experience, in this case the planners failed to assign any naval combat vessels as escorts. The vast naval armada that had carried the Fourteenth Army to the Philippines a month earlier had long since departed for other duties. Perhaps the Japanese considered this operation more like a river crossing than a true amphibious exercise, thus the absence of naval support.

But the most significant problem with their approach was that they had badly overestimated their own prowess and, more-over, underestimated the determination of their opponents. To land a single infantry battalion more than 10 miles behind enemy lines and expect that unit to go on the attack, cut the main supply route of a corps and then seize a huge mountain defies all logic. The entire operation was based on two faulty assumptions: that the Filipinos were collapsing, and that the Japanese penetration of I Corps' main line of resistance would allow for a quick linkup. The Japanese planners apparently believed that all that was needed to tumble the I Corps was an amphibious landing.

The only map of the coast that Japanese planners could find was 1:200,000 scale, completely useless in locating landing beaches on a rugged shoreline. To better prepare for the invasion, the planners sent several planes roaring along the coast, hardly 100 yards from the shore, to take pictures. Mapmakers then produced an aerial photograph on which planners sketched a seaborne route from Moron south to Caibobo Point, and an offshoot of another route to Quinauan Point and Agloloma Bay. To add to navigational difficulties, the coast along the west side of Bataan blended into Mariveles Mountain so well that it was difficult to distinguish headland from cove even during the day. From the sea, the coast presented a formidable appearance, with very high, timbered banks rising to tall mountains. At night, distinguishing a headland from a cove would prove nearly impossible.

Colonel Tsunehiro's 2nd Battalion, 20th Infantry (reinforced), embarked from Mayagao Point north of Moron on the night of January 22 and immediately sailed into trouble. The 900 men encountered strong tides, pitch-black skies and rough seas. Throughout the night, initial Japanese attempts to land at the predetermined site—Caibobo Point—met with failure. Allied troops manning listening posts on the island had heard boat engines barely 200 yards out to sea, but it was so dark that the observers could not see a thing.

As the barges nosed closer to shore, personnel from the grounded 17th Pursuit Squadron fired on the invaders with their .50-caliber machine guns. The barges presented their vulnerable sides to the guns when they tried to back away, and the heavy bullets chewed through the nearest craft and cut down many of the Japanese infantrymen. The barrels of the 17th Pursuit's machine guns glowed red as thousands of rounds arched over the water at the packed barges. Men operating a battery of 75mm guns ranged the boats and then fired for effect. Many of the Japanese survivors abandoned the doomed craft and swam to barges farther offshore. After rescuing the bedraggled survivors, the Japanese sailed south. By now the navigators were badly confused and the boats scattered.

Next the Japanese edged to the east and found a more hospitable piece of terrain—Quinauan Point—although they still had no idea where they were. There, Japanese troops splashed ashore on the rocky beach without meeting any opposition. Their boats rattled and banged against rocks, and the soldiers shouted and sang as they landed. Although the American airmen could hear the Japanese, the defenders were set up along the wrong beaches to do much about it. Meanwhile, 600 Japanese proceeded to climb Quinauan's nearly vertical dirt cliffs. For the moment, the invaders were safe—they had landed where no one thought they would.

A second group of 300 Japanese landed at Longoskawayan Point, 11 miles south of the intended landing spot. They came ashore at a ridge running off the hill mass of Mariveles Mountain, only 3,000 yards from Mariveles Harbor. If they could grab the key terrain there—617-foot-tall Mount Pucot—they could gain control of the high ground, which might enable them to block the main road along the west coast, dominate Mariveles Harbor and control the road out of Mariveles with their light artillery. Of course, they would have to be reinforced, for 300 soldiers could not do that much on their own. Mount Pucot sat on Lapiay Point, just north of Longoskawayan and only 1,000 yards from the strategically important West Road.

When the empty landing craft headed back toward the Japanese ships, they came across a U.S. Navy PT-boat. Ensign Barron W. Chandler commanded patrol torpedo boat PT-34, 70 feet long, 20 feet wide and powered by three Packard engines. Four torpedo tubes and four .50-caliber machine guns in two twin mounts were its main armament. Chandler had just finished a routine patrol off Subic Bay when he sighted an unidentified craft two miles off Canas Point. As the two boats converged, the unknown craft blinked a dim, unintelligible series of white dots and dashes. Chandler changed course, increased speed and closed on the vessel. Still not sure what it was, Lieutenant John D. Bulkeley, the squadron commander, yelled "Boat ahoy." The answer was immediate. Japanese machine-gun bullets ripped through the boat from 25 yards' range, hitting Chandler in both ankles.

The PT-boat's .50-caliber guns rattled into action at 0442 hours, joined by automatic rifle fire from engine room personnel, who fired over the sides. The Japanese landing craft increased speed to 18 knots and headed for Bagac Bay. PT-34 circled the 47-foot craft three times, all the while firing into its vulnerable flanks. Under this pounding, the Japanese craft sank lower and lower before eventually disappearing beneath the waves.

Sixteen minutes after the first shot was fired, only Chandler's boat remained in the immediate area. It was too dark to look for survivors, but PT-34 stayed in the area for the next 90 minutes, searching for more Japanese boats. When the Americans moved closer to shore in their search, friendly machine-gun and 3-inch shore battery fire forced them out to sea.

Just before dawn, Lieutenant Bulkeley sighted a second landing barge three miles offshore, and PT-34 headed out at full speed to investigate. The enemy craft increased its speed to 15 knots and pushed north. PT-34 overtook the Japanese and opened fire from 400 yards, a more prudent distance than in the previous engagement. After a tracer round hit the Japanese barge's fuel tank, the boat started to burn and drift.

As PT-34 closed the distance, the barge tried to ram it. The American sailors threw a couple of hand grenades at the vessel, taking the fight out of the Japanese. Then Bulkeley boarded the enemy barge—which turned out to be empty except for one dead and two wounded Japanese, one of them an officer. Bulkeley was collecting the muster record of the landing party and the operations plan when the boat sank beneath him. He managed to tread water and keep his two prisoners afloat until the sailors on PT-34 fished them out.

Because of the tide, heavy seas and darkness, the Japanese—relying on inadequate maps and now widely separated from one another—had come ashore at two different points, neither of which was specified in the plan. Disorganized and lost, they had only one advantage over the Americans—they had come ashore where no one expected them to.

Even that slim advantage soon evaporated. American and Filipino beach defenders and local reserves located and then attacked the invading troops. They soon had them contained. The airmen and Constabulary troops were not sufficiently trained or equipped to be able to evict the invaders, but the Japanese were too few in number to be able to break out of their beachheads. General Kimura was unwilling to abandon them to their fate, but his reinforcement attempts were piecemeal and ineffective.

A single company of Japanese infantry from the 1st Battalion, 20th Infantry, with two small artillery pieces boarded landing craft at Olongapo on January 26. They also loaded extra food and ammunition for their comrades at Quinauan. Amazingly, the Japanese had not learned about the 300 men who had landed farther south at Longoskawayan. Under the light of a disappearing first quarter moon, the rifle company shoved off from Olongapo's docks at midnight, cruised out of Subic Bay and made the 30-mile trip in three hours.

Once again, poor seamanship, a dark night and difficulty with spotting landmarks along Bataan's coast muddled the attackers and brought them 2,000 yards short of their objective. From offshore, the points and bays so easily identified on maps merged into a solid mass of woods, appearing as an unbroken curved shoreline. Some Filipino artillery rounds splashed near the Japanese, a few boats ran aground on reefs, and the bulk of the ammunition could not be landed. Like its predecessors, this company was now lost, on its own and quickly blocked by American and Filipino troops.

Up to that point, Japanese efforts to land and cut the West Road had been a mess, and the situation did not improve as time went on. The Japanese now decided once again to reinforce their original failures. As before, however, too few troops were given too large a mission. The planners decided on January 27 to use the rest of the 1st Battalion, 20th Infantry, to reinforce Quinauan Point and seize Mariveles Mountain. Major Mitsuo Kimura's battalion moved to Olongapo and embarked for the trip to Quinauan. There was little time to plan or rehearse, since Kimura received his orders on January 31 and had to sail the next evening.

The 500-man battalion had been in trouble even before it left friendly shores on February 1. On January 28, a Filipino patrol on Bataan's east coast had found a mimeographed order on the body of a dead Japanese officer, revealing enemy intentions to reinforce the western landings and drive to Mariveles Mountain. The decision to reinforce the Quinauan effort had been made only the day before. Confirmation of Japanese intentions came on January 30, when Philippine Scouts captured a Japanese aerial mosaic of the west coast, indicating that the enemy's ultimate objective was the capture of the West Road.

There were also signs of pending reinforcements at Quinauan Point itself. At dusk on February 1, a Japanese ship sailed very close to the point, as if to draw fire. Some observers on the shore thought it was a minelayer or minesweeper, and the American troops could see sailors aboard scanning the coast through binoculars. The Americans took immediate action to counter the expected landings. Staff officers alerted observers along the west coast and dispatched one of the two American light-tank battalions to the threatened area. The 3rd Battalion, 45th Infantry (Philippine Scouts), on Quinauan Point emplaced heavy and light machine guns on both the north and south shores of the peninsula. Philippine Scouts of the 2nd Battalion set up 12.30-caliber machine guns to cover Silaiim Bay and the sea.

The crews of Curtiss P-40 fighters, concealed under jungle foliage, went on alert just after dark. Ground crews fueled the planes and armed them with three 100-pound anti-personnel bombs under each wing, as well as .50-caliber machine-gun ammunition. Mechanics rolled the planes from their protective revetments along jungle paths to the airfields, where they stood ready for immediate takeoff. Here was a chance for the defenders to take the initiative and lash out at the Japanese before they could land. Everyone waited tensely. The weather was good—the skies were clear and the moon was up.

With his plan already compromised, Major Kimura encountered still another serious problem once his flotilla sailed. Three U.S. Navy signalmen perched in a treetop observation post spotted the boats in the light of a full moon. They sounded the alarm via a direct telephone line to Wainwright's I Corps command post. The carefully laid defense plan—the first coordinated air-sea-land action of the campaign—then slipped into gear. Navy PT-boats sped into the area, and the Philippine Scouts' 26th Cavalry Regiment boarded Bren-gun carriers and buses and left the I Corps reserve for Caibobo Point.

Four P-40s from the 17th Pursuit Squadron roared off from dirt airstrips, climbed over Mariveles Mountain and dropped toward the sea to attack the 12 or more Japanese barges. The first P-40 swept over the trees, its Allison engine screaming, then flashed over the water and dropped six fragmentation bombs squarely amid the lumbering troop-laden barges. "Oh, it was a wonderful sight," recalled Private Henry S. Winslow, a 21-year-old Iowan who watched from the shore. "We knew we were really giving it to them. It was a wonderful feeling."

The low-flying pilots dropped down for a second pass and subjected the barges to murderous .50-caliber fire from their six wing-mounted guns. Five of the barges sank, carrying most of the equipment- and ammunition-encumbered troops with them. The P-40 blitz came as a shock to the Japanese, who had been confident of their aerial superiority in the area.

All the American aircraft returned to base, landed safely and rearmed for another strike. Ground personnel serviced the P-40s, which continued to fly sortie after sortie. The ground crews were amazed to see the planes encrusted with salt spray kicked up from the sea. Excited pilots regaled the mechanics with stories about the bright moon lighting the sea as if it were day. After eight sorties—flown singly as soon as a plane was rearmed—four fresh pilots replaced the original four and took off for yet another strike.

Down along the coast, Filipino 155mm guns of E Battery, 301st Artillery, and then Philippine Scout 75mm cannons of D Battery, 88th Artillery, found the range of Kimura's barges. They were joined by the heavy .50-caliber ground-mounted machine guns from Philippine Scout and U.S. Army Air Forces units. The rain of shells and heavy machine-gun fire cut swathes in the Japanese infantry crowding the tightly packed barges. When the Japanese drew closer to shore, Philippine infantry added their light machine-gun and rifle fire to the uproar. So did soldiers of the Filipino 12th Infantry. Tracers ricocheted in every direction from the barges and boats and the sea itself.

Corporal Robert Vogler was serving as second gunner on a .50-caliber gun, one of three that had been collected by the 17th Pursuit Squadron and were now dug in on the beach barely 18 inches above the high-water mark. "They brought in the barges with a launch and then threw them sideways and we opened up on them," Vogler later recalled. "It was shooting at less than a hundred yards. Beautiful!" Tracers and ball ammo punched in at water level and exploded out the other side. The gunners had earlier changed the ratio of balls to tracers and were now shooting one tracer to every three ball rounds. The heavy slugs wreaked havoc in the wooden-sided barges.

Lieutenant Vincent E. Schumacher's PT-32 got into the battle somewhat late, firing machine guns and two torpedoes at the Japanese minelayer *Yaeyama*, which was supporting the attack. The crew had seen gun flashes along the coast, and despite the fact that the PT-boat's hull was jury-rigged with wires and braces, Schumacher and his crew headed for the fight. *Yaeyama* pinned PT-32 with a bright searchlight and began firing two-gun salvos. PT-32 responded with a starboard torpedo at 4,000 yards and a port torpedo at 3,000 yards. "At this time, there was an explosion below the searchlight," Schumacher later reported, "definitely not gunfire, and debris came up into the searchlight beam."

Actually, the minelayer had dodged the torpedoes but taken a direct hit on her bow by a dud round from shore-based artillery. After losing half their force before even touching shore, the battered Japanese turned about and limped north. The barges turned away from Quinauan Point shortly after midnight.

Either because of his tenacity or because his damaged boats could not make the return trip to Moron, his closest safe harbor, Kimura beached the survivors at Silaiim Point and joined his one company already there. They were the last Japanese who would come ashore. Filipinos and Americans spent the next morning finding and killing isolated enemy troops who had survived the sinking of their barges and made it to shore.

Many of the invading troops who had landed uninjured and with equipment were still full of fight. It would take another two weeks of savage fighting by MacArthur's best troops to root out the remaining Japanese. American and Filipino infantrymen as well as artillery and light tanks ground down the Japanese holding the three separate beachheads. When the battle was over, two Japanese battalions had been annihilated. Ravines overflowed with enemy dead, and bloated corpses drifted in the surf. "The most unforgettable thing," remarked one American, "was the stench of the dead bodies in the tropical heat."

More than 1,400 Japanese died in the attempt to invade Bataan, and their plan to cut of the I Corps had failed miserably. It was a bloody rebuff in a campaign that was otherwise marked by spectacular Japanese successes.

Death of Convoy PQ-17

By Raymond A. Denkhaus

G ermany's ill-fated invasion of the Soviet Union in June
1941 gave England an unlikely and problematic ally.
Unlikely because Great Britain's government was ardently
anti-Communist, and problematical because of the vast distances
involved in supplying aid under the protection of an already
hard-pressed Royal Navy.

Political differences aside, British Prime Minister Winston
Churchill felt that any nation warring with Germany was already
an ally and deserved aid, from Britain as well as the United
States. England's commitments elsewhere around the globe precluded providing manpower or seizing the initiative. For now, the
only aid readily available was a constant flow of supplies.

Originally, an informal agreement provided for the delivery
of all goods to Soviet ships at British and American ports. The
responsibility for ferrying supplies back to the Soviet Union
would then rest entirely with the Soviets. But there were not
enough ships in the Soviet navy to handle such a monumental
task, and eventually the convoys to the Soviet Union came to
consist mainly of British and American ships.

Axis domination of the Mediterranean left only two Allied supply routes to the Soviet Union open. One, through Iran, required a sea journey of more than 13,000 miles. The second was a more practical northern route of less than 2,500 miles, but it crossed the cruelest sea of all, the Arctic Ocean. This Arctic route became known as the Murmansk Run.

Sailing around the northern tip of Norway, the convoys would be exposed to one of the largest concentrations of German U-boats, surface raiders and aircraft anywhere in the world. Attacks by more than a dozen subs and literally hundreds of planes at one time would not be uncommon. Strict orders forbade the halting of any ship for even a moment for fear of being attacked by prowling German U-boats, and individuals who fell overboard or survivors seen adrift on the waters had to be ruthlessly ignored. In the first two years of the run, more than one-fifth of the supplies sent to Murmansk would be lost.

Late in August 1941 a small, unnumbered convoy of seven ships made the trip from Iceland to the Soviet port of Archangel in 10 days without incident. The convoy, which had been hurriedly assembled, made the trip both as an experiment and as a gesture of good faith.

That September a military mission was sent to work out a formal aid program for the beleaguered Soviets. Negotiations at first were difficult. The Soviets dismissed all discussion concerning aid and demanded the immediate opening of a second front. They were convinced that only an offensive somewhere else could reduce the pressure the Germans were putting on them.

Several times the talks broke up after bitter disagreement. Marshal Josef Stalin often pointed out that while the Soviet Union was saddled with the burden of carrying 90 percent of the war, all the British were offering was "the loss of a few ships in support of the common cause." It was only after it looked as if the negotiations would break down altogether that the Soviets were finally willing to listen to aid proposals. The British and American representatives agreed to furnish all the planes, tanks and other war materiel that the Soviets felt they needed. For an industrial giant like the United States, the manufacturing would be the easy part; getting the goods safely halfway around the world would prove more difficult.

Originally, the Allied convoys went unnamed and unnumbered. After several round trips were successfully completed, a coding system was established. All convoys bound for the Soviet Union were designated "PQ," and those returning were designated "QP."

At first the Germans had to ignore the Allied crossings because they had few warships available to track the supply convoys. By the end of 1941, seven convoys had delivered 750 tanks, 800 planes, 2,300 vehicles and more than 100,000 tons of general cargo to the Soviet Union. Convoy PQ-8 was attacked by a U-boat but safely reached Murmansk on January 19, 1942. By early February 1942, 12 northbound convoys including 93 ships had made the journey with the loss of only one ship to a U-boat.

Although the early convoys encountered little German opposition, they still had to traverse the treacherous Barents Sea, part of the Atlantic Ocean. Winter brought nearly four months of unbroken darkness, which helped conceal the convoys from the enemy but made navigation difficult. Polar ice also pushed down from the north, forcing all ships to make a closer voyage to German-held Norway. The subzero winds howling off the polar cap could easily reach hurricane velocity and whip waves to a height of 70 feet. At such temperatures, sea spray froze immediately and created a top-heavy covering on anything exposed to it. The ice had to be chipped away to prevent the Allied ships from capsizing. Binoculars iced up, as well as guns and torpedoes. Freezing decks could become mirror-smooth, making it impossible for the crewmen to walk on them.

Any man who fell into the sea during the Arctic winter was as good as lost. On January 17, 1942, the British destroyer *Matabele* was torpedoed and sunk. Although a rescue ship arrived on the scene within minutes, only two survivors out of a crew of 200 were safely pulled from the water. The rest had all frozen to death.

Visibility was also frequently a problem. When the warmer waters of the Gulf Stream blended with the frigid Arctic waters, the result was often an unimaginably thick fog and occassionally blinding snow. Ships had to drastically reduce speed to prevent collisions. Escorting or intercepting the convoys became even riskier.

The Germans did not remain inactive in the Arctic for long. British commando raids along the Norwegian coast had convinced Adolf Hitler that sooner or later Britain would choose that country to begin its invasion of Europe. "Every ship that is not in Norway," said the Führer, "is in the wrong place."

While Hitler did not want to expose the newly launched battleship *Tirpitz* to action in the Atlantic, he had agreed to Grand Admiral Erich Raeder's request that *Tirpitz* be moved to the safety of the Norwegian fjords. The battleship not only would help deter a British invasion but also would be available to pounce on passing convoys. Hitler's permission for the move carried a proviso, however: Until the British carriers covering the convoys were neutralized, *Tirpitz* would not be risked on prolonged operations at sea. The Allies were unaware of the restrictions placed on *Tirpitz*'s movement.

The mighty *Tirpitz* had arrived in the northern waters on January 16, 1942. She was later joined by the cruiser *Admiral Hipper,* the pocket battleships *Admiral Scheer* and *Lützow,* and many attending destroyers. In early March, convoys QP-8 and PQ-12 narrowly missed being intercepted by the newly arrived enemy battle squadron.

The Germans soon began to achieve some coordination in their attacks on the Allied convoys. PQ-13, which sailed for the Soviet Union on March 20, lost five ships to German dive bombers and torpedo planes. Two ships were lost to U-boats and one to a force of marauding destroyers. In the attempt to beat back the enemy surface ships, the escorting cruiser *Trinidad* was sunk by one of her own rogue torpedoes.

The pack ice soon began to retreat, and the convoys were able to pass north of Bear Island and farther away from the hostile coasts. But summer also brought its own perils. It was the time of the midnight sun, when the days were nearly endless and darkness never really came. Under those conditions, concealment from a vigilant enemy was all but impossible. German long-range bombers and surface ships had little trouble locating and attacking the convoys. The greater travel distance of the northern route also added several days to the voyage.

Despite the dangers and hardships, the Allies were unanimous in their desire to keep the Soviet Union in the fight. They feared that if the Soviets were knocked out of the war, as the Russians had been in 1917, the entire weight of the German army would be unleashed in the West before the United States was really ready to fight. The British had no choice but to grit their teeth and continue to honor their pledge to send supplies to the Soviets through the ports of Murmansk and Archangel, even at the risk of shortchanging their own forces, which were stretched thinly around the world.

Realizing the strategic importance of the supplies flowing to the Soviets, Germany planned to make the trip so costly in lives and ships that the Allies would be forced to abandon any further attempts. They assembled a force of more than 260 aircraft and about 30 U-boats to greet any convoys that attempted the voyage.

Despite the increased danger from the Germans and protests from some within the Admiralty, political commitments forced PQ-16 to set out as scheduled in May 1942. A total of seven ships were lost during the run, all but one to aircraft. Clearly, Germany was gaining the upper hand in the Arctic, and sooner or later there would be a real disaster—but it was impossible to determine where and when.

By the end of June 1942, PQ-17, the largest and most valuable convoy in the history of the run, was formed up and ready to sail for Murmansk and Archangel. Its cargo was worth a staggering $700 million. Crammed into bulging holds were nearly 300 aircraft, 600 tanks, more than 4,000 trucks and trailers, and a general cargo that exceeded 150,000 tons. It was more than enough to completely equip an army of 50,000. Although some argued that PQ-17's run should be postponed until the shorter days of winter, it was considered politically prudent to continue supplying Russia without interruption, and the convoy left as scheduled.

Leaving Reykjavik, Iceland, on June 27, 1942, PQ-17 was an impressive sight. Thirty-five cargo ships—22 American, eight British, two Russian, two Panamanian and one Dutch—were escorted by six destroyers and 15 other armed vessels. One ship, S.S. *Empire Tide,* was a catapult-armed merchantman that carried a Hawker Hurricane fighter which could be launched to intercept enemy aircraft and perform reconnaissance. A cruiser force, consisting of HMS *London* and *Norfolk,* USS *Tuscaloosa* and *Wichita,* and three U.S. destroyers, steamed 40 miles north of the convoy to provide close cover. As the ships moved out in single file, Lieutenant Douglas Fairbanks, Jr., serving aboard *Wichita,* observed the move. The actor wrote that the ships "waddled out to sea like so many dirty ducks ... everyone who was watching paid a silent tribute and offered some half-thought prayer." Once out to sea, the ships took up their appointed positions in nine columns and plodded ahead at only 7 or 8 knots. Straight away, two ships were lost; one ran aground, and the other, suffering from engine trouble, was ordered back to the harbor.

For additional protection, the British Home Fleet was set to sail from its base at Scapa Flow on the following day. It was to trail PQ-17 at a distance of 200 miles and provide distant cover. The fleet included the battleship HMS *Duke of York,* two cruisers and 14 destroyers reinforced by the battleship USS *Washington* and the carrier HMS *Victorious.*

Unknown to the men of PQ-17, details of the convoy's size and importance were already in the hands of German Intelligence. The patrolling submarine U-456 spotted the convoy as soon as it reached open water.

Early on July 1, 1942, a German reconnaissance plane arrived just as PQ-17 was passing a returning convoy, QP-13. Because of the intermingling of ships and escorts as the two convoys passed each other, the German pilot incorrectly reported the convoy's size. In an effort to clarify the situation, the Germans dispatched U-255 and U-408 from their Ice Devil Group. After sorting things out, the Germans decided to ignore the returning convoy and to concentrate on the heavily laden PQ-17. Spared by the Germans, QP-13 unfortunately sailed into a friendly minefield in the Denmark Strait and lost four ships.

Although PQ-17 was closely shadowed by U-boats, visual contact between the Germans and the Allied convoy was suddenly broken when the icy polar winds flowing over the warmer waters created a vast and welcome fog. Visibility was severely restricted for the ships of the convoy, as well, but PQ-17's crews took comfort in the fact that if they could not see, then neither could they be seen by the enemy.

Although every crewman hoped that the protective fog would remain, in the still, bright afternoon the fog began to lift, and another long-range German scout plane appeared. Veterans aboard the convoy vessels knew that it would circle well out of gun range and remain only long enough to replot course and speed.

Now the men of the convoy waited for the inevitable attack. At 6:30 p.m. on July 2, seven Heinkel He-115 torpedo bombers struck. Loosely organized and lacking determination, the planes were driven off before any ships could be destroyed. Concentrated anti-aircraft fire kept the attackers at bay and prevented them from making accurate passes. After losing two planes, the Germans dropped their torpedoes well outside effective range and returned to their base.

It was not until the third day that the Germans scored a hit. The victim was the American Liberty ship *Christopher Newport*. Severely damaged, she began taking on water and was finally given up. Despite the loss, the men of the convoy felt that they had resisted brilliantly. They were confident that together with their escort they could complete the rest of the journey in good order.

All went well until the following afternoon, when elements of the Luftwaffe tried to press home another attack. Again, stubborn anti-aircraft fire drove the planes off. Later that same day, a flight of 25 planes was observed splitting into two groups before attacking—an attempt to divide the murderous defensive fire. With the convoy gunners busy defending against level bombers overhead, several torpedo planes, flying just above the water, were able to get in close. They launched at least 20 torpedoes, but only three found their mark. The Soviet tanker *Azerbaijan* was hit, but her crew managed to control the damage, and she eventually made it to port. Not so lucky were the merchantmen *Navarino* and *William Hooper;* damaged beyond repair, they both went down.

Back in London, the First Sea Lord, Admiral Sir Dudley Pound—nervous, war-weary and possibly suffering from an undiagnosed brain tumor—monitored developments. His sporadic intelligence reports, supplied by Ultra intelligence intercepts, confirmed that *Tirpitz* had slipped her moorings at Trondheim on July 3 and appeared to be moving out to sea. Due to the delays in decoding all incoming transmissions, it was impossible for the Admiralty to know exactly where *Tirpitz* was, only where she had been.

Tirpitz was only shifting berths, but the move was enough to put the Admiralty into action. It was obvious to Admiral Pound that *Tirpitz* and her battle group were undertaking a strike position. Without knowledge of Hitler's stipulation concerning British carriers, Pound was gripped by an overwhelming fear. Even with just a cursory look at his charts, he easily calculated that *Tirpitz*, steaming at 30 knots, could successfully evade the Home Fleet, overpower the cruiser force and slaughter the merchant ships.

Without confirmation of *Tirpitz*'s exact whereabouts, Pound believed the enemy force could already be closing on the convoy at high speed. His only alternative to maintaining the convoy was dispersal. The admiral called an emergency meeting of his naval operations staff, but his mind was already made up. Surrounded by about a dozen officers, Pound asked each one in turn which action they would pursue in light of the latest intelligence. Vice Admiral Sir Henry Moore, vice chief of the naval staff, recommended that if, and only if, the convoy was to be dispersed, there was no time to waste. The longer the delay in giving the order, the less sea room was available for dispersal, because the ships had to avoid the ice. Every other officer was against dispersal at that time. Pound politely thanked the men for their opinions, turned to an aide and said, "The convoy is to disperse."

The stunned escort commanders received the Admiralty's orders in the form of three rapid and poorly worded messages.

First message: "2111 ... Most Immediate and Secret. Cruiser Force withdraw to Westward at high speed...." Second message: "2123 ... Immediate. Owing to threat of surface ships, convoy is to disperse and proceed to Russian ports...." Third message: "2136 ... Most Immediate. Convoy is to scatter...."

PQ-17 was stripped of all protection and abandoned. Admiral Pound had decided to save the warships and let the merchantmen fend for themselves. Individual ships stood a better chance of survival against superior surface forces than vessels that were crowded together in the restrictions of a convoy. But scattering in the narrow confines north of the Arctic Circle would prove fatal. After confirmation of the orders was received, the men of the convoy could only stare in disbelief as their protection turned at high speed to join the cruiser force some 40 miles away.

Many of the escort commanders felt that the Admiralty must have hard proof that *Tirpitz* and her battle fleet were on the prowl and could be expected at any moment. They erroneously believed that the escorts had been ordered to move away in a maneuver to draw out *Tirpitz* for a showdown. One final message read: "Escort to merchant ships ... sorry to leave you like this ... good luck ... looks like a bloody business...."

Lieutenant Fairbanks wrote, "It was such a terrible feeling to be running away from the convoy at a speed twice theirs and to leave them to the mercies of the enemy...." While every man aboard the merchant ships was a volunteer and had expected a hazardous run, none had bargained for a journey such as this.

Before the last of the escorts had disappeared over the western horizon, the ships of the convoy began "starring"—breaking up their well-disciplined lines. Some fanned out to the north toward the ice edge, some due east toward Novaya Zemlya, and some southeast, directly toward the Russian ports. The American ships were seen lowering their colors as if in surrender. But they were only defiantly replacing their faded and tattered flags with bright, new oversized ones. For the Americans in the convoy it was Independence Day, July 4, 1942.

When news of the dispersal was reported to German naval headquarters, Admiral Raeder ordered *Tirpitz* to make ready to sail. At noon on July 5, 1942, *Tirpitz*—along with *Scheer, Hipper* and six destroyers—set sail to intercept PQ-17. Still uncertain of the location of the Allied covering force, and with reports of successful attacks on the Allied merchantment beginning to come in from U-boats and aircraft, Raeder then reconsidered. Apparently there was no need to risk the pride of the German navy. *Tirpitz* was ordered back to port at 9:30 p.m. The destruction of PQ-17 was to be left to the forces already engaged.

At Whitehall, 2,000 miles away, the decoders suddenly fell silent. *Tirpitz*, re-anchored, was now receiving all her messages overland. Only one wireless intercept from the German naval command came in, informing the U-boats near the convoy that no German surface ships would be operating in their area and they were free to continue their attacks. That information was hurriedly forwarded to Admiral Pound in hopes that he would recall the escorts and regroup the convoy. But it made no difference. The admiral knew that his orders had been sent and were probably already being acted upon. By now the ships were well within the range of German aircraft, and they could no longer be protected by the Home Fleet. As far as Admiral Pound was concerned, the matter was closed. The order to scatter would not be rescinded.

The slaughter had begun about 8:30 a.m. on July 5. Soon the Arctic airwaves were filled with frantic distress signals from stricken ships. A British freighter, *Empire Byron*, was among the first victims, going down after being torpedoed by a U-boat. Next to go was an American ship, *Carlton*. Then a flight of nine dive bombers concentrated on *Daniel Morgan* and the freighter *Washington*, while U-boats accounted for another American vessel,

Honomu. Before semidarkness mercifully put an end to the massacre, PQ-17 also lost *Bolton Castle, Paulus Potter, Earlston, Pankraft, River Afton, Aldersdale, Zaafaran, Fairfield City* and *Peter Kerr*.

The attacks continued for three more days without respite. Roving aircraft caught up with and sank Pan Atlantic, while prowling U-boats, working alone or in small wolfpacks, dealt death blows to *John Witherspoon, Alcoa Ranger, Olopana and Hartlebury*. One ship, *Winston Salem*, miraculously evaded numerous attacks only to be intentionally beached on the island of Novaya Zemyla, where she floundered until some of her cargo was salvaged. July 9 passed without incident; however, on the 10th, enemy planes caught *Hoosier* and184*El Capitan* while they were making a desperate run for landfall southeast of Murmansk. They, too, were pounded to pieces and sent to the bottom within 100 miles of safety.

Two little-known incidents illustrate the merchant ships' dramatic struggle for survival in the Arctic. During the height of the attacks on July 5, the armed trawler *Ayrshire* made a desperate move. Serving as escort for *Silver Sword, Ironclad* and *Troubadour*, she led them in a mad dash directly into the ice barrier. Once anchored, the ships' crews hurriedly painted their superstructures white to camouflage the vessels. Then, moving slowly along the ice edge and skirting the eastern extremes of the Barents Sea, the four ships eventually made for port.

Another incident involved the men of the naval armed guard serving aboard *Washington*, who actually chose to make the last leg of their trip to the Soviet Union in open lifeboats. *Washington* was carrying more than 600 tons of high explosives when she came under dive-bomber attack on July 5. Several hits had set the deck cargo ablaze, and with the flames raging out of control, the order to abandon ship was given. The gun crews loaded into two lifeboats and pulled away from the fiery wreck as fast as they could. When another ship tried to save them, the survivors repeatedly waved off all rescue attempts. They reasoned that they would simply be leaving one target for another and voted to remain adrift. It was their hope that once in the lifeboats they would be ignored by the attacking Germans. Within hours, just as anticipated, they witnessed the sinking of their would-be rescuers, hit by three torpedoes. Rigging sails and rowing in shifts, they reached the Soviet Union after 10 freezing days.

Air attacks by the Luftwaffe had temporarily closed the port of Murmansk, further disrupting deliveries of supplies, and the remaining ships of PQ-17 were rerouted. Only two ships made it across the White Sea to be unloaded at Archangel on July 9. Over the next few days, more stragglers came limping in, but it would take until July 28 for the last of the survivors of PQ-17 to arrive.

The toll taken on the abandoned convoy was horrendous. Only 11 of the 35 merchantmen that left Iceland finally made it to the Soviet Union. Fourteen of the sunken ships were American. More than two-thirds of the convoy had gone to the bottom, along with 210 combat planes, 430 Sherman tanks, 3,350 vehicles and nearly 100,000 tons of other cargo. More than 120 seamen were killed and countless others were crippled and maimed. The financial loss exceeded half a billion dollars.

For the Royal Navy, the massacre of PQ-17 and the abandonment of the convoy was one of the most shameful episodes of the war at sea. Details of the losses were kept from the public until after the war. The British decision to withdraw its protection from the convoy strained Anglo-American relations. Admiral Ernest J. King, chief of U.S. naval operations, was so enraged that he was very reluctant to have American and British ships continue operating together. Churchill lamented the fate of PQ-17 and wrote in his memoirs years later, "All risks should have been taken in the defense of the merchant ships."

To make matters worse, the suspicious Soviets refused to

believe that 24 ships from one convoy had been sunk. They openly accused their Western allies of lying about the disaster, and remained oblivious to the dangers and hardships endured by the merchantmen and escorts alike. No thanks were ever extended for the safe delivery of 5,000 tanks and more than 7,000 fighters and bombers. The Soviets never acknowledged that the 4 million tons of supplies that did arrive through the Arctic ports and the Persian Gulf may have kept their forces from being defeated by the Germans in the summer of 1942.

Shaken by the colossal losses taken by PQ-17, Churchill and President Franklin D. Roosevelt, over strong Soviet protest, postponed the sailing of PQ-18 until autumn. When the convoy did sail, it was protected by 53 warships, including two submarines and the aircraft carrier Avenger. Once again, the Germans mounted a major effort to prevent the delivery of supplies and weapons. They managed to sink 13 ships of PQ-18. Bowing to pleas from within the Admiralty and in the wake of such unacceptable losses, all further sailings were suspended until winter.

With the exception of several months in 1943, when the Battle of the Atlantic was at its peak, the convoys to the Soviet Union ran from 1941 until the war's end. Campaign ribbons were awarded for service in almost every other theater of the war, but not one was awarded for service in the Arctic. Before the fighting ended, however, Allied seamen had taken 1,526 individual ships in 77 convoys on the Murmansk Run. Nearly 100 ships were lost to enemy action and the unyielding weather. Allied losses in the Arctic eventually exceeded those in the North Atlantic sea lanes, and before the war ended the Arctic route had accounted for nearly 37 percent of all Allied surface ships sunk in all theaters of the war.

After the tremendous losses incurred by PQ-17, the Admiralty developed improved defensive tactics for convoys, including assigning greater numbers of escort vessels for each convoy as well as using radar, sonar and improved weaponry aboard the escort vessels. Because of the Allies' improved defensive tactics and its own worsening military situation after 1942, Germany would never again be able to dominate the northern seas. Later convoys would still be subject to attack, but no other convoy, before or since, suffered such death and destruction as PQ-17.

1943

Deadly Luftwaffe Strike in the Adriatic

By Eric Niderost

On the afternoon of December 2, 1943, 1st Lt. Werner Hahn piloted his Messerschmitt Me-210 reconnaissance plane over the port of Bari, in southeastern Italy. Cruising at 23,000 feet, his aircraft made a telltale contrail as he streaked across the sky, but Allied anti-aircraft crews took little notice. Still unmolested, the German pilot made a second pass over the city before turning north toward home. If Hahn's report was promising, the Luftwaffe would launch a major airstrike against the port.

Bari was a city of some 200,000 people, with an old section of town that dated back to the Middle Ages. Old Bari, clustered on a fist of land that jutted out into the Adriatic, boasted such famed landmarks as the Castello Svevo, a brooding medieval fortress dating to Norman times, and the Basilica San Nicola, which allegedly contained the bones of St. Nicholas.

In contrast, new Bari had broad boulevards and modern buildings. These new buildings included a sports facility nick-named "Bambino Stadium," which had been built by Italian dictator Benito Mussolini as a reward to the citizens for producing the most babies in a specified period of time. Bari—old and new—

had been fortunate, suffering little damage because the Allies had earmarked the city as a major supply port from the start.

As 1943 drew to a close, Bari's medieval torpor and somnolent grace were shaken off by the influx of Allied shipping into its harbor. Tons of supplies were offloaded almost around the clock, transforming the once quiet town into a hive of activity. On December 2, at least 30 Allied ships were crowded into the harbor, packed so tightly they almost touched.

The port was under the jurisdiction of the British, in part because Bari was the main supply base for General Bernard Law Montgomery's Eighth Army. But the city was also the newly designated headquarters of the American Fifteenth Air Force, which had been activated in November of that year. The Fifteenth's primary mission was to bomb targets in the Balkans, Italy and especially Germany. Fifteenth Air Force commander Maj. Gen. James H. "Jimmy" Doolittle had arrived in Bari on December 1.

The Americans had championed daylight precision bombing, but the Eighth Air Force in England was suffering terrible casualties in order to prove the theory valid. Luftwaffe strength was increasing, not decreasing, over Germany. The Fifteenth Air Force was intended to take some of the pressure off the beleaguered Eighth.

In addition to the usual war materiel, ships moored at Bari carried aviation fuel for Doolittle's bombers and other much-needed supplies. Selection of Bari as the Fifteenth Air Force headquarters-about 75 miles from the Fifteenth's primary airfields at Foggia-meant a large infusion of staff personnel. About 200 officers, 52 civilian technicians and several hundred enlisted men were being brought into the city.

Totally absorbed by the task of getting the Fifteenth Air Force off the ground, the Allies gave little thought to the possibility of a German air raid on Bari. The Luftwaffe in Italy was relatively weak and stretched so thin it could hardly mount a major effort. Or so Allied leaders believed.

German reconnaissance flights over Bari were seen as a nuisance. At first, British anti-aircraft batteries fired a half-hearted round or two, but eventually they ignored the German flights altogether. Why waste ammunition?

Responding to rumblings about lax security measures, British Air Vice Marshal Sir Arthur Coningham held a press conference on the afternoon of December 2 and assured reporters that the Luftwaffe was defeated in Italy. He was confident the Germans would never attack Bari. "I would regard it as a personal affront and insult," the air marshal haughtily declared, "if the Luftwaffe would attempt any significant action in this area."

Not everyone was so sure that the German air force was a broken reed. British army Captain A. B. Jenks, who was responsible for the port's defense, knew that preparations for an attack were woefully inadequate. But his voice, as well as those of one or two others, was drowned out by a chorus of complacent officers. When darkness came, Bari's docks were brilliantly lit so unloading of cargo could continue. Little thought was given to the need for a blackout.

In the harbor, cargo ships and tankers waited their turn to be unloaded. Captain Otto Heitmann, skipper of the Liberty ship SS *John Bascom,* went ashore to see if the process could be speeded up. He was disappointed in his quest, but he might have been even more concerned had he known what was aboard SS *John Harvey.*

John Harvey, commanded by Captain Elwin F. Knowles, was a typical Liberty ship, scarcely different from the others moored in the harbor. Much of her cargo was also conventional: munitions, food and equipment. But the ship had a deadly secret cargo. Approximately 100 tons of mustard gas bombs were on board.

The bombs were meant as a precaution, to be used only if the Germans resorted to chemical warfare.

In 1943 there was a possibility that the Germans just might use poison gas. By that point in the war, the strategic initiative had passed to the Allies, and Germany was on the defensive on all fronts. Adolf Hitler's forces had sustained a major defeat at Stalingrad, and they had lost North Africa as well. The Allies were now on the Continent, slowly inching their way up the Italian peninsula.

Hitler, it was said, was not a great advocate of chemical warfare, perhaps because the Führer himself had been gassed during World War I. He was, however, ruthless and might be persuaded to use gas if he believed it would redress the strategic balance in his favor. Intelligence reports suggested that the Germans were stocking chemical weapons, including a new chemical agent called Tabun.

American President Franklin D. Roosevelt issued a policy statement condemning the use of gas by any civilized nation, but he pledged that the United States would reply in kind if the enemy dared to use such weapons first. *John Harvey* was selected to convey a shipment of poison gas to Italy to be held in reserve should such a situation occur.

When the mustard gas bombs were loaded aboard *John Harvey*, they looked deceptively conventional. Each bomb was 4 feet long, 8 inches in diameter and contained from 60 to 70 pounds of the chemical. Mustard is a blister gas that irritates the respiratory system and produces burns and raw ulcers on the skin. Victims exposed to the gas often suffer an agonizing death.

The poison gas shipment was shrouded in official secrecy. Even Knowles was not formally informed about the lethal cargo. Perceptive members of the crew, however, must have guessed the voyage was out of the ordinary. For one thing, 1st Lt. Howard D. Beckstrom of the 701st Chemical Maintenance Company was on board, along with a detachment of six men. All were expert in handling toxic materials and were obviously there for a purpose.

John Harvey crossed the Atlantic without incident, successfully running the gantlet of German submarines that still infested the ocean. After a stop at Oran, Algeria, the ship sailed to Augusta, Sicily, before proceeding to Bari. Lieutenant Thomas H. Richardson, the ship's cargo security officer, was one of the few people on board who officially knew about the mustard gas. His manifest clearly listed 2,000 M47A1 mustard gas bombs in the hold.

Richardson naturally wanted to unload the deadly cargo as soon as possible, but when the ship reached Bari on November 26, his hopes were dashed. The harbor was crammed with shipping, and another convoy was due shortly. Dozens of vessels were stacked up along the piers and jetties, each waiting its turn to be unloaded. Since the lethal gas was not officially on board, *John Harvey* was not about to be given special priority.

For the next five nerve-racking days, *John Harvey* rode peacefully at anchor at Pier 29 while Captain Knowles tried vainly to get British port officials to speed things up. This was difficult, because he was gagged by the secrecy that surrounded the gas shipment. How could he get officials to act when he was not even supposed to know that he was carrying the mustard gas in the first place?

While Knowles fretted, German reconnaissance pilot Hahn had returned to base. His positive report about conditions at Bari set in motion a raid that had been discussed and planned some time before. The Bari attack was the product of a planning session between Luftwaffe Field Marshal Albert Kesselring and his subordinates. The Allied airfields at Foggia were discussed as possible targets, but Luftwaffe resources were stretched too thin to permit the effective bombing of such a large complex of targets.

It was Field Marshal Wolfram von Richthofen, commander of

Luftflotte 2, who suggested Bari as an alternative. A cousin of famed World War I ace Manfred von Richthofen, the field marshal was an experienced officer who had served in Poland and the Soviet Union as well as in the Battle of Britain. His advice, Kesselring knew, was sound. Richthofen believed that if the port was crippled, the British Eighth Army's advance might be slowed and the nascent Fifteenth Air Force's bomber offensive delayed. Richthofen told Kesselring that the only planes available for such a task were his Junkers Ju-88 A-4 bombers. With luck, he might scrape together 150 such planes for the raid.

When the strike force was mustered, there were only 105 Ju-88s available for the mission. But the element of surprise, coupled with an attack at dusk, might shift the odds in the Germans' favor. Most of the planes would come from Italy, but Richthofen purposely wanted to obfuscate matters by using a few Ju-88s from Yugoslavia. If the Allies thought the entire mission originated from there, they just might misdirect retaliatory strikes to the Balkans.

The Ju-88 pilots were ordered to fly their twin-engine bombers east to the Adriatic, then swing south and west. British anti-aircraft would probably expect an attack—if any—to come from the north, not from the west. The Ju-88s were also supplied with Duppel, thin strips of tinfoil cut to various lengths. The tinfoil registered like aircraft on radar screens, producing scores of phantom targets.

The aim of the German pilots was to arrive over Bari around 7:30 p.m. Parachute flares would be released first to light the way for the attacking aircraft, and the Ju-88s would come in low, trying to get under Allied radar that was already confused by the Duppel.

The Germans arrived at Bari on schedule. First Lieutenant Gustav Teuber, leading the first wave, could hardly believe his eyes. The docks were brilliantly lit; cranes stood out in sharp relief as they unloaded cargo from the ships' gaping holds, and the east jetty was packed with ships.

Scores of Ju-88s descended on Bari like gigantic birds of prey, their attack illuminated by the city's lights and German flares. The first bombs hit the city proper, great geysers of smoke and flame marking each detonation, but soon it was the harbor's turn. Some 30 vessels were riding at anchor that night, and each ship's crew had to respond to the emergency as best they could. Surprise was total, and some ships had to function without a full complement, since many sailors were on shore leave.

The German flares gave sailors the first inkling of the impending attack. Aboard *John Bascom,* the second officer, William Rudolf, saw the flashes and alerted Captain Heitmann. *John Bascom*'s gun crew sprang into action, joining the barrage that shore batteries were now hurling into the sky. Tracer bullets laced the air, but the anti-aircraft fire was largely ineffective.

There was no time to cut anchor cables and get underway; crews along the east jetty watched helplessly while a creeping barrage of German bombs came ever closer to their vulnerable vessels. *Joseph Wheeler* took a direct hit and exploded into flames; *John Motley* took a bomb in its No. 5 hold. *John Bascom,* anchored next to *John Motley,* was next in line for punishment.

John Bascom shuddered under a rain of bombs that hit her from stem to stern. One of the explosions lifted Captain Heitmann off his feet and slammed him against the wheelhouse door. Momentarily stunned, his hands and face bloody, Heitmann saw the body of Nicholas Elgin sprawled nearby, blood pumping from a head wound, his clothes torn off by the force of the blast.

The ship's bridge was partly destroyed, the decks were buckled and debris was everywhere. There was nothing left to do but abandon ship. Ignoring his own wounds, Heitmann ordered the crew into the single undamaged lifeboat. By now, the entire harbor was a hell on earth, where yellow-orange flames leaped into the air, producing dense columns of acrid smoke. Ships were in various stages of burning or sinking. When flames reached munitions-laden holds, some exploded. The surface of the water was covered by a viscous scum of oil and fuel, blinding and choking those unlucky enough to be in the water.

Meanwhile, the crew of *John Harvey* was engaged in a heroic battle to save their ship. The vessel still was intact and had sustained no direct bomb damage. Nevertheless, she had caught fire, and the situation was doubly dangerous with the mustard gas bombs aboard. Captain Knowles, Lieutenant Beckstrom and others on board refused to leave their posts, but their heroism was ultimately in vain.

Without warning, *John Harvey* blew up, disappearing in a huge, mushroom-shaped fireball that hurled pieces of the ship and her cargo hundreds of feet into the air. Everyone on board was killed instantly, and all over the harbor the force of the concussion knocked men off their feet. The blast sent out multihued fingers of smoke like a Fourth of July fireworks celebration and made the harbor as bright as day.

The men aboard USS *Pumper,* a tanker carrying aviation fuel, were witnesses to *John Harvey*'s last moments. Air initially rushed into the vortex of the blast, then the concussion radiated out to knock the tanker 35 degrees to port.

Meanwhile, Heitmann and his surviving crew managed to reach the tip of the east jetty, around a lighthouse that was located at its north end. He had about 50 men. Many were badly wounded, and some were so badly burned that the slightest touch brought agony. At first the lighthouse area seemed a refuge, but it soon became apparent it was more of a deathtrap. A sea of flames cut Heitmann and his men off from following the jetty's long spine into the city, where they might have been relatively safe.

While the sailors waited to be rescued, Ensign K. K. Vesole, commander of *John Bascom*'s armed guard detachment, was having difficulty breathing. Many of the other men were gasping, but it was Vesole who noted something strange about the smoke. "I smell garlic," he said, without realizing the implications of his remark. A garlic odor was a telltale sign of mustard gas. The gas had become liberally intermixed with the oil that floated in the harbor and lurked in the smoke that permeated the area.

Mustard gas-laced oil now coated the bodies of Allied seamen as they struggled in the water, and many swallowed the noxious mixture. Even those not in the water inhaled liberal doses of gas, as did hundreds, perhaps thousands, of Italian civilians. A launch dispatched from *Pumper* rescued Captain Heitmann and the other *John Bascom* survivors from the east jetty, but their troubles were just beginning.

The German raid began at 7:30 p.m. and ended 20 minutes later. German losses were very light, and they had succeeded beyond their most sanguine expectations. Seventeen Allied ships were sunk and another eight were damaged, causing Bari to be dubbed the "second Pearl Harbor." The Americans sustained the highest losses, losing the Liberty ships *John Bascom, John L. Motley, Joseph Wheeler, Samuel J. Tilden and John Harvey*. The British lost four ships, the Italians three, the Norwegians three and the Poles two.

The next morning survivors woke to a scene of utter devastation. Large parts of Bari had been reduced to rubble, particularly the medieval old town. Portions of the city and the harbor were still burning, and a thick pall of black smoke hung in the sky. There were more than 1,000 military and merchant marine casualties; about 800 were admitted to local hospitals. The full extent of civilian casualties may never be known. Conservative estimates hover around 1,000, though there were probably more.

Fortunately, Bari was the site of several Allied military hospitals and related support facilities. Some were housed at the Bari Polyclinic, built by Mussolini as a showcase of Fascist health care. The Polyclinic was home to the 98th British General Hospital and the 3rd New Zealand Hospital, among others. Those facilities received many of the mustard gas victims that began to appear.

Casualties from the raid began pouring in until the hospitals were filled to overflowing. Almost immediately some of the wounded began to complain of "gritty" eyes, and their condition worsened in spite of conventional treatment. Their eyes were swollen, and skin lesions began to appear. Swamped with wounded of all descriptions and still not realizing they were dealing with poison gas, hospital staffers allowed victims to remain in their oil-and-gas-soaked clothes for long periods.

Not only were the victims severely burned and blistered from prolonged exposure, but their respiratory systems were also badly irritated. The mustard gas casualties were wracked with coughs and had real difficulty breathing, but the hospital staff seemed helpless in the face of this unknown ailment. Men started to die, and even those who did recover faced a long and painful convalescence. Temporary blindness, the agony of burns and a terrible swelling of the genitals produced both physical and mental anguish.

As the victims began to die, the doctors started to suspect that some kind of chemical agent was involved. Some physicians pointed fingers at the Germans, speculating that they had resorted to chemical warfare after all. A message was sent to Allied headquarters in Algiers informing Deputy Surgeon General Fred Blesse that patients were dying of a "mysterious malady." To solve the mystery, Blesse dispatched Lt. Col. Stewart Francis Alexander, an expert on chemical warfare medicine, to Bari.

Alexander examined the patients and interviewed them when appropriate. It was beginning to look like mustard gas exposure, but the doctor was not sure. His suspicions were confirmed when a bomb-casing fragment was recovered from the bottom of the harbor. The fragment was identified as an American M47A1 bomb, which was designated for possible delivery of mustard gas. The Germans could be eliminated as suspects; in this case, the Allies were to blame.

Alexander still did not know where the mustard bombs had originated. The doctor tallied the number of mustard deaths in each ship, then plotted the position of the ships in the harbor. Most of the victims came from ships anchored near *John Harvey*. British port authorities finally admitted off the record that they knew John Harvey was carrying poison gas. Alexander drew up a report detailing his findings, which was approved by Allied Supreme Commander General Dwight D. Eisenhower.

Secrecy still dogged the whole affair, however. Eventually, the British and American people were told of the devastating Bari raid, but the part played by mustard gas was kept from them. British Prime Minister Winston S. Churchill was particularly adamant that this aspect of the tragedy remain a secret. It was embarrassing enough that the raid occurred at a port under British jurisdiction. Churchill believed that publicizing the fiasco would hand the Germans a propaganda coup.

Although the gas was mentioned in official American records, Churchill insisted British medical records be purged and mustard gas deaths listed as the result of "burns due to enemy action." Churchill's attempts at secrecy may have caused more deaths, because had the word gone out, more victims, especially Italian civilians, might have sought proper treatment. Axis Sally, the infamous propaganda broadcaster, learned the truth and taunted the Allies. "I see you boys are getting gassed by your own poison gas," she sneered.

There were 628 mustard gas casualties among Allied military and merchant marine personnel. Of these, 69 died within two weeks. Most victims, however, like Captain Heitmann of *John Bascom*, fully recovered. But the figures do not include the uncounted Italian civilians who must have been exposed to the deadly chemical. There was a mass exodus of civilians out of the city after the raid. Some were probably gas victims who died for want of proper treatment.

The deaths and injuries were terrible tragedies, but Bari was a strategic disaster as well. The port was completely closed for three full weeks after the terrible incident. On January 12, 1944, General Mark Clark's Fifth Army launched an offensive, part of an overall push that included the Anglo-American landings at Anzio some days later. Elements of the Fifth Army crossed the Rapido River and established a bridgehead, only to be forced to withdraw due to lack of supplies. Bad weather was the official cause of the supply problems, but the closing of Bari was probably a major factor.

The Fifteenth Air Force suffered setbacks as well because of the German success at Bari. Just two days after the raid, the Fifteenth had been scheduled to act in concert with the Eighth Air Force in a combined offensive against Germany. The Bari raid sharply curtailed the Fifteenth's participation in that offensive. In fact, the Fifteenth Air Force did not make a major contribution to the war until after February 1944.

The Bari raid was a twofold disaster. On one hand, it was truly a second Pearl Harbor, one of the most notable Luftwaffe exploits of the war. But it was also the only poison gas incident of World War II, a tragedy made worse by the perceived exigencies of wartime secrecy.

Allied Aerial Destruction of Hamburg

By David H. Lippman

The weather that July in Hamburg had been very hot, mostly dry. Two days before, a heavy thunderstorm had rumbled through, but the rain evaporated in the heat. On Saturday, July 24, 1943, the citizens of Hamburg were taking a rest from the heat and the backbreaking strain of World War II.

All across Germany's leading seaport, Hamburg's 1.75 million people enjoyed her cafes on the Alster and Elbe rivers, the huge zoo and the Ufa-Palast cinema, the Reich's largest. Once again Hamburg was free of air raids. To the average citizen, it must have seemed unlikely that the city would ever be bombed.

But Hamburg was about to be destroyed.

The architect of that destruction was Air Chief Marshal Sir Arthur "Bomber" Harris, head of British Bomber Command. The stocky Harris had great intelligence, enormous determination and an unyielding hatred of Germany. His aim as chief of Britain's bomber offensive was to destroy Germany's cities.

By 1943, Bomber Command's four-engine Avro Lancaster bombers could deliver 8,000-pound bomb loads on German cities nightly, guided to their targets by radar. The U.S. Army Air Forces

(USAAF) flew daylight missions and made precision attacks on German factories. Round-the-clock bombing was becoming a reality.

On May 27, 1943, Harris picked a target for the RAF. Because of the short summer nights, they targeted a city relatively close to Britain. Hamburg was Germany's second largest city, producing warships like Bismarck and churning out U-boats—400 during the whole war. Hamburg was protected by flak, rings of searchlights and night fighters, all controlled by a string of radar stations. But Harris had a new secret weapon, code-named "Window," to use on Hamburg. British scientists said Window would blind the Nazi defenses.

Harris' plan to bomb Hamburg, Operation Gomorrah, was simple: Hit Hamburg by day and night, dropping at least 10,000 tons of bombs and destroying the city. The Royal Air Force, accustomed to area bombing by night, selected the center of Hamburg, just north of the Alster River, as its target. The Americans, who planned to hit Hamburg by day with precision attacks, chose giant factories south of the Alster.

On July 22, the only question remaining was what the weather would be like. Harris and Brig. Gen. Frederick L. Anderson, commander of the U.S. Eighth Air Force's 4th Bombardment Wing, met with meteorologists and learned that skies were clearing. Harris set the attack to begin at precisely one minute after midnight on Sunday, July 25. Bomber Command would dispatch 792 planes loaded with a variety of ordnance, ranging from 4-pound incendiary "sticks" to 8,000-pound high-explosive bombs that looked like giant dustbins.

Window also was prepared. The new device seemed an unlikely weapon to RAF crews. It consisted of bundles of metalized paper strips—each bundle had 2,200 strips—made of coarse black paper with aluminum foil stuck to one side.

Operation Gomorrah began at precisely 9:45 p.m., when a

Short Stirling bomber of the 75th New Zealand Squadron took off from RAF Mepal in Cambridge. The last bombers took off at 11 p.m. Pathfinders dropped marker bombs—a mix of benzol, rubber and phosphorus that detonated at preset heights, set off by a barometric fuse—to blaze the route to Hamburg. Flying conditions were perfect as bombers advanced at 160 mph, using radar fixes to stay on course. The stream of aircraft was 203 miles long.

The Luftwaffe picked up the advancing British planes on its radar and sent up twin-engine Messerschmitt Me-110 and Junkers Ju-88 night fighters to intercept. The British reached their assembly point at about 12:20 a.m. and began dropping Window, which turned out to be a brilliant device.

British scientists had theorized that the strips of metalized paper floating in the air would swamp German radar with false echoes. The idea was not new. Japanese naval aircraft had used such a weapon—called Giman-shi, or "deceiving paper"—during night attacks on Guadalcanal. Adolf Hitler's scientists had developed their own, called Duppel, in Berlin and tested it. The test was so successful that the Germans were afraid it would fall into British hands and be used against them. Incredibly, Reichsmarshall Hermann Göring, chief of the Luftwaffe, not only ordered all research on Duppel stopped but forbade development of a counter to the device.

Now, from Lancasters and Handley Page Halifaxes, bundles were hurled out flare chutes into the freezing dark, a wearying task. In all, 7,000 bundles were dropped.

Down below, Luftwaffe radar stations that had been easily plotting RAF bomber streams were flooded with false returns. Hostile planes were everywhere. The whole defense system was blinded.

German ground controllers panicked. All Luftwaffe planes were ordered to simply fly toward Hamburg and find their own targets. Rolf Angersbach, in a Dornier Do-217, obediently headed for the city and found himself surrounded by slow-moving radar contacts . . . but no planes. After firing his guns all over the sky, he was ordered to land to tell his bosses what was going on. Angersbach later recalled that he found everyone "helpless and bewildered."

Not every Luftwaffe pilot was flummoxed. A Lieutenant Bottinger shot down one Halifax bomber. But 740 planes roared on untouched toward Hamburg. Ahead of them flew the Pathfinders. Bombardiers looked down through their H2S radar sets, which were unaffected by Window, to find Hamburg glowing beneath them. There were no clouds, and a gentle wind blew. Bombing conditions were perfect.

At precisely 12:57 a.m., the lead de Havilland Mosquitoes opened their bomb doors and dropped 39 yellow and red target indicators, marking out a 4-by-3-mile rectangle over downtown Hamburg. Minutes later, the main force of Lancasters arrived to find the German defenses defeated by Window.

"The master searchlights and all the others were waving aimlessly about the sky like a man trying to swat a flying ant in a swarm. All the crew were delighted," said Flight Lt. G. F. Pentnoy. For 50 minutes, RAF crews bombed the city in security.

German night fighters hung at Hamburg's edge, hoping to hit a bomber. The main force lost only three bombers over Germany's most heavily defended city. The attack seemed incredibly easy.

Down below, it was nightmarishly different.

In the confusion of the evening, the air raid alarms had been set off at 9:30 p.m., followed by the all-clear at 10, and then set off again at 12:33 a.m. The Hamburg police logged their 319th air raid alarm of the war at 12:51 a.m. as the target indicators skittered down in the night, each looking like a large fireball in the sky. Within minutes, the target indicators and 30-pound incendiaries started exploding, and people dived for the air raid shelters.

Most of Hamburg was burned to ashes. Firefighters, reserve

police and Hitler Youth, the backbone of Hamburg's civil defense, were overwhelmed. More than 54 miles of street frontage was burning. Karl Kaufmann, the district party leader, sent for reinforcements, and as many as 86 brigades were working in 692 teams by the end of the night.

The bombing was concentrated and continuous. Within minutes, the city's telephone lines were snapped and police headquarters was hit. Kaufmann had to take his maps and message forms to Gestapo headquarters. Fire Chief Otto Zaps could not get through the wrecked streets.

Nonetheless, Hamburg fought back. City flak defenses were jammed by Window but still fired off 50,000 rounds. Traugott Bauer-Schlichtgeroll of the 267th Heavy Flak Battalion was dismayed that his radar had gone crazy. As the other defenders blazed away anyway, the 17-year-old gunner looked uneasily at the blood-red sky over Hamburg.

Whole neighborhoods were going up in flame. The Rathaus, the Nikolaikirche, the central police station and the telephone exchange were all gone. So was the Ufa-Palast cinema. Helpless firefighters stood by, unable to save the great theater because armor-piercing bombs had burrowed through the streets and sliced the water mains.

Police later estimated 1,500 dead, many more injured and thousands homeless. The RAF had dropped 184 flares, 263 target indicators, 1,346 tons of high explosives and 938 tons of incendiaries.

Overhead, the last bomber to fly over the burning city that night, a Halifax of No. 102 Squadron, turned for home at 1:55 a.m. Flight Sergeant E. M. Cartwright said the RAF crews could see the fires of Hamburg behind them for much of their flight home.

The return trip was fairly easy. The crews dumped more Window bundles. One Lancaster flew over flak at Cuxhaven and was brought down. Another was caught by a lone German fighter. The bombers started landing at 3:19 a.m., and the final plane, a Canadian bomber, came in at 5:15 a.m. Only 12 bombers were lost. Eighty RAF crewmen were dead, and seven had been captured.

In Hamburg, the sirens warbled the all-clear signal at 3:02 a.m., and citizens trooped out to the streets to find Window strips blowing around. They also found scenes of horror. Otto Mahncke saw sailors rescuing people from a burning house, passing them from balcony to balcony. Suddenly the house collapsed, and everyone fell into the ruins.

Order seemed to break down. Mahncke tried to save a woman trapped in a burning house but failed. As he left, he saw policemen at a nearby station not doing anything to help. All over Hamburg, people searched for their ruined homes and lost families. Dawn brought little daylight, since burning fires cast a huge pall of smoke across the city.

The Nazi civil defense machine rumbled into action. At 4:10 a.m. the fire department logged, "Situation of Major Catastrophe declared," which placed every man and woman working in the city under Nazi Party control. Firefighters from Bremen, Kiel, Neumunster, Oldenburg and Eidelstedt were on their way, joined by Ukrainian Wehrmacht recruits from Training Corps VIII. In all, 35,000 men were soon at work quelling blazes. The fire department logged at 8:50 a.m., "Eight large areas of fires are still without firefighting forces."

While Hamburg firefighters labored to fight fires without phones or water, another assault was coming. The U.S. Eighth Air Force was going to hurl 323 Boeing B-17 Flying Fortresses and 3,230 airmen at Hamburg that afternoon, targeting the Blohm & Voss U-boat yards and the Klockner Aero-Engine Factory. Briefings and aircraft preparation took all morning at 15 airfields. Each B-17 was loaded with 10 500-pound high-explosive bombs or 16 250-pound incendiaries and 1,850 gallons of aviation octane.

Takeoff was at 1 p.m. Unlike the RAF fliers, Americans flew in close formation all the way over and all the way back. Much of the time after takeoff was spent marshaling the wings of graceful Flying Fortresses into tight boxes and out over the North Sea.

About 10 percent of the American planes had to abort—the U.S. crews were still gaining experience—but the rest rumbled over the North Sea under clear skies, climbing to 28,000 feet. Gunners in exposed positions pounded their fingers on their guns, trying to maintain their circulation in the freezing temperatures.

The Luftwaffe was having problems, too. The Germans sent 24 Messerschmitt Me-109 fighters to attack an incoming force that was presumed to be American bombers. It turned out to be a diversionary raid of British Douglas A-20 Havoc bombers heavily escorted by Supermarine Spitfires. The RAF lost seven Spitfires, and the Luftwaffe lost two Me-109s, but the B-17s were not touched.

Finally, the Luftwaffe realized what was happening and hurled Me-109s and Ju-88s at the American force. But the B-17s changed course, and the Luftwaffe only had them in radar contact for four minutes. As a result, the Americans swept in on Hamburg from the southwest with little aerial interference but facing heavy flak.

As the Americans homed in on Hamburg, 30 Me-109s swooped in. But the tough B-17s were able to take great punishment and stay in the air. When the Americans reached their initial point, the pilots saw a fantastic sight—Hamburg burning under a dense pall of smoke. One crewman, unaccustomed to the effects of RAF bombing, thought it was a thunderstorm. Others thought it was a smoke screen.

As the American planes closed in, so did German flak. It was the densest the Americans had yet seen. At 4:34 p.m., the lead planes opened their bomb bay doors and, 40 seconds later, released their loads. The Blohm & Voss yard was completely covered by smoke.

The American assault lasted 12 minutes, mostly because one wing dropped its bombs late. As soon as the bombs were gone and photos had been taken by bombsight cameras, the B-17s corkscrewed east and regrouped for the journey home. Ninety B-17s delivered 186 tons of bombs, but 78 planes suffered flak damage.

As the Americans approached, Hamburg had gone to "Danger 15"—the highest alert level, meaning air attack due within 15 minutes—to prepare for its first bombing by the USAAF. Smoke and flame interfered with U.S. efforts. Some bombs fell far short and killed cows in fields south of the city. Others missed the U-boat shops at Blohm & Voss. But more bombs wrecked important buildings, including the Blohm & Voss casting foundry, and destroyed ships.

Bombs tore apart oil tanks and apartment blocks, but others fell harmlessly into the Alster River. Two of Hamburg's U-boat yards and minor industrial areas were damaged, and 20 people were killed. The raid was not a great success, but Hamburg had not been given a chance to recover. All across the city, groggy firefighters returned to their work, while engineers struggled to restore phone lines. Luftwaffe bomb disposal squads wrestled with delayed-action bombs dropped the previous night.

Everyone knew the Americans would return. But first they had to make it back to England.

The Luftwaffe regrouped fast. It refueled its fighters, which then took off again and scored quickly. Eleven American planes were straggling due to damage—none of those reached home. Meanwhile, the rest of the formations flew home under heavy attack. Gunners blazed away, littering their planes with spent shells. Some hit their own planes. The 379th Bomb Group alone fired off 63,544 rounds of ammunition.

"They [the Germans] threw up everything that had a propeller," Lieutenant Howard Cromwell remembered. "They came in from every direction. . . . I only did three or four raids and this was certainly the worst one for fighters."

After the Me-109s departed, the Luftwaffe sent in their night fighters. The Me-110s took on B-17s for the first time. The Americans lost 15 B-17s, with 36 killed and 104 taken prisoner. The Luftwaffe lost six fighters.

That evening, Bomber Harris, learning that Hamburg was still covered by smoke, decided to send his Lancasters to Essen but keep nerves jangled in Hamburg with a high-speed nuisance raid by Mosquitoes. While the wooden planes did little damage, Hamburg residents got little sleep.

In Hamburg, all the local military district's assets had been called out. The Hitler Youth, Marine and Hamburg brigades posted warnings, carried messages through blitzed streets, and boiled tea and cabbages at soup kitchens.

The next day, July 26, the Americans returned in force. Two bomber wings again hit the Klockner and the Blohm & Voss factories. Takeoff was at 9 a.m., and many Americans were flying on only five hours of sleep. The Luftwaffe responded with heavy fighter attacks, to which the Americans put up a determined defense. But a number of B-17s, flown by exhausted crews, turned back.

Hamburg greeted the USAAF with heavy flak and a smoke screen. The bombers hit their targets precisely at noon, and the attack lasted one minute, a tribute to tight formations. Some 91 tons of high explosives and 27 tons of incendiaries fell on Hamburg.

Down below, Hamburg had been trying to get back to work when the bombs hit. Many factory workers were absent, still digging out, but at least 150 citizens were killed. Fires started in soybean oil tanks and lanolin factories, and a 500-pound bomb hit the Neuhof power station, one of Hamburg's two biggest. The station was out of action for a month. Hamburg had lost 40 percent of its power.

The Americans flew home without much interference. Most Luftwaffe pilots were defending against a simultaneous air attack on Hanover. Only two B-17s were lost in the second Hamburg strike, but 22 were lost over Hanover.

That night was quiet. The RAF had flown bombing runs for three nights. The next day was also quiet. The Americans needed a rest, too. In Hamburg, the Germans began to evacuate homeless people and roll in additional mobile flak batteries of 88mm guns. Fires started by the RAF three days before continued to burn.

That evening, Bomber Harris ordered the RAF to hit Hamburg again. This would be the most important raid of the battle. The RAF would attack the city by flying from east to west, taking a roundabout route over Lübeck to confuse the Germans. More incendiaries would be used to lighten the bombloads in favor of fuel.

A total of 787 bombers were hurled at Hamburg, and some high-ranking officers made the trek to see the effects of Window for themselves, among them General Anderson of the Eighth Air Force. The Lancaster he flew in, R5868, is now preserved at the RAF museum in Hendon.

Takeoff was near sunset, and only 41 planes aborted. Most of the bombers now had Window chutes, and dropping the aluminum foil was becoming a matter of routine.

The Luftwaffe was trying to cope with Window's effects. Night fighters were ordered to fly at higher altitudes and broadcast what they were doing as a running commentary to help fellow night fighters. Even so, the Luftwaffe shot down only five RAF bombers on the journey in. At Lübeck, the Luftwaffe flak did not open up. It is believed the local commander was holding fire so as not to reveal his blacked-out city, hoping the RAF would bomb elsewhere.

The RAF did. The first yellow target indicators of July 28 went down on Hamburg at 12:55 a.m., under clear skies. The main force of 729 planes swept in, and soon pilots saw "a great fountain of burning debris thrown up for what seemed to be thousands of feet."

"As far as I could see was one mass of fire," said Sergeant W. G. Lamb of No. 460 Squadron. " 'A sea of flame' has been the description and that's an understatement."

Down below, the Germans opened up with their new flak guns but scored few hits. They were handicapped by Window, heavy smoke, lack of electricity and an order to limit fire to a maximum altitude of 5,500 meters (18,000 feet). Above that point, German fighters could operate freely, a new Luftwaffe tactic that would later prove successful. That evening, however, the new tactic was not too effective. Another failed German tactic was to light decoy flares that might be mistaken for target indicators, but German flares were red and British flares were yellow.

The last bomb fell at 1:47 a.m., and the RAF headed home, having dropped 2,326 tons of bombs and lost 21 planes—2.8 percent—a staggering success. In Hamburg, most fire engines were on the west side of town extinguishing three-day-old blazes from the first raid when "Danger 15" was sounded at 11:40 p.m. Incendiary bombs started fires across the city. Then the Hamburg citizens heard a shrill howling in the streets.

The howling was something that had never before been recorded. The Germans named it Feuersturm or "firestorm." High temperatures, low humidity, concentrated bombing that started a large number of fires and the fact that Hamburg's firefighters were all on the west side of town were all factors in the spread of the firestorm. The firefighters struggled to reach the area but could not get through the wreckage.

The impact was tremendous. Within 15 minutes of the RAF attack, most fires were blazing unchecked. As the fires linked and grew, they needed more and more air. Temperatures reached 1,400 degrees as the blaze actually began to suck all the air out of the city.

The firestorm spread over a 4-square-mile area and hit 16,000 apartment-block frontages totaling 133 miles, most of them older buildings. Beneath these buildings were air raid shelters, where many people died either from heat or from asphyxiation. Some fled.

As Kate Hoffmeister, 19, fled, she found that the Eifestrasse asphalt had melted. People were trapped, lying in the sticky goo, screaming. Hoffmeister, herself burned, slid down a bank and hid under a wool blanket. Her father, aunt and two uncles died.

Erika Wilken and her husband Willi took shelter in a public toilet and soaked cloths with water from the tanks. A phosphorous bomb fell directly outside, setting off panic and flame. The only way out was through the fire. Erika and her husband hid at the back for a while, then ran through the fire, barely burned.

All across Hamburg, the firestorm sucked air to feed itself. The fire raged three miles up, and winds were moving at 150 miles per hour. As the heat hit clouds overhead, a greasy, black rain started falling. On the ground, the intense heat set many people afire.

Many people saved themselves by diving into canals or taking refuge in open spaces like soccer fields. Others survived in public shelters that had gas- and smoke-tight doors. But there were few of those. In most shelters, the firestorm drew out the oxygen and replaced it with carbon monoxide. Others were felled by flying timbers or falling bricks or were even dragged off into burning buildings by the wind. In all, more than 40,000 people perished in the three-hour firestorm.

Around 4 a.m. the wind gradually dropped, and firefighters were able to set up a perimeter. Even so, the firestorm center was still too hot for rescue workers to enter.

Hermann Kroger and his firefighting team felt fresh air enter their shelter at 6 a.m. Traute Koch, 15, emerged from her burrow to find large heaps of rubble where there had been houses, and what appeared to be tailor's dummies everywhere. She said to her mother, "Mummy, no tailors lived here and, yet, so many dummies lying around." Traute's mother told her not to look too closely. The "dummies" were corpses.

Kaufmann sealed off the firestorm area to civilians and deployed armed guards. Using loudspeaker vans, he ordered Hamburg citizens not engaged in essential work to leave the city. Many left Hamburg on foot; 15 of Hamburg's 18 railway stations were out of action.

The massive and complex Nazi apparatus came to Hamburg's aid. Sixteen thousand liters of milk, beer and coffee were supplied, along with half a million loaves of bread. Trucks and trains were commandeered to evacuate refugees. Hamburg University students transported 63,000 people. Others were taken on ships or Luftwaffe Junkers Ju-52 transports. Most left on foot, pushing or pulling carts loaded with personal goods.

In one respect, Bomber Harris had succeeded. Hamburg could no longer function. Harris still was not finished, however. He left Hamburg alone the night of the 28th because there was too much smoke for accurate bombing. But on the morning of Thursday, July 29, Harris ordered one more strike on the wounded city. Seven hundred eighty-six Lancasters thundered down runways that evening.

The Luftwaffe had begun to figure out how to deal with Window. Its radar operators began to separate aluminum foil strips from Lancasters. More searchlights were brought in. The RAF lost 31 bombers on that raid.

Hamburg was easy to spot. Pathfinders saw fires still burning and spewed target indicators at 12:40 a.m. Crews were stunned at the sight of vast tracts of Hamburg that lay beneath them, burning and smoking from a two-day-old raid. A New Zealander said, "The whole area glittered like the sun shining on early morning dew."

Seven hundred bombers dropped 2,323 tons of bombs over Hamburg in about an hour. Despite Kaufmann's orders, Hamburg was still full of people—essential workers, firefighters, the elderly and the infirm.

Massive fires broke out in Barmbek, a residential district, and other areas not hit the previous few nights. Hamburg's exhausted firefighters simply tried to contain the edge of the blaze. About 800 people died.

Harris wanted to hit Hamburg again, but the Air Ministry wanted strikes on Italy instead, to tip that demoralized country into surrender. Hamburg got four days and three nights of rest.

The last Hamburg strike was August 2, 1943, with 737 bombers that ran smack into a massive thunderstorm, the worst many pilots had ever encountered. Four hundred bombers plowed through lightning to hit the city, but there was no order in the attack. Bombs rained down on all kinds of different areas, damaging a vegetable oil factory and the opera house. The auditorium was burned out, but the stage, loaded with bread, was undamaged.

The last aircraft to bomb Hamburg was a Vickers Wellington captained by Flight Lt. J. C. Morton of No. 466 Squadron, who released his incendiaries at 2:55 a.m. on August 3. The RAF lost 33 bombers. The last plane to return from the raid, a 75th New Zealand Squadron Stirling flown by Pilot Officer Clifford Logan, wobbled down at RAF Mepal at 6:30 a.m.

In Hamburg, Kaufmann and his aides went straight to work. Convict labor was sent to defuse unexploded bombs. Concentration camp prisoners and Wehrmacht men slowly moved into the ruined firestorm area to extract corpses, which were buried in mass graves. No attempt was made to identify the victims.

Evacuees received free rail transport to relatives' homes across the length and breadth of Germany. War production in Hamburg slowly began to return to normal, though it never quite reached that goal.

Casualties were estimated at 45,000, most of those during the firestorm. Fifty-six percent of Hamburg's residential units were destroyed, along with 436 public buildings.

Kaufmann begged Hitler to visit Hamburg to buck up morale. The Führer refused. Instead, Reichsmarschall Hermann Gˆring, who had boasted that if one bomb fell on a German city he could be called "Meier," visited the ruins. He decorated some flak gunners, met with city officials, then toured the wreckage. Hamburg citizens, gathered about hoping to return to inspect their smashed homes, greeted Göring with taunts of "Well, Hermann Meier, what have you got to say now?"

The Turning Points of Tarawa

By Joseph H. Alexander

The first of four turning points in the Battle of Tarawa occurred at 8:55 A.M. on D-Day, November 20, 1943, when the ragged lines of eighty-seven American assault amphibian vehicles (officially "landing vehicle tracked," or LVTs) approached Betio Island's fringing coral reef. Both sides watched intently. Could these strange "little boats on wheels," as a Japanese survivor of the battle would describe them, negotiate the coral wall at low tide? In a series of nearly ninety violent collisions, the LVTs hit the reef, slowed, then crawled over the barrier to rumble the remaining quarter-mile ashore with their landing force of 1,500 Marine Corps riflemen and combat engineers. At this improbable sight, one Japanese *rikusentai* (naval infantryman) exclaimed, "The god of death has come!"

Yet the Japanese had surprises of their own to spring. The Americans were astounded to find that the Imperial Navy defenders had survived the greatest bombardment of the war to that point with most of their major weapons and all of their fighting spirit intact.

Both sides had much at stake. For the United States, defeat at

Tarawa could derail the newly conceived Central Pacific campaign and fatally undercut national confidence in the largely untested doctrine of amphibious assaults against heavily defended beachheads. Tarawa for the Japanese was a proving ground as to whether their isolated garrisons could keep American invaders at arm's length until the Combined Fleet could sortie from Truk and force the long-sought "Decisive Battle."

The American side of this landmark battle has been told often: Here for the first time is the Japanese perspective, pieced together from the few survivor's accounts, translations of Japanese war diaries and unit histories, captured documents, and ULTRA radio intercepts.

Compared to the more notorious Japanese bastions of Truk and Rabaul, little-known Tarawa seemed an unlikely site for the first large-scale, opposed amphibious assault of the war. The British Crown Colony of the Gilbert Islands, of which Tarawa was a part, had been an easy conquest for Japanese naval forces in the second week of December 1941. Small terms of *rikusentai* seized Makin and Tarawa without opposition, then departed, leaving only observation units and light security forces. But the Gilberts ceased being a backwater in August 1942, when the Americans executed a submarine-launched raid on Makin in order to relieve Japanese pressure on the Guadalcanal beachhead. While tactically inconclusive, this two-day raid galvanized Imperial General Headquarters (IGHQ) into building up forces in that distant quarter. Within a week, the Yokosuka 6th Special Naval Landing Force, fifteen hundred strong, sailed for Tarawa. In six weeks construction troops had a bomber strip under way on Betio, the key island of Tarawa Atoll.

There remained much to do in preparation for an American invasion. During autumn 1942, Army Chief of Fortifications Lt. Gen. Tokusaburo Akiyama toured Japanese island outposts from the Lesser Sundas in eastern Indonesia to the Gilberts and found disturbing levels of unpreparedness. Sobered by the American invasion of Guadalcanal, Akiyama found the Gilberts, truly the farthest outposts of the empire, to be equally vulnerable to an unexpected offensive. He also stated the obvious: Tarawa, with its central location, bomber strip, and natural defense features, was the key to the Gilberts.

To the extent possible, IGHQ accorded Tarawa's defensive preparations top priority and supplied generous amounts of naval troops, weapons, fortification materials, and labor. Betio became a formidable citadel, and the garrison's operational mission evolved to simply resisting an American landing for a minimum of three days, until the Combined Fleet could arrive.

Adm. Mineichi Koga flew his flag as commander of the Combined Fleet on board the superbattleship *Musashi* in Truk harbor at this time. In August 1943, Koga issued his Third Stage Operational Policy, which included *Hei* Plan #3, counterattack guidelines should the Americans invade the Gilberts. In that event Koga hoped to take advantage of his geographic position to assemble submarines, surface forces, air units, and a counter-landing force from throughout the Pacific.

Koga's *Hei* plan had flaws. The Combined Fleet was already critically low on fuel. Further, the Imperial Navy suffered from a lack of strategic intelligence. An American offensive was in the wind—but where? Twice Koga sortied his fleet into the Central Pacific in response to false alarms, consuming precious fuel to no avail. When Adm. William F. Halsey landed the 3d Marine Division on Bougainville on November 1, 1943, Koga decided to reinforce Rabaul with his heavy cruisers and—most critically—the last 173 qualified naval aviators in his command. Halsey's daring carrier-based air raids on Rabaul in early November damaged eight Japanese cruisers and killed about 150 pilots. This emasculated the Combined Fleet for the winter. Koga still had the fleet carrier *Zuikaku* with him at Truk, but without its air group he would not risk his superbattleships. The Tarawa garrison likely never knew it, but from this point they were truly on their own.

The Americans would face an all-navy force in the Gilberts. In February 1943, IGHQ had redesignated Tarawa's original *rikusentai*, the Yokosuka 6th, as the 3rd Special Base Defense Force, with responsibility for manning the bigger guns and most of the fourteen tanks. Then came the 111th Construction Battalion, commanded by Lt. Isao Murakami. With Betio's bomber strip already well under way, Murakami's large, talented force—similar in organization and can-do spirit to the American naval "Seabee" battalions—began building gun emplacements, magazines, and command posts. Murakami's force had stopped in Kwajalein en route to take on board the first two (of four) 8-inch guns. Antiaircraft systems went up first; then the big coastal defense emplacements, followed by bunkers and pillboxes. Then it was time for more fighting men.

On March 17, 1943, Comdr. Takeo Sugai arrived on Betio Island with his newly formed Sasebo 7th Special Naval Landing Force. Tarawa would be the first and last fight for the Sasebo 7th. Formed in Japan, on Kyushu, only six weeks earlier, the unit contained a mix of combat veterans, new volunteers, and old hands recalled to service. Those men whose reports of Tarawa have survived reflect this variety of combat experience. Commander Sugai, a Naval Academy graduate who would prove to be a resolute combat fighter, was off the active rolls as recently as 1940, serving as a professor in a Kobe merchant marine school. Warrant Officer Kiyoshi Ota served in the landing force that seized Hainan Island in 1940. Petty Officer Chuma, a trained antiaircraft gunner, served previously in Batavia, Saigon Makasssar, and the Celebes. Petty Officer First Class Tadao Onuki, a tank commander at Tarawa, was a truck driver in the expedition by the Japanese Fourth Fleet that seized Rabaul from the Australians in 1942. All hands—veterans and rookies alike—benefited from intensive weapons training at the Tateyama Naval Gunnery School near Yokosuka before embarkation.

Freshly promoted Rear Adm. Keiji Shibasaki took command of these disparate elements at Tarawa on July 20, 1943. Shibaski hit the ground running. Troops trained all day, then helped build fortifications and obstacles half the night. Training invariably involved live firing exercises. To ensure fire discipline among his many machine gunners along the shoreline, Shibasaki ordered the fronts of the pillbox embrasures sealed shut to force the crews to concentrate only on their assigned field of fire, typically enfilade fire along the seaward sides of barbed wire entanglements or other obstacles.

Shibasaki is often remembered for his boast to the native Gilbertese that "a million Americans cannot take Tarawa in a hundred years." He may well have said that, but his purpose surely would have been to boost the morale of his own garrison— several thousand young Japanese sailors on a crowded equatorial island at the very farthest reaches of the empire, waiting for the inevitable American invasion. Already sickness had taken a toll. Shortly before the battle Shibasaki had to send Lieutenant Murakami back to Japan with several hundred acutely ill troops.

Shibasaki faced other problems trying to integrate the defense of Betio. His career experiences would hardly have made him (or any flag officer) an expert in the complex details of fire control, heavy ordnance, mine warfare, tactical communications, air operations, or fortifications engineering. Sensing this, the navy division of IGHQ dispatched in August 1943 a "defense combat team" of experts under the distinguished Namizo Sato, dean of the Naval Mine School. Sato would have served Shibasaki better had he stayed more than just a few days at Tarawa, but he had little incentive to linger: The place was hot, unhealthy, and subject to bombardment. While the garrison dutifully planted antiboat mines along the obvious landing points on Betio—the southern, western, and eastern beaches—they left the northern shore for last and never mined the lagoon entrance in the belief their coastal defense guns would command that narrow passage. But Shibasaki ran out of time. The invasion occurred while he still had more than 3,000 mines waiting to be sown.

Shibasaki's hopes of further enhancing Betio's defenses were frustrated when U.S. submarines increasingly began to interdict Japanese cargo ships along the extended route from the home islands to the Gilberts. From August to November, Shibasaki looked in vain for a special delivery of 25mm dual-purpose (anti-air and antiboat) machine cannons and—especially—*cement*. Warrant Officer Ota admitted during his initial POW interrogation that "the weak point in the defensive installations was that all the pillboxes were not as yet converted [from logs] to concrete."

U.S. Navy ULTRA intercepts reveal that Shibasaki expected the cargo ship *Mikage Maru* on November 20. His concern for the safe arrival of this ship (with its presumed cargo of weapons and cement) amid the gathering storm of preliminary bombardments may account for the strange sight that greeted the vanguard of the U.S. Southern Attack Force as it cautiously approached Tarawa from the west the night of November 19. Betio was suddenly pinpointed by a series of flashing signals in a strange code from the equivalent of masthead lights. The garrison evidently thought their ship was at hand. Instead it was the enormous American task force, steaming dead toward the island.

Despite this unpleasant shock, the Japanese opened the battle before dawn on the 20th. There were 4,601 of them on Betio: 2,571 *rikusentai,* 30 mechanics in the 755th Air Group detachment (abandoned in haste the previous day by their pilots), and 2,000 civilians in the 111th Construction Battalion. The landing force component of the U.S. Southern Attack Force consisted of the 2nd Marine Division, which numbered around 19,000 men. Of course these 5,000 would execute the amphibious assault on D-Day, and a total of 7,000 more would hit the beach—or try to—before D-plus-3.

Sentries on Betio lit the darkness with a red warning flare. At 5:07 A.M., the big eight-inch guns opened up on the American ships, including the vulnerable transports, still full of troops and unwittingly anchored well within range (due to strong currents and inaccurate navigational charts). But the Japanese crews couldn't capitalize on their advantage. In the only really effective gunnery sequence of a long, frustrating morning, U.S. battleships opened a devastating counter-battery fire that blew up a magazine, destroyed three of the guns, and damaged a fourth. In a matter of minutes, all four of Shibasaki's prized eight-inch batteries had been taken off the board. The lagoon entrance was suddenly accessible to the enemy.

Shibasaki notified his superior commanders at 5:59 A.M. that an American task force was bombarding the island and launching landing craft. Thirty minutes later Admiral Koga activated *Hei* Plan #3 to counterattack the Gilberts. Nine longrange submarines were already under way from the Carolines to the Gilberts, alerted by preliminary sightings of the converging American task forces. In the Carolines, Col. Manjiro Yamanaka, commanding a 1,500-man army regiment known to Japanese strategic planners as the Ko Detachment, received urgent orders to prepare for embarkation on board two destroyers for a counter-landing operation in the Gilberts.

When early dawn revealed the southern horizon covered with fifty American warships, including three battleships (plus five escort carriers out of sight over the horizon), Commander Sugai assembled his subordinates and conducted a ceremonial burning of the Sasebo 7th's colors. There would be no retreat, no surrender, for the *rikusentai*.

Stung by the abrupt loss of his main batteries, Shibasaki

ordered his secondary coastal defense guns—four 140mm shielded mounts, and a half dozen pedestal-mounted 80mm deck guns—to open up on the enemy fleet. Yet Shibasaki was poorly served by his coast-defense gunners. Against dozens of U.S. ships clearly within range, arrayed broadside, and barely making steerageway as they bombarded the island, the Japanese gunners could record only a long series of near-misses.

Ordnance failures further frustrated the Japanese. As American landing craft approached the island, the Japanese fired shells with airburst fuses calculated to inflict maximum damage on troops—but the shells had been overloaded with explosives which vaporized the shrapnel, simply "dousing [the invading Marines] with hot sand." One of the 140mm batteries nailed the USS *Ringgold* (DD 500) dead center with two rounds—but both shells proved to be duds. Give this reprieve, *Ringgold* would contribute materially to the second turning point of the battle several hours later.

Shibasaki's relief from these setbacks came from a strange quarter. American inexperience in coordinating carrier air strikes and naval gunfire led to two deadly lapses wherein all firing ceased for roughly thirty minutes at a time. The lapses gave the Japanese defenders ample time to shake off the effects of the pounding and move forces and ammunition from the south shore to the threatened north shore—negating some of the tactical surprise the Americans had earned by attacking through the lagoon to approach Betio from the north.

During the second pause—from 8:55 A.M. to 9:25 A.M.—*Ringgold* and her sister ship, the U.S.S. *Dashiel* (DD 659), in Fire Support Section Four honored the cease-fire order angrily. As the only gunships in the lagoon, they could see that the Marine assault waves were still twenty-five minutes from touchdown on the beach. Shibasaki grasped the opportunity to rush more troops from the south shore to the endangered northern coast. Petty

Officer Onuki used the lull to maneuver his Type 95 light tank out of deep cover and into a good firing position overlooking the north shore.

At 9:35 A.M., the communications ship *Katori Maru* in Kwajalein recorded this urgent message from Shibasaki:

> Enemy is approaching all over the shore north of the pier, inside atoll, with more than 100 amphibious tanks within visible sight. Later, 200 or more landing craft observed. Inside the atoll . . . four or more destroyers and minesweepers have entered and are making bombardment to cover the landing force. Other parts of the fleet are outside the atoll. . . . Several tens of carrier planes and float planes are used by enemy for air superiority. All of our forces are in high morale, having decided to fight until death.

"We could see the American landing craft coming toward us like dozens of spiders scattering over the surface of the water," said Warrant Officer Ota. But Shibasaki and Sugai berated their troops out of their shock. Now the Americans were fully within range of every weapon on the island. The guns of the *rikusentai* would not disappoint their commanders. Fire lashed out at the Americans from a hundred narrow embrasures and ports. Onuki commenced firing the 37mm gun from his tank turret. "There we broke our silence," he said. "Under roaring fires, enemy craft wrecked, American soldiers went down one after the other, went falling into the sea."

Petty Officer Chuma's Type 88 dual-purpose 75mm gun had proven ineffective against the enemy's fast-flying aircraft, but now, firing horizontally, fifteen rounds per minute, the crew had a field day against the slower LVTs and landing boats. Chuma's pedestal-mounted gun was one of four on the island's northwest shore that would eventually be overrun by infantry. But for a glorious hour that morning, these gunners accounted for most of the destroyed American landing craft. The U.S. Marines lost only eight LVTs in the initial shocking assault, but at least half of these blew up, with great slaughter, from direct hits by Chuma's coolly-firing battery.

On the northeastern shore that morning, a 127mm dual-purpose gun crew displayed equal virtuosity, sinking consecutively four landing craft as they approached the reef laden with light tanks. While cheered by this success, Shibasaki could only curse his fate that the same gun had been out of action an hour earlier when other enemy landing craft delivered fourteen Sherman medium tanks to the reef, where they rumbled over the coral and advanced through the shallow water beyond. One Sherman foundered in a submerged bomb crater, but the others made it ashore unmolested by anything greater than small-arms fire.

Once ashore, however, the Shermans encountered the *rikusentai*'s well-served field guns and light tanks. A single 75mm mountain gun knocked out three Shermans as they rumbled inland, unescorted by riflemen. One plucky Japanese light tank, engaged in a losing duel with a Sherman near the western shore, launched a dying, final 37mm round, a phenomenal shot, right down the barrel of the opposing tank. The Sherman survived, minus its main gun, and served in the reduced capacity of an armored machine gun. The Japanese had never seen tanks this large, but their spirited defense whittled away at the Shermans until only two were left operational by dusk on D-Day.

Throughout the fire of all these field guns, and fully integrated with the vicious cross-stitching of the Japanese machine guns, fell hundreds of rounds of well-aimed indirect fire. American survivors would curse the effectiveness of Japanese mortar fire on D-Day. In fact, the Japanese had *no* mortars on Betio, just the squat but deadly Type 92 70mm howitzers and the ubiquitous

50mm grenade-throwers. (The Americans erroneously—and dangerously—called the latter "knee mortars." In fact, if fired from the knee, their recoil would break a man's leg, as some U.S. troops with captured weapons found out the hard way.)

The American gamble of converting lightly armored, mechanically frail logistic vehicles into assault craft worked to the extent that 1,500 Marines forced a shallow series of toeholds along the north shore—identified by the landing force as Red Beaches One, Two and Three, from west to east. But with their LVTs increasingly knocked out of action by point-blank fire and their reserve troops piled up along the reef in deeper-draft boats, the Americans realized the battle would now be won or lost by their ability to get sufficient forces ashore via the 500-yard wade from the reef to avoid being overwhelmed by local counterattacks. Over the next twenty-four hours, three separate battalion landing teams tried to reinforce the beaches on both sides of the pier by such desperate wading. Japanese machine gunners, maintaining their disciplined fire sectors, had a tabletop shooting gallery against the Americans struggling through the shallows. Hundreds of Marines fell to this unremitting fire; those who made it ashore often arrived weaponless and in tactical disarray.

As D-Day sped toward its early tropical sunset, the U.S. commanders knew they were in great danger. Fifteen hundred of the 5,000 Marines who had crossed the reef that day lay dead or badly wounded. The survivors clung to scattered pockets, out of communication with one another, and grimly aware they faced an equal number of Japanese whose forte was night fighting.

At this critical point, in the late afternoon of D-Day, occurred the second turning point of the battle of Tarawa. Western military historians have surmised for the past half-century that Admiral Shibasaki died on the third day of the battle and that the expected Japanese counterattack did not materialize the first night because the heavy bombardment shredded Japanese wire communications. Translation of detailed Japanese accounts, however, reveals the surprising fact that Shibasaki died the first afternoon, along with his entire staff. This loss clearly affected the ability of the Japanese to orchestrate a counterattack the night of D-Day.

The coup de grace came from the fortunate USS *Ringgold* and her sister destroyer. Both ships steamed dangerously close to the north shore, enjoyed uncommonly good communications with the Marines on the eastern flank, and delivered well-directed 5"/38 fire on a day otherwise marked by inexact naval gunfire support. From his improvised defensive position, Warrant Officer Ota estimated the ships to be only a thousand yards offshore, marveling that "with the naked eye we could clearly see the American sailors on the destroyers' decks."

According to Japanese accounts, Admiral Shibasaki realized by midafternoon on D-Day that his concrete command post was the only safe refuge for his hundreds of wounded men. In a humane but fateful decision, he ordered his entire staff to evacuate the shelter and follow him across the island to an alternate site. The two destroyers, firing for some time at Japanese gun positions within the same target area, received sudden reports from their shore fire-control party of enemy troops in the open. The ships switched to multiple salvos of airburst-fused 5"/38 shells, any one of which could have made quick work of exposed troops. Japanese accounts indicate a "large-caliber shell" caught Shibasaki in the open, killing him instantly.

The garrison's communicators studiously avoided reporting Shibasaki's death. At 4:30 that afternoon, the *Katori Maru* received its last message from the garrison, which simply reported: "Enemy under support of fleet and aerial bombing have entered . . . the harbor and are continuously landing men and materials. We are fighting them near the north-south line leading to the pier."

The early death of Shibasaki and his staff left Commander Sugai in command of the Betio defenses, but Sugai was bottled up in his deadly "pocket" in the northwest. Lt. jg Tamikichi Taniguchi, commanding the Second Company of the Sasebo 7th, was likewise in dangerously close contact with the assortment of Marines on the western beach.

Only Lt. jg Goichi Minami, commanding the Third Company on the east, had it in his power to win or lose the battle the first night. The U.S. Marines were particularly vulnerable on that flank—barely 600 troops scattered along a shallow enclave running west from the Burns-Philp Wharf at the eastern edge of Red Beach Three past the base of the main pier to the precarious position, at the edge of Red Beach Two, of Col. David M. Shoup, commanding the assault forces ashore. Lieutenant Minami easily had three times that number, counting both *rikusentai* and armed construction workers, and he had only to penetrate 400 yards along the beach to cut off the lifeline of the pier and overrun Shoup. No major American force in the Pacific War was ever as vulnerable as the exhausted elements of the 2nd Marine Division that first night at Tarawa. But young Minami, in his initial exposure to combat, was no substitute for the fiery Shibasaki. Japanese forces remained essentially immobilized at the moment of their greatest opportunity.

The third turning point of the battle occurred shortly before noon on the second day along the western end of the island, designated by the Americans as Green Beach. This phase of the battle took place between two company commanders, Lieutenant jg Taniguchi of the Sasebo 7th, and Maj. Michael P. Ryan, commanding an unlikely assortment of survivors ("Ryan's Orphans") from four different landing teams. Taniguchi's men still occupied a daunting series of pillboxes, gun emplacements, and camouflaged foxholes, but their fields of fire were oriented westward. Ryan attacked north to south from his initial toehold on the western edge of Red Beach One. More significantly, Ryan, in the expediency of close combat, had discovered the deadly combination of fire and maneuver that would spell the doom of Japanese garrisons in the Central and Western Pacific for the remaining two years of the war. Sherman tanks covered by infantry, improvised assault squads of flamethrowers and demolition experts, and a shore fire-control party with a working radio. Responsive naval gunfire spelled the critical difference. Ryan's team called in major-caliber naval fire within fifty yards of the Marines. In less than an hour the Americans had swept the entire west coast. The 2nd Marine Division finally had a covered beach over which to land reinforcements fully intact.

Ryan's achievement became a critical turning point in the battle, because the Japanese could not recover from the annihilation of Taniguchi's company and the subsequent loss of Betio's broad western shoreline. Its loss meant the Japanese would henceforth be blind to American reinforcements approaching Betio from the west. The Americans' constant aerial strafing, naval bombardment, and increasingly effective shelling from the artillery of the landing force prevented Sugai and Minami from executing any deployments to reinforce the west during daylight. This must have been keenly galling to Commander Sugai. The Marines presented absolutely perfect targets—paddling ashore for over an hour in eighty-four rubber boats from the western reef, backlit throughout by the setting sun—yet no Japanese were in a position to fire an aimed shot with any weapon, not even a rifle.

The final turning point in this bloody contest occurred the third night, when Commander Sugai and Lieutenant jg Minami finally mustered forces on the eastern flank to counterattack the same 1st Battalion, 6th Marines who had landed with such impunity the previous evening.

This was a sensibly planned, well-orchestrated series of night attacks—not at all the sake-soaked *"Banzai!"* charges typically characterized by western historians. Initial probes found the seams between American units and the location of their automatic weapons. This accomplished, a force of some 500 to 700 *rikusentai* then struck those sectors of the Marine lines at 4:00 A.M. Such a concentrated attack delivered along the north shore the first night could have devastated the American landing force. By the third night, however, the Marines had tipped the balance in their favor.

Prearranged naval gunfire and artillery concentrations blanketed the eastern approaches; star shells kept the battlefield in constant illumination. More than half these Marines had fought the Japanese in the Solomons; their lines bent but did not break. Individual troops proved their mettle in primeval hand-to-hand fighting with knives and bayonets. The attack failed at great loss to the Japanese. Warrant Officer Ota's account is instructive:

> Each man was so loaded down with hand grenades we could hardly walk . . . 'READY!' We disabled the safeties on our hand grenades. 'ATTACK!' We rushed all together here and there. I completely forgot my wounded knee. The dark night was lighted as bright as day. There were heavy sounds of grenade explosions, the disordered fire of rifles, the shrieks, yells, and roars. It was just like Hell. The night battle was over in half an hour. Altogether, about 750 of us had entered the night attack. Almost all were killed, but I was somehow still alive.

The failure of their counterattack broke the back of the Betio defenders. A few hours of residual fighting on the fourth morning cleaned out the last pockets of resistance. Many of the surviving *rikusentai* chose to die at their own hands. Warrant Officer Ota and Petty Officer Onuki somehow survived having their respective bunkers scorched with flame-throwers and flattened by charges of TNT and were captured.

Elsewhere in the Gilberts, the U.S. Army's 27th Division overran Butaritari Island in Makin Atoll; a Marine reconnaissance unit landed by rubber boats from a transport submarine to wrest Apamama Atoll from its small Japanese garrison; a fresh Marine landing team ran a force of 175 *rikusentai* to ground on Buariki Island, Tarawa Atoll, and, in savage jungle fighting reminiscent of Guadalcanal, killed them all on November 27. The U.S. Central Pacific Force had recaptured the entire Gilbert Islands in exactly two weeks.

Admiral Koga's *Hei* Plan #3 had failed. Only his fleet submarines achieved any degree of success, notably the sinking of the escort carrier USS *Liscome Bay* (CVE 56) off Makin by *I-175*. But the Southern Attack Force sank *I-35* off Tarawa on the fourth day of the battle, and other U.S. forces sank *I-40* in the northern Gilberts two days later.

Koga, shaken to his roots by the devastation wreaked earlier on his carrier pilots and heavy cruisers at Rabaul, never stirred from Truk. His decision to ignore the threat to the Central Pacific and reinforce the northern Solomons in effect cost him not only his chance for the "Decisive Battle" in the Gilberts but led as well to his being outflanked and forced to vacate Truk by the subsequent (and nearly immediate) U.S. invasion of the Marshalls. IGHQ would retain Koga in command of the Combined Fleet, however, until his death in a plane crash shortly after the Marshalls campaign. The Fourth Fleet's emaciated force of destroyers and light cruisers never left the Marshalls. Colonel Yamanaka's Ko Detachment deployed from Ponape to Kwajalein, but waited there in vain for final orders to execute their counter-landing in the Gilberts. Admiral Koga canceled *Hei* Plan #3 on December 4.

Admiral Shibasaki and his men fulfilled their side of the plan in spades, holding the American landing force at bay for the requisite three days. The last *rikusentai* very likely died with eyes searching the western horizon in vain for the sight of the expected Japanese battleships. Shibasaki received a posthumous promotion to vice admiral; the emperor commended the doomed garrison. They had paid a fearsome price: 4,455 died. The bulk of the 146 prisoners captured by the Marines on Betio were Korean laborers; only nineteen were Japanese. Two were survivors of the sunken submarine *I-35;* several others were civilian members of the 111th Construction Battalion—carpenters, masons, a barber, some "pick and shovel men." Only eight were *rikusentai* from either the Sasebo 7th Special Naval Landing Force or the 3d Special Base Defense Force. The 2,571 *rikusentai* at Tarawa thus suffered a fatality rate of 99.7 percent.

The *rikusentai* nevertheless sold their lives dearly. The American landing force sustained 3,400 casualties (including 1,115 killed) in three days, roughly 30 percent of the assault elements of the 2nd Marine Division who were able to land while the battle still raged. This savage fighting in such a compressed time and space—more than 5,500 Japanese and Americans killed in seventy-six hours within a space smaller than that occupied by the Pentagon building and its parking lots—would remain the haunting hallmark of the battle.

Tarawa became a pivotal milepost in the Pacific War. The Americans learned from their many mistakes, validated their previously unproven amphibious doctrine, and rolled "on to westward," an increasingly invincible juggernaut. The Japanese tried desperately to devise countermeasures, including the increasing use of special suicide attack units, but never again would they hold an American landing force in such dire jeopardy as they did the first night at Tarawa.

War's Greatest Tank Duel

By Pat McTaggart

The incessant artillery fire had cost many of the soldiers yet another sleepless night. None of the veterans could recall such a constant din of battle since the war had started, yet they went about the business of preparing their armored mounts for the coming attack with little complaint.

As the sun began to rise over the steppes on Monday, July 12, 1943, the elite of the two most powerful armies in Europe unknowingly made ready to meet each other in a headlong clash of armor that would become the largest single tank engagement the world has ever seen.

The Battle of Kursk had begun eight days earlier on July 4, when Generaloberst Hermann Hoth launched his Fourth Panzer Army in an afternoon attack on three Soviet armies positioned on the southern sector of the Kursk salient. The next day, the entire line erupted in a spasm of explosions and death. The numbers of men and materiel involved in the battle were staggering. Some 900,000 German soldiers, supported by 2,700 tanks and assault guns, 10,000 artillery pieces and 2,000 aircraft, faced 1,300,000 Red Army troops, backed by 3,600 tanks, 20,000 artillery pieces and 2,400 aircraft, on a front approximately 300 miles in length. The salient, formed as a result of the 1942 Soviet winter offensive, was barely 100 miles across at its widest point.

German planners, most notably Field Marshal Erich von Manstein, has envisioned a classic two-pronged attack on the flanks of the salient. In the south, Hoth's Fourth Panzer Army, aided by Armeeabteilung (Detachment) Kempf, would slice through General Nikolai F. Vatutin's Voronezh Front with 1,500 armored vehicles, while Generaloberst Walter Model's Ninth Army, with 1,200 tanks and assault guns, would smash General Konstantin K. Rokossovsky's Central Front in the north. The two forces were to meet at Kursk, with a secondary armored thrust meeting some 30 miles to the east of the city. If all went well, the salient would be pinched off and nine Soviet armies would be destroyed.

The plan might have worked, but for the fact that Soviet intelligence had penetrated the German general staff and was receiving top-secret messages issued by the Oberkommando der Wehrmacht (OKW), the German armed forces high command, faster than the German commanders in the field.

Manstein envisioned a May attack. However, Adolf Hitler's indecision concerning the date, coupled with the Soviet intelligence coup, gave the Red Army time to prepare for the operation that the Germans had code-named Zitadelle (Citadel). Instead of achieving a quick, decisive breakthrough, the German panzer formations would find themselves faced with a series of defensive belts. Immense minefields, concentrated batteries of antitank guns (known as PAK Fronts), and the determination of the Soviet soldier would also be deciding factors in the outcome of the battle.

Hitler had postponed Zitadelle for almost two months while he waited for a new generation of armored vehicles to come off the assembly lines. The Porsche Tiger, nicknamed "Ferdinand," or

"Elefant," and the newly developed Mark V Panther medium tank were expected to combine with the already proven Henschel version of the Tiger to flatten Soviet defenses and to annihilate any Russian counterattacks.

However, these "miracle" weapons did not live up to Hitler's expectations. They had been produced too quickly, and several defects, which could have been found during testing, went undiscovered in the rush to get them to the front.

A fault in the Panther's engine and fuel systems caused several deadly fires on the battlefield, while vulnerable tracks and a weak drive system soon immobilized many of the Ferdinands. Another "minor" defect, not taken into account by the engineers at home, was the fact that the Ferdinand, which was really a heavily armored, self-propelled 88mm gun, rather than a true tank, possessed no secondary armament.

Without any machine guns to protect them, immobilized Ferdinands became easy prey for Soviet tank-killer infantry groups.

There were other surprises for both sides during the first few days of the battle. Hoth's July 4 midafternoon attack caught the Soviets off guard. Two armored fists, composed of General der Panzertruppe Otto von Knobelsdorff's XLVIII Panzerkorps and Obergrüppenführer (SS General) Paul Hausser's SS Panzerkorps, were able to take essential observation points for the opening of the general offensive set for the next day.

As German gunners prepared their artillery pieces in the early hours of July 5, the eastern sky lit up with a deadly fireworks display. Seconds later, Soviet shells were falling on assembly areas and artillery positions all along the German line. For the Landser (German infantry) waiting in their trenches to start their own attack, the Soviet barrage was psychologically damaging. They looked at one another and asked the same questions "Can this be a coincidence? Do they know we are coming?" The uncertainty continued to haunt them as they dug deeper into the sandy Russian earth, trying to escape the hail of steel falling from the sky.

Marshal Georgi Zhukov, master tactician of the Soviet defenses at Kursk, almost won the battle before the ground operations could get underway. As Luftwaffe bombers sat on their runways, armed and fueled for an early morning strike, hundreds of bombers and fighters from the Soviet Second and Seventeenth Air Armies were already heading toward the German airfields.

Disaster was narrowly averted due to the presence of new German "Freya" radar equipment that picked up the massed Soviet formations only minutes away from their targets. Luftwaffe General Hans Seidemann immediately assembled the fighters of his VIII Fliegerkorps. They swerved through the bombers already on the runways, taking off in a desperate attempt to meet the Soviet threat.

Seidemann's fighters successfully intercepted the Soviet planes, forcing them to flee. He estimated that 120 Soviet aircraft were destroyed during the initial contact. Although that figure may be questioned, even Marshal Zhukov stated that "aerial support was insignificant and, to be frank, ineffective. Our strikes at the enemy airfields at dawn were too late."

Despite superior Soviet intelligence, the outcome of the battle was far from certain. Precise planning for a battle is only good until the first shot is fired. The innumerable variables in war weather, commander temperament, troop and technical quality make for a constant change of conditions in which no one can truly predict the outcome. Kursk was no exception to that rule.

Model's Ninth Army immediately ran into trouble in the north. The main assault was directed at Lt. Gen. Nikolai P. Pukhov's Thirteenth Army, with secondary strikes on Thirteenth Army's junction with Forty-eighth Army and Seventieth Army. Massed anti-tank fire and the extensive Russian mine-fields took a heavy toll of German armored vehicles.

Model's objective for July 5 was the town of Olkhovatka, fewer than 12 miles from his jump-off positions. It was not until July 7 that his armored spearheads finally reached the outskirts of the town. A fanatic defense of the heights around Olkhovatka finally stopped the Germans dead in their tracks.

Three Soviet tank corps (III, XVI and XIX) were rushed to the area to reinforce the defenders. Model then switched his main axis of attack 12 miles to the east. The railroad junction at the village of Ponyri thus became the focus of a bitter battle that once and for all dashed any hopes of further German advances in the north.

Generaloberst Hoth's Fourth Panzer Army, attacking in the south, achieved better results in the early days of the assault. The XLVIII Panzerkorps (made up of the 3rd and 11th Panzer divisions, Grossdeutschland Panzergrenadier Division, 332nd Infanteriedivision [I.D.] and two-thirds of the 167 I.D.) and II SS Panzerkorps (Leibstandarte SS Adolf Hitler, Das Reich and Totenkopf [Death's Head] divisions, SS Panzer divisions and one-third of the 167th I.D.) were able to smash through Lt. Gen. Ivan M. Chistyakov's Sixth Guards Army's first defense line in about two hours.

However, a sudden rainstorm, which flooded several gullies in the area, and well-placed minefields stopped the advance, allowing Chistyakov's troops to retreat to a second defensive belt. As Hoth's panzers pressed their attack on Chistyakov's line, Vatutin sent Lt. Gen. Mikhail E. Katukov's First Tank Army, along with the II and V Guards Tank Corps, into the battle in an effort to stop the Germans.

By July 7, the Fourth Panzer Army was involved in a battle of attrition as its armored corps attempted to batter its way forward. Soviet tank units hit the flanks of the armored thrust in sharp engagements that left the countryside littered with smoking wrecks. The Leibstandarte reported 123 enemy tanks destroyed in three days of battle, but the Germans also sustained substantial losses.

Vatutin kept pressing the enemy, but he was hearing disturbing news from his tank commanders. The Germans had devised a new weapon a tank destroying aircraft that was wreaking havoc on Soviet armored formations. Four squadrons of Henschel Hs-129s, led by Hauptmann (Captain) Bruno Meyer, were attacking the Russian armor with 30mm cannon mounted below the aircraft fuselage.

Another experimental group, composed of Junkers Ju-87G Stukas armed with a 37mm cannon under each wing, was commanded by Hauptmann Hans-Ulrich Rudel. Describing the action at Kursk, Rudel noted, "In the first attack, four tanks exploded under the hammer blows of my cannons; by evening, the total rises to twelve." By the end of the war, Rudel would become the undisputed "tank buster" in the world with 519 confirmed kills.

On the Soviet side, the sturdy Ilyushin Il-2 ground-attack aircraft, equipped with two N-37 or P-37 anti-tank cannon, made life just as miserable for the German panzer crews. The vast array of new or experimental equipment on both sides was very impressive, but the outcome of the battle would, as always, hinge on the determination and the blood of the men fighting on the ground.

Hoth continued the attack. Zhukov and Vatutin knew that OKW orders specified the seizure of the town of Oboyan as a major objective for the Fourth Panzer Army. If the Germans succeeded in capturing the town, which was a vital supply railhead for the southern sector of the salient, Vatutin's entire front would become unhinged. Recognizing the danger, Zhukov ordered Lt. Gen. Alexei S. Zhadov's Fifth Guards Army, along with Lt. Gen. Pavel A. Rotmistrov's Fifth Guards Tank Army, to make a forced march of 190 miles to meet the German thrust. In the meantime,

Chistyakov's Sixth Guards Army and Katukov's First Tank Army would have to hold the Germans at bay.

Hoth planned to use XLVII Panzerkorps and II SS Panzerkorps to take Oboyan, while Armeeabteilung Kempf protected his right flank against the threat of a counterattack from Zhukov's reserve forces. The fighting in front of Oboyan was the fiercest yet seen. With the help of a massive Luftwaffe bomber attack, Hausser's SS divisions were able to tear a wide gap in the Sixth Guards Army's defenses.

Near the village of Beregovy, a company of the Leibstandarte, commanded by Obersturmführer (1st Lt.) Rudolf von Ribbentrop, son of the German foreign minister, broke through a Soviet anti-tank belt. Supported by panzergrenadiers, Ribbentrop's tanks raised havoc among the Russian defenders, causing many units to abandon their positions.

Vatutin ordered General Katukov to stop the Germans at any cost. Katukov sent two armored infantry regiments into the breach, but both regiments were quickly destroyed. One eyewitness reported, "After two hours, all that was left of them was their [regimental] numbers."

Other attacks on Hausser's flanks also ended in disaster, but they bought the Soviets time to regroup. Panic struck several Russian units, but military council representatives and political commissars managed to halt the rout. New defensive positions were occupied while the Germans were dealing with Katukov's spoiling attacks.

At Voronezh Front headquarters, Vatutin received a direct order from Josef Stalin. His Military Council representative, Nikita S. Kruschev, read the brief message, "On no account must the Germans break through to Oboyan." The order pinned Vatutin to the Oboyan area and gave him little room for maneuver. Zhadov and Rotmistrov were on the way, but in the meantime, the Soviet line would be stretched to the limit. It would be a very close thing.

Heavy fighting enveloped the area for the next few days. Zhukov fed reinforcements into the battle as they were needed, while gathering his main reserves for a massive counterstrike. The counterattack, set for July 12, would be a coordinated assault against both Hoth and Model.

Zhadov and Rotmistrov's advance units began arriving in the area on July 10 and were dispersed in the groves and gullies that dotted the countryside behind the main battle area. After force marching 190 miles, the vehicles of the two armies needed a thorough going-over before they could strike, and the men, who had been on the move for three days, needed time to rest. Soviet mastery in camouflaging materiel and men prevented German air reconnaissance from detecting the arrival of the Russian reinforcements.

Meanwhile, Hausser and Knobelsdorff kept hammering away at the Soviet defenses in front of Oboyan. The panzer divisions were gaining ground, but they were also taking serious casualties from the well-entrenched defenders.

At Fourth Panzer Army headquarters, Hoth decided to change the axis of his attack in an attempt to cut his losses while bypassing the main Oboyan defensive belt. He planned to send Knobelsdorff's XLVIII Panzerkorps around the western edge of the town, while Hausser's SS Panzerkorps wheeled east to Prokhorovka, finally linking up with Knobelsdorff north of the Oboyan railhead. Armeeabteilung Kempf would still cover the right flank against the inevitable Soviet counterattack. If the plan worked, Hoth's forces would be able to fan out on the broad plains beyond Oboyan and fight the classic tank battle that the German army had perfected over the years.

In disobeying his specific instructions from OKW, the panzer general caught Zhukov and Vatutin flat-footed. The II SS Panzerkorps, overcoming stubborn resistance, managed to breach Chistyakov's Sixth Guards Army's line in several areas. As the Leibstandarte and Das Reich divisions moved toward Prokhorovka, units of the Totenkopf Division assaulted Soviet positions along the Psel River.

Sturmbannführer (Major) Karl Ullrich, commanding the 3rd Battalion of the 6th Panzergrenadier Regiment/Totenkopf, led his men forward despite the deadly fire coming from the heights on the opposite bank. As artillery and machine-gun fire raked the advancing SS grenadiers, they appeared ready to break.

Ullrich personally led his distraught men in a final assault on the Soviet positions, capturing the village of Krasny Oktyabr and establishing a bridgehead on the enemy bank. Victory seemed to be within Hoth's grasp as he steadily poured his meager reserves through the gaps in the Russian line caused by Hausser's troops.

Knobelsdorff's corps was also making progress against Katukov's First Tank Army. Grossdeutschland and 3rd Panzer Division inflicted heavy casualties on the Soviets as they advanced. The 3rd Panzer reported taking 1,700 prisoners as it sliced through the Russian defenses.

Katukov and Chistyakov were once again forced to throw reserves into the battle as soon as they arrived. Soviet counterattacks, uncoordinated and costly as they were, helped slow the German advance somewhat. Nature also intervened with showers that turned the ground into a sloppy morass that hindered men and machines alike.

Zhukov was playing a dangerous game in planning to coordinate his northern and southern attacks on the same day. While Chistyakov and Katukov pleaded for more reinforcements, Fifth Guards Tank Army and Fifth Guards Army were preparing to strike. Vatutin's front would just have to hold for one more day.

On the morning of July 11, Hausser and Knobelsdorff renewed the attack. Under a protective umbrella of Stukas and

Messerschmitts, the panzers continued to batter the Soviets. By the end of the day, Sixth Guards Army had been all but destroyed, and Katukov's First Tank Army was severely mauled. Units of the Fifth Guards Army, thrown into the battle as a stopgap measure, had also been decimated in the day's fighting.

The only good news of the day for Vatutin was to be found on his left flank, where a spirited resistance by the Seventh Guards Army and the Sixty-ninth Army had slowed Armee-abteilung Kempf to a crawl. Hoth's plan of a two-pronged attack on the Soviet armor was in serious trouble thanks to the courage and sacrifice of those two armies.

Meanwhile, Katukov, at First Tank Army headquarters, kept calling Vatutin, asking the same question: "Where are the armored corps of Fifth Guards Tank Army?" Finally, he received the reply that he had desperately been waiting for. "They are on their way," the message from the Voronezh front headquarters said. The die was finally cast, and the outcome of the entire Zitadelle operation would be settled on the following day.

Obersturmführer Ribbentrop remembers the morning of July 12 as being "a very beautiful day, but there was a sense of uneasiness about it. Here and there, an artillery shell exploded, and some machine-gun fire could be heard fairly close by. In the clear blue sky, we could see aircraft circling lazily."

Ribbentrop's company had started Zitadelle with 22 tanks on July 5. He had just seven left as he prepared to move toward the showdown at Prokhorovka.

Less than 10 miles away, Captain Peter A. Skripkin went through essentially the same routine as Ribbentrop. Skripkin commanded the 2nd Battalion, 181 Brigade of the XVIII Tank Corps in Rotmistrov's Fifth Guards Tank Army. The battalion would be at the forefront of the tank army's surprise attack.

Around 8 a.m., Hausser's force of more than 600 panzers began moving up the narrow defiles leading to Prokhorovka. At the same time, Rotmistrov's command, totaling some 850 tanks, raced forward, hoping to catch the Germans unaware.

Great clouds of dust, churned up by the massive armored forces, obscured the vision of both sides. While Hausser's corps headed straight for Prokhorovka, Rotmistrov's units sped toward the German flank.

Both sides spotted each other simultaneously, but the Soviets had the advantage of racing down the hills blocking the German flank and closing with the SS divisions quickly. The Tiger's awesome 88mm gun, which had been used so successfully in picking off Soviet armor at long range, was nullified by the Russian charge. Before the end of the day, more than 1,500 of the world's best tanks would be engaged in close combat on a narrow front bordered by the Psel River on one side and a railway embankment on the other.

Ribbentrop's radio crackled. Panzeralarm came across the wire as the first Russian tanks came over a hill crest. He acted swiftly, positioning his depleted company on the reverse slope of a small hill in the valley. "I saw tanks, T-34s, approaching down the hill," he said. "They were 800 meters away; an ideal range for a good shot. Suddenly, I noticed more enemy tanks coming at our flanks. They were between 150–200 meters away. I counted 15, 20, 30, 40 of the T-34s before I quit. Russian infantry were riding on their sides. I ordered the company to open fire, and my gunner destroyed a T-34 about 50 meters from us. Then all hell broke loose."

The Russian commanders knew that the 76mm guns on their T-34s were only effective at close range against the massive armor of the Tiger and Panther tanks. Disregarding early losses, they continued to close with the Germans, using the superior cross-country speed of their tanks to narrow the gap between themselves and the enemy.

Captain Skripkin's unit ran into a group of Tigers as it

attacked from the left bank of the Psel River. Knowing that he had to close quickly, he yelled, "Forward, follow me!" to the rest of his battalion before plunging into the midst of the German formation. Within minutes, he had destroyed two of the Tigers.

General Rotmistrov, watching the battle from a hill near Prokhorovka, noted: "The tanks were moving across the steppe in small packs, under cover of woodland and hedges. The bursts of gunfire merged into one continuous mighty roar. Soon the whole sky was shrouded by the thick smoke of burning wrecks. On the black, scorched earth the gutted tanks burnt like torches. It was difficult to establish which side was attacking and which side was defending."

The battlefield resembled a scene reminiscent of the huge cavalry clashes of the 19th century. Tanks charged headlong at each other, firing at point-blank range. Smoke and dust made it nearly impossible to tell friend from foe.

Ribbentrop had already destroyed several T-34s when his own tank was hit by Soviet fire. His gunner was wounded, and the firing optics in his tank were so damaged that the panzer was no longer battle worthy. Four of the seven tanks in his company had already been destroyed in the intense fighting. Commandeering another panzer, Ribbentrop continued the battle, infiltrating a wedge of Soviet tanks and destroying several of them at a range of less than 20 meters before pulling back.

Rotmistrov kept feeding waves of tanks into the gap between Hausser and Armeeabteilung Kempf. Kempf's III Panzerkorps, commanded by General der Panzertruppe Hermann Brieth, was still some 12 miles away at midday. He was advancing, but the pace was slow in the face of heavy Russian resistance. Kempf had almost 300 panzers in his detachment; enough to tip the scales in favor of the Germans at Prokhorovka. As it was, his panzers might just as well have been on the moon.

With Rotmistrov's tank corps pressing his flanks, Hausser was forced to divert a portion of his spearhead forces to meet the Russian attack. The Soviets continued to drive deep into the German columns, suffering heavy losses in the process. When driven back, the Russian commanders immediately regrouped and charged again, giving no respite to the enemy.

One such attack breached a hastily formed defensive line and allowed several T-34s to maul the soft-skinned vehicles of a panzergrenadier battalion. The battalion adjutant, Obersturmführer Werner Wolff, formed a counterattacking force from the remnants of a company commanded by a sergeant. More than 30 T-34s were destroyed by Wolff's infantry in close combat, temporarily halting the threat.

For both sides, the battle was fought with great heroism. Captain Skripkin's T-34 was hit by two shells from a nearby Tiger. Wounded, Skripkin was pulled from the smoldering vehicle and taken to the relative safety of a shell crater. Skripkin's driver, Aleksandr Nikolayev, noticed an approaching Tiger and returned to his damaged tank. Starting the engine, Nikolayev rammed the crippled T-34 into the German at full speed. Both tanks were destroyed in the massive explosion that followed.

Rotmistrov's opponent, Generaloberst Hoth, was well forward in the battle area as the tanks continued to clash. He received steady reports of the heavy losses being inflicted by both sides as he watched the battle through a trench telescope.

The scene that presented itself to Hoth was one of utter chaos. Burning tanks, some with blackened corpses lying grotesquely beside them, dotted the landscape. Stukas and Il-2s circled like birds of prey, waiting for an opening in the smoke before diving to add more destruction to the armored forces below.

By late afternoon, it was clear to Rotmistrov that he had blunted the German attack and had forced Hausser's Panzerkorps into a defensive posture that was becoming almost impossible to overcome. Each side had lost more than 300 tanks and although the Soviets had not been able to destroy the SS Panzerkorps, the Germans' end-run attempt to take Prokhorovka had failed.

The Russian general ordered his tank and infantry units to withdraw from the field in order to regroup for the expected resumption of the German offensive on the 13th. Indeed, Hoth was already planning his next move when word reached him of the extent of the massive Russian attack against Model in the north. When the situation became clearer, the panzer general knew that there was no chance that his forces could link up with Model's Ninth Army.

Later that evening, the commanders of Army Groups Center and South, Field Marshals Kluge and Manstein, were on their way to the Führer's headquarters in East Prussia. Two days earlier, the British and Americans had invaded Sicily. The specter of the collapse of the Italian government had convinced Hitler that Zitadelle should be called off.

Orders were already being issued for Hausser's Panzerkorps to disengage the enemy and to prepare to move to Italy in case of a surprise Allied landing on the mainland. When Hitler told the two field marshals his decision, they were dumbfounded. Like most of Hitler's decisions, however, the order was irrevocable.

The Battle of Prokhorovka was over. Hausser's Panzerkorps remained on the battlefield, but it was a battlefield of mass destruction and very little worth. Survivors of the battle aptly describe the area as the "gully of death."

As a strategic operation, Zitadelle should never have taken place after its initial postponement. German forces in a defensive mode could have exacted a terrible toll from Russian armies attacking their well-entrenched positions. Instead, it was the Germans who were bled white in front of the Soviet defenses. Despite his own losses, Zhukov had enough reserves left to begin going over to the offensive on the morning of July 12.

The courage of both the Russian and German combatants

made the battlefield a mass grave for thousands of brave soldiers. The highly trained German panzer crews who were lost in the battle were irreplaceable. Prokhorovka marked the end of the myth of German armored invincibility. With the end of the battle, the Germans lost the strategic initiative on the Eastern Front forever.

Gallant Sortie Survived

By Peggy Robbins

The fact that future president of the United States John F. Kennedy was a naval hero in World War II is known by millions, but today relatively few know enough about Kennedy's remarkable exploit to have any idea how extraordinary it really was.

In early 1942, the PT-boat (patrol torpedo boat) service came to the attention of the American public when Lieutenant John D. Bulkeley received the Medal of Honor for commanding the PT that rescued General and Mrs. Douglas MacArthur and their young son from Manila and slipped them to the north coast of the southern Philippine island of Mindanao. The PT-boats, extremely light and maneuverable, had proved themselves so effective in the waters around the Philippines that it was decided to employ them in the South Pacific. The boats could move at over 40 knots per hour; they could, with muffled engines, slip in on targets, fire torpedoes, and then speed away fast enough to outrun pursuers.

In June 1942, Jack Kennedy, who had received his commission as an ensign in the U.S. Navy some months earlier, was one of thousands who reported to the U.S. Naval Reserve Midshipmen's School at Northwestern University in Evanston, Ill., to prepare for sea duty. So, as he said later, he was in the right place at the right time when Lieutenant Bulkeley and John Harllee, executive officer at the Navy's new PT school at Melville, Rhode Island, visited Northwestern looking for reserve officers to man the PT-boats. Kennedy was eager to get into combat, and he had had much experience in sailing despite his very boyish looks. As soon as he finished his training at Northwestern, he was promoted from ensign to lieutenant junior grade and, on orders, he hurried to the Melville school, where he had an advantage in rank over the majority of his fellow officers who were recent university graduates.

Kennedy did well in his studies seamanship, navigation, gunnery, engineering, and the handling of torpedoes. He did so well that Harllee wanted him to remain at the school as an instructor. Kennedy objected, but was assigned to a squadron and made skipper of a training boat, PT-101. At Melville he acquired the nickname "Shafty" in reference to his request for overseas duty; having been denied, he had complained, "I've been shafted."

Kennedy was later ordered to the Solomon Islands in the South Pacific as an officer replacement. Delighted, he left San Francisco on a transport on March 6, 1943, and in due time arrived at Tulagi, the prewar capital of the British Solomon Islands Protectorate. Tulagi, a narrow, hilly island lying just off the southwest coast of larger Florida Island, had been seized by the Japanese in May 1942 and, three months later, recaptured by Americans as part of the invasion of Guadalcanal. Most of the PT base operations were centered on Tulagi, and the PTs, when they were not out on a strike, were moored beneath the bushes all along the shores of Tulagi and Florida, hidden from Japanese planes.

Kennedy was soon faced with the tasks of selecting a new

crew and getting the old 77-foot PT-109, which had already been in combat for months, in shape for the offensive that was ahead. He took his 10-man crew from replacements who had just arrived from Melville. His first log entry as skipper was dated April 26, 1943 "moored in usual berth" and that day he set to work training the men and cleaning and repairing the boat. He worked side by side with the crew. When PT-109 went into dry dock, Kennedy donned shorts and labored at scraping and sandpapering her bottom and applying a fresh coat of the forest-green paint that was used on PTs for camouflage in the island waterways. Skipper Kennedy was well-liked by the crew of PT-109 from the start.

In a few days, the PT and her crew were in shape to begin difficult dusk-to-dawn patrols, firing on Japanese transports and barges and mauling Japanese shore installations. Radioman John E. Maguire, a 26-year-old New Yorker, later recalled: "Our skipper Jack Kennedy was . . . a gangling kid who said he was 26 (which he was), but I always thought he was younger. . . . He was a millionaire. . . . His father was an ambassador. . . . Once, when a ship's carpenter bawled hell out of him for accidentally spilling water on him, the lieutenant just stood there in his skinny green shorts and said, 'Excuse me,' and let it go at that. That carpenter did a lot of gulping when he found out the kid was PT-109's skipper." As captain of 109, Kennedy was no pushover. He demanded and received full compliance with his orders and never for a minute lost control of the boat's operation.

By the end of May, Tulagi was buzzing with preparations for the invasion of New Georgia in the western Solomons. Ships of all kinds, destroyers, cargo ships, landing craft, were steaming up from Guadalcanal and the New Hebrides toward the invasion area, and the vessels at Tulagi had been ordered to move ahead to the Russell Islands, to the west and about a third of the distance to New Georgia.

After a period of patrol duty in the Russells, PT-109 returned to Tulagi in mid-June to have her three engines replaced. After the refitting, she was sent first to Guadalcanal and then ordered back to the Russells. Preparations for the New Georgia invasion had progressed and a base for PT operations was set up on the north coast of Rendova, one of the larger of the Solomons. On June 30, several landings were made on Rendova. The night before the landings, PT-109's mission was to patrol the area between the Russells and New Georgia and, with her torpedoes, help defend the convoys from Japanese attack.

The weather that night became increasingly violent, and only clever seamanship saved 109 as she labored through mountains and valleys of water. A PT-boat accompanying 109 sent up a distress signal. Kennedy headed his heaving boat through the savage waves toward the other PT and got close enough to hear her skipper yell that his boat had a big hole in her hull. Kennedy, hanging onto 109's wheel to keep standing, managed to get his boat close enough to a destroyer on its return trip from New Georgia to get a bilge pump for the stricken PT. But as 109 was maneuvering away from the destroyer, a wave slammed into her port side and jarred a torpedo out of its tube. The torpedo slammed into a heavy depth charge, which was knocked from its perch. The depth charge in turn smashed through the deck and into the crew's quarters, landing on the bunk above Motor Machinist's Mate Edmund T. Drewitch. Drewitch was flung about the violently rocking quarters, his nose smashed, two front teeth broken, and his right kneecap split. At the suffering Drewitch's insistence, PT-109 delivered the pump to the other boat, remained nearby until a rescue tender arrived and then took him to a hospital in the Russells.

In mid-July 109, with two new members added to her crew, was ordered to proceed to the PT forward operating base on Rendova, which was in the center of the main Pacific battle then being fought. PT-109 was one of 18 to 20 PTs moored at Rendova. The PT men spent their days surrounded by the sights and sounds of war and their nights patrolling the dark narrow waters between islands, continually harassing enemy movements. PT-109 successfully accomplished its missions despite some close calls, dangerous situations and mostly minor woundsuntil August.

On August 1, 1943, Kennedy and his crew were relaxing at Rendova and "attending to special business." After many nights at sea, they were scheduled to take the night off. New crew members had taken the place of two men who had recently been wounded seriously enough to be hospitalized, and they were mingling with the others. The "special business" had to do with an experiment in PT-boat weaponry. Someone had come up with the idea that 109 needed a powerful foredeck gun to make her a better match for her next engagement with a Japanese steel barge. Kennedy had somehow secured possession of an old Army 37mm anti-tank gun and moved it to 109 in a Higgins boat. "Only our skipper could have managed that," remarked one member of Kennedy's crew. The men had hauled the anti-tank gun and some 2-by-8 planks aboard, and, with the help of a carpenter, were installing it.

The men hardly had time to rest before Lieutenant Kennedy was notified that there was firm reason to expect that the Japanese would be moving in force toward Kolombangara Island that night. Six destroyers and all available PTs were prepared for action. Soon after that, Rendova's air raid siren wailed, and then the cry "Condition Red!" mingled with the sound of machine-gun fire from Japanese planes tearing down toward the palm trees. According to official reports, 25 Japanese dive bombers raked Rendova Harbor during the attack. The machine guns of all the PT-boats responded; several planes were hit, and at least one crashed in the harbor. Early in the attack, Kennedy rushed into 109's cockpit, ordered the engines started, and yelled to Maguire that he should cast off. While 109's machine gun continued to blaze, Kennedy steered away from the concentration of boats through the debris-littered harbor and zigzagged until the all-clear signal sounded before returning to the base. One PT had been blown up, another was sinking, and several more were damaged.

Later that afternoon, Kennedy attended the daily conference of boat captains at operations headquarters. With the other skippers he was told: "The Japs mean business this time. Tonight we'll have to use everything we have." At least four enemy destroyers were scheduled to move from Bougainville Island to Blackett Strait on Kolombangara's west side and head on to Vila on the island's southern tip.

There were 15 PTs in operating condition, and the commander divided them into four divisions, with each division led by one of the four boats that had radar sets. PT-109 was in Division B under Lieutenant Henry J. Brantingham in PT-159. As the senior skipper, Brantingham was leader of all PT groups as well as Division B.

The gathered skippers were told that there was no time to lose; they must get ready in a hurry. As Kennedy rushed back to PT-109, he encountered Ensign George Henry Ross, an acquaintance from Melville and the executive officer of the PT the Japanese had sunk that day. Ross now had no boat. "Jack, how about letting me ride with you tonight?" he asked Kennedy. "Do you know how to fire a 37mm anti-tank gun?" Jack responded. "Hell no," Ross replied, "but I can learn fast." Kennedy said, "Okay, come on."

The PTs departed Rendova at 6:30 p.m. on August 1, their torpedo tubes full, their guns aimed at the sky, and their helmeted crews alert and tense. The four boats of Division B had the greatest distance to go to reach their designated patrol stations on the Kolombangara coast, and moved out first. By the time they entered Blackett Strait, the night was pitch-black. PT-109 reached her station about 8:30 and soon began patrolling at idling speed to reduce the size of her wake, which, if seen, could guide Japanese planes to her. The boat had lost radio contact with PT-159, as had the majority of the 15 PTs in the group. Most of the PT skippers, including Kennedy, did not know that Brantingham's boat and one other PT had already engaged the enemy, whose destroyers—*Amagiri*, *Hagikaze*, *Arashi* and *Shigure*—had nearly blown them out of the water. The tactical plans for the night's PT operation were lost in confusion. PT-109 could only continue patrolling. The four destroyers would deliver 900 troops and 120 tons of supplies to Vila that night while successfully dodging a total of 30 torpedoes launched by the PTs.

Radioman Maguire later wrote: "I looked for a long time out across the bow of PT-109 into the night and squinched hard ahead, trying my best to glimpse some shape or movement on the seas. . . . It was the black heart of a squally night . . . no moon, no sound at sea. . . . Somewhere out there elements of the Japanese Imperial Fleet were hard about their business; we'd been hunting them so long. . . . Somewhere above were Jap floatplanes, the kind that followed the wakes of our PTs and splattered our plywood decks to splinters. Somewhere around us were jungle islands filled with Japanese. . . . Skipper Kennedy was at my left in the cockpit . . . at my right elbow, jammed into the starboard gun turret, was Motor Machinist's Mate 2nd Class Harold Marney. To keep our movements silent, we held the middle engine low and throttled the starboard and port engines down to neutral. Aft, the rest of the crew were having just as bad luck as we, trying to find something to shoot at. The sea was silent. . . ."

Then Marney yelled, "Ship at two o'clock!" and Kennedy and Maguire suddenly saw "something fast and big" bearing down on them "[an enemy] destroyer moving like lightning!" Kennedy yelled, "Sound general quarters!" and sounded the engine-room buzzer, signaling engineer Patrick McMahon to throttle starboard and port engines full ahead. McMahon did not have time to respond. Up on the bow, Ross was trying to fire the newly installed 37mm fieldpiece. He had gotten the projectile in but had no time to fire it. Amagiri was closing fast on PT-109.

Maguire remembered: "The destroyer hit us.... Its bow crushed into our side about three feet in front of Marney's turret, sweeping him down into the sea and under the [destroyer's] propellers. He didn't even have time to scream. The wheel was yanked out of Kennedy's grasp and he went slamming down on his back; I could hear him gasping on the deck when he hit. I went down, too.... I could hear the planks and decking crack apart.... Kennedy called, 'Are you all right, Mac?'

"The destroyer didn't even slow down. Its bow carried along our starboard side, shearing away the middle two-thirds of PT-109. Our boat snapped in two, and we never saw the after half again. Kirksey, our gunner, went with it." Torpedoman Andrew Jackson Kirksey was a 25-year-old native of Reynolds, Georgia; he had a son born three months after he had enlisted.

PT-109's fuel tanks exploded. McMahon, who had no warning of danger, was engulfed in a river of flame and then, with the blazing stern pulled down by the engines' weight, was plunged into the black watery depths. Although badly burned and completely without the use of his arms, he managed to fight his way to the surface.

Kennedy, Maguire (who had been flung against the day-room canopy) and Seaman 1st Class Edgar Mauer, whose right shoulder had been badly bruised, were still on the bow. The skipper, who feared another explosion from the heat of the fire, yelled, "Everybody in the water!" Maguire's rubber life belt failed to inflate, and Kennedy waited for him to get another; then the three vaulted into the water at a point where the flaming fuel on the surface had been largely pushed away by Amagiri's wake. Ross, who had already hit the water, was clinging to a log with several others.

Gunner's Mate Charles Harris had jumped into the water seconds before the destroyer hit 109. "I dove over the torpedo tube and went under," he recalled. "Next thing I knew, I was in the water, surprised to see I had my life jacket on; flames were exploding all around me, but I wasn't right in them. Suddenly, I heard McMahon calling for help; he was in the flames. . . . I tried to move toward him, but my left leg wouldn't move. . . . I had hit it against the torpedo tube, diving in."

Harris yelled for Kennedy: "Skipper! Skipper! Can you give McMahon a hand? He's burned bad." Harris treaded water by McMahon while Kennedy, who was some distance away, swam toward them, calling out every few minutes to encourage them to "Hold on!" and to check their location. When he reached them, McMahon lay helpless in the water. Kennedy grabbed McMahon's kapok and started towing him back to the part of 109 that was still floating, and to which he had told the others in the water to return. The exhausted Harris said, "Go on, Skipper, I've had it," and dropped behind. "He snapped and fussed at me," Harris recalled. "He said I was putting on a hell of a shameful exhibition for a fellow from Boston." Harris, furious that the Skipper didn't seem to realize how much his leg hurt, swore at Kennedy but he started swimming again. Kennedy gripped his arm and held him above the surface while Harris removed his kapok, took off his sweater and jacket, and put his kapok back on. Then, alongside Kennedy, who was still towing McMahon, he slowly made it back to the boat. Kennedy called out to Kirksey and Marney over and over, but there was no answer.

The 11 survivors resting on the remains of PT-109 were in various physical conditions. McMahon, the most seriously injured, drifted in and out of consciousness. His face, right side and arm were burned black, and his whole body was banged-up, but he did not complain. Thirty-three-year-old William Johnson, a native of Scotland who had grown up in Massachusetts, had been scheduled for rotation home when he was assigned to 109 instead; now he lay battered black and blue and half-dead from swallowing gasoline. Kennedy helped Johnson in every way he could, as he did the others.

Before long, the bow of the boat, which had drifted some distance from where it had been hit by the destroyer, turned turtle. It continued to float, but Kennedy figured it would likely sink during the coming night. The orphaned sailors had no food, no water, no medical supplies, and they were adrift in enemy waters. He told the men they would have to leave the bow and swim to a group of small islands to the west, about 3[h] miles away. Two or three of the men still had their handguns, and Kennedy had salvaged a Thompson submachine gun, a .38 revolver, three .45s, nine clips and a ship's lantern. That was all they would take with them. Alog in the water and a plank from the anti-tank gun mounting also might help. "I'll take McMahon," Kennedy said matter-of-factly.

At 2 p.m. on August 2, after the other men were in the water, Kennedy took the two straps of McMahon's kapok, which he wore over his Mae West, tied them together, and eased the burned man into the water. Then Kennedy got into the water and put the straps between his clenched teeth. Swimming face down and using the breaststroke, he towed McMahon along almost above him. Most of the other men, including all the ones who were poor swimmers, hung onto the log and, by kicking, moved along, too.

"An hour went by," McMahon recalled. "The skipper would pull me and then rest a while to get his breath, and I could hear him coughing. . . . I knew he was in no great shape himself, after being thrown down by the ramming . . . but he was desperately swimming for both of us and not counting the cost. When he'd stop to rest he'd ask me, 'Are you okay?' He kept my spirits up."

About 6:30 p.m., the PT survivors reached a tiny island they called "Plum Pudding," which was about 100 yards long and less than 70 yards wide. It boasted only six coconut trees and some brush, but there were no Japanese. The men dropped to the ground under the palm trees and rested. After a few minutes, Kennedy told the others they were too far south of Ferguson Passage, the nearest place where there was hope of seeing other PT-boats on patrol. He intended to swim into Ferguson Passage beyond the next island, tread water and try to signal to a boat on night patrol. "With that, which we could hardly believe," wrote Ed Mauer, "Kennedy hitched up his shorts, put on a vest, tied a .38 around his neck, picked up the ship's lantern, gave us a quick wave of his hand, walked into the sea, and, carrying the lantern in his kapok, started swimming toward Ferguson Passage."

Kennedy's training on Harvard's swimming team served him well. He reached the passage and treaded water for hours, holding up his lantern, without seeing a patrol boat. He then decided to swim back to Plum Pudding Island. His men, on the beach watching for him, saw him caught in the current and swept past the island. "He flashed the lantern once and yelled, and we went out on the coral reef to try to reach him," Mauer said, "but, oh, he was gone!"

Mauer continued: "Then, in the morning, I saw a ghost. There was the skipper, crawling out of the sea on his hands and knees. We ran to him and carried him. He was throwing up and he barely moved. He had been in the water 12 hours and he was feverish. We carried him up the beach, where he passed out."

By this time, a report had reached PT headquarters in Rendova and been confirmed by a hidden coastwatcher that PT-109, commanded by Lieutenant John F. Kennedy, had been destroyed in action with no survivors.

Kennedy lay sick on the beach at Plum Pudding most of a day and night, and then told the men they would all have to move to a larger island with more trees. They were even out of water on Plum Pudding. Torpedoman Ray Starkey recalled: "It was the same grueling swim as before. Kennedy took McMahon, pulling his life jacket with his teeth, and the rest of us held onto our log and kept pushing. But this time Kennedy was much weaker. He moved slowly, like a man caught in slow-motion film, and we knew he was in great pain." Kennedy had an old back injury that had been greatly aggravated when he had slammed into the deck of PT-109.

Starkey continued, "It took us three hours to cover the mile to that island. The skipper looked terrible. His feet were blistered and swollen, and he threw up a lot from the saltwater he swallowed pulling McMahon. Some of the men found coconuts, banged them open and gulped down the milk so fast they got sick. We tried to eat some live snails, but they were punk. It rained a torrent that night and everybody went around licking water off tree and bush leaves. It tasted very bitter. The next morning we found out whyall the leaves were covered with bird dung. We named the place 'Bird Island.' "

Still without food and water, the men on Bird Island were getting weaker and weaker. Kennedy and Ross decided to check out Nauru Island, on the passage only a half-mile away. "Kennedy and I swam side by side for Nauru that night," Ross wrote. "I guess you couldn't have found a sorrier sight than the two of us, just inching ahead. It took more than an hour for us to get there. . . . We half walked and half crawled across Nauru. We found a smashed landing barge with a cask of water and some old hardtack biscuits. Delicious!"

Kennedy and Ross stayed awake all night on the passage side of the island, hoping to hear the sound of PTs, but none was heard. "Next sunrise, Kennedy was prowling around and found a one-man dugout canoe hidden under some palm trees. That night he was out there in the passage, endlessly searching for PTs. . . .

So he paddled back to the other island and took the men a keg of water and some hardtack. It was the first food they'd had since our boat was rammed."

Returning to Nauru, Kennedy's canoe went under in a tropical squall and left him struggling in open water. "Fortunately," Ross continued, "two natives in a war canoe spotted him and dragged him to shore. . . . They were bushy-haired fellows with bones piercing their noses. For a long time both Kennedy and I tried unsuccessfully to communicate with the natives in pidgin English. He said, 'RendovaAmerican,' over and over, and finally they understood. Kennedy split a coconut with a sheath knife and on the polished interior shell scratched a message: '11 Alive Nauru Island Native knows posit and reefs Kennedy.' He gave the coconut shell to the natives, said 'Rendova! Rendova!,' and they got back in their war canoe and started toward Rendova. Kennedy and I were so exhausted we passed out. I thought he was finished."

The native had shown Kennedy and Ross where a two-man canoe was hidden, and late that night, Kennedy said they must go out in the passage again. Ross was opposed to that, but Kennedy insisted, so they paddled out. They were caught in a howling storm, and 5-foot-high waves swamped the canoe. They were banged around in the reef tide and slashed by the sharp coral edges, then tossed into the shoal water. They managed to crawl onto the sand.

In the morning the two men were awakened by a noise and found "four big, mean-looking natives" standing over them. To their surprise, one said in English with a British accent, "I have a letter for you, sir." Kennedy opened it and read: "To the Senior Officer, Nauru Island. I have just learned of your presence on Nauru Island. I am in command of a New Zealand infantry patrol operation on New Georgia. . . . I strongly advise that you come with these natives to me. Meanwhile, I shall be in radio communication with authorities at Rendova, and we can plan to collect balance of your party. Lieutenant Evans."

"I jumped up and slapped the big boys on the back," Ross recalled. "We all laughed. I hadn't laughed in five days." One of Ross's arms was very swollen because of infected coral cuts.

The natives took Kennedy and Ross to the island where the others were. The "brown life-savers" had brought food for all of themyams, pawpaws, rice, potatoes, boiled fish and C rations with roast beef hash. The starving sailors could hardly wait while the natives fashioned spoons out of palm fronds and dishes from coconut shells. As soon as the meal was over, Kennedy stood upwhich in itself was not easy because his feet and legs were in bad condition from coral slashesand said matter-of-factly, "I'm going to get the rescue boat now."

The natives stretched him in the bottom of their canoe and covered him with old rags and palm leaves in case they were spotted by the Japanese. Anenemy plane buzzed them and then went on. The canoe stopped at Gomu, where Lieutenant Evans was waiting. Evans told Kennedy that a rescue boat was on the way from Rendova and would pick up his men. Kennedy, however, was to be taken directly to headquarters and put in the sick bay. Kennedy firmly refused that plan. He was responsible for his men. He knew the area. And he would pilot the boat to their rescue. Kennedy did just that. Before many hours had passed, all 11 survivors of PT-109 were getting medical care in a sick bay in Tulagi Harbor. All recoveredsome rapidly, some in time.

The end of the PT-109 incident was by no means the end of Lieutenant John F. Kennedy's naval service in the war in the Pacific, but this remarkable exploit best illustrates his capable, courageous and compassionate leadership. Perhaps the greatest tribute to Kennedy's performance during the disaster is the fact that not one word of criticism was ever mixed with the lavish praise of his conduct by every man who served on the PT. Engineer Bill Johnston ended his praise with an expression of feeling that seems to have been shared by the others: "Lieutenant Kennedy was one hell of a man....I didn't pick him for my skipper, but I kept thanking God that the Navy had picked him for me."

Terrible Lessons Learned

By Martin F. Graham

At 11 a.m., July 11, 1943, in the Tunisian city of Kairouan, Brigadier General Charles L. Keerans was handed a decoded message from 82nd Airborne Division Commander Major General Matthew Ridgway. Keerans, assistant division commander, took the message with anticipation. Little had been heard from the front inthe 36 hours since the start of the invasion of Sicily.

Spearheading the invasion were the 3,405 members of Colonel James M. Gavin's 505th Parachute Regimental Combat Team (PRCT), who had left Kairouan at dusk on July 9 for their maiden combat jump. Since their departure, only bits of information on their fate had trickled down through the ranks of those "All Americans" remaining behind.

Many rumors had been circulating throughout that Muslim holy city: the 505th PRCT had been captured en masse, or the 505th had been slaughtered as soon as it landed. The suspense had heightened in the early afternoon of July 10, when word reached members of the 504th PRCT that their jump on Sicily had been indefinitely postponed.

Keerans was as much in the dark as the other members of the 504th when he was handed Ridgway's message on the morning of the 11th: "Mackall tonight. Wear white pajamas." This was Ridgway's code for Keerans to send in the 504th. It was the call to action that Keerans had been waiting for. He immediately contacted Colonel Reuben H. Tucker, 504th commander, to begin preparations for the jump.

On July 10, 24 hours into the invasion, even Ridgway knew little more than Keerans concerning the whereabouts of Gavin and most of his command. Since only one-third of the 82nd had jumped on July 9, Ridgway chose to land on Sicily with amphibious troops in order to ensure contact with his force from Kairouan. Once on shore he immediately headed for the area north of Gela, the 505th's objective. In the next few hours he managed to collect fewer than 50 paratroopers. Ridgway also failed to establish radio contact with either Gavin or his battalion commanders.

Returning to the command boat Monrovia, Ridgway persuaded U.S. Seventh Army commander General George S. Patton to postpone the 504th's jump, scheduled for that night, until more could be learned about the fate of the 505th.

Ridgway was deeply troubled by the situation he found on Sicily. He had used all his personal and professional influence over the previous months to maneuver his division into the position of being the showcase of American airborne troops. All aspects of the airborne invasion of Sicily had been carefully planned and rehearsed in every detail since the 82nd arrived in North Africa on May 10, 1943. Yet more than 36 hours after its initial action, Ridgway could only muster about 10 percent of the men who had jumped. Little did the division commander realize that the situation would worsen over the next 24 hours.

The Allied high command had identified Sicily as an important strategic objective during the Casablanca conference in January 1943. It would offer airfields and staging areas as a step-ping stone to the invasion of southern Europe. Also, the high command believed that control of Sicily might hasten an Italian surrender.

Army Chief of Staff General George C. Marshall had planned to delay the first major airborne action until the invasion of France, months away. He later changed his mind, assigning the 101st Airborne Division to take part in the invasion of Sicily, Operation Husky. He again reversed himself, electing to replace the 101st with the 82nd. Although Ridgway later denied it, some observers felt that, since Ridgway was one of "Marshall's boys," he had used this personal relationship to influence the chief of staff's decision to send the 82nd to North Africa to prepare for the invasion.

General Dwight D. Eisenhower, the Allied supreme com-mander, appointed a special adviser, British Maj. Gen. Frederick A. M. Browning, for the airborne planning of Operation Husky. When Ridgway learned that the 82nd would play what amounted to a mop-up role in Browning's plan, he did everything he could to have it modified. His lobbying paid off, and the All Americans were given a much more important part.

Since Sicily is roughly shaped like a triangle, with one apex on the south-east side, Eisenhower's invasion plan called for a pincer movement against that corner of the island before dawn on July 10, 1943. American troops would land west of the apex and British troops to the east. Prior to the amphibious landings, airborne troops would land inland from the beachheads to cap-ture strategic roads and bridges and to set up defensive positions blocking the enemy's ability to send reinforcements to the front.

A shortage of transport planes made it necessary to divide the airborne operation into four phases: two prior to the amphibious landings of July 10 and two over the following three days.

In two separate missions, the British 1st Airborne Division, the Red Devils, were to capture and hold various bridges around Syracuse and destroy coastal batteries, to hasten the advance of British General Bernard L. Montgomery's Eighth Army. British glider troops would be sent in before the amphibious assault and parachutists two to three days later.

The primary objective of the 505th PRCT was to seize 16 pillboxes and blockhouses on a piece of high ground, Piano Lupo, seven miles northeast of the landing beaches. Secondary objectives were to deny the enemy the use of the Ponto Olivio airfield, secure roads leading to the beaches, disrupt enemy communications, conduct ambushes against targets of opportunity, and create general havoc in the enemy's rear.

Tucker's 504th PRCT would jump at the Farello airfield west of Gela after it was secured by the 505th.

Gavin's combat team (the 505th Parachute Infantry Regiment [PIR]; 3rd Battalion, 504th PIR; 456th Parachute Field Artillery Battalion [PFAB]; and airborne engineer, signal, medical, and naval support units) began forming around the 266 C-47s neatly lined up on runways surrounding Kairouan in the late afternoon of July 9. The mission would take place at night to avoid Axis aircraft, which controlled the skies over Sicily.

Each trooper struggled with his individual load of more than 100 pounds of equipment, including the main and reserve parachutes, rifle or carbine and several days' supply of ammunition, grenades and rations. Some men also carried .45-caliber Colt pistols, bazookas, communication radios, mine detectors, light machine and submachine guns, mortars and demolition kits.

As they waited, most read the message Gavin circulated to all members of his combat team:

"Soldiers of the 505th Combat Team: Tonight you embark upon a combat mission for which our people and the free people of the world have been waiting for two years.

"You will spearhead the landing of an American force upon

the island of Sicily. Every preparation has been made to eliminate the element of chance. You have been given the means to do the job and you are backed by the largest assemblage of air power in the world's history.

"The term American Parachutist has become synonymous with courage of a high order. Let us carry the fight to the enemy and make American Parachutists feared and respected throughout all his ranks.

"I know you will do your job. Good landing, good fight, and good luck."

Ridgway had his own words of encouragement for the young colonel who would be leading his troops into battle for the first time: "We're counting on you and your men. We know damned well you can get the job done. Now give 'em hell over there!"

Although Kairouan is only about 250 miles from Sicily, airborne planners chose a 420-mile route to avoid passing over the Allied amphibious fleet. From Tunisia, the C-47s were to proceed southeast to Chergui Island, where they would veer to the east. Guided by bright searchlights on Malta, the planes were to turn left and head directly north to the southeast corner of Sicily, traveling in the narrow corridor between the American and British amphibious fleets. Once in sight of the coast, the C-47s would again turn left, remaining away from the coast to avoid antiaircraft fire. When they reached the area where the Acate River enters the Mediterranean, they were to turn right and head for the drop zone northeast of Gela.

The planes would fly in formation at 200 feet to avoid radar detection, a height at which a sudden gust of wind or a minor navigational error could send a plane to a watery grave. Most of the pilot members of the 52nd Troop Carrier Wing had never been exposed to anti-aircraft fire and were inexperienced in carrying airborne troops. Even in the best of weather conditions, the flight would be extremely difficult for green pilots. And the weather would prove to be far from acceptable.

The C-47s began taking off at 8:35 p.m., July 9. While Gavin's plane waited on the runway, an air corps lieutenant poked his head in the door and asked, "Colonel Gavin? Is Colonel Gavin here?"

"Here I am," he said.

"I was told to tell you that the wind is going to be 35 miles an hour, west to east," stated the lieutenant. "They thought you'd want to know."

Training jumps were usually canceled when the wind reached 15 mph, and the top safe air speed for parachutists was considered to be 20 mph. There was little the combat team leader could do at this stage of the operation, however. Flight problems surfaced quickly. Pilots had difficulty finding Chergui Island. High winds broke up the formations. To avoid midair collisions, the formations were widened to a point where they ceased to exist.

Thrown off course, most pilots could not locate Malta even though the searchlights burned brightly. Once the inexperienced navigators realized they had missed Malta, they ordered the pilots to turn left. Three disoriented planes decided to return to North Africa. Before reaching land, one ran out of fuel and crashed into the sea, killing all aboard.

Looking out his window, Gavin could see that they were flying over an armada of ships. Realizing that the planes had missed the corridor between the American and British amphibious fleets, Gavin held his breath, fearing friendly fire. Luckily the ships' guns remained silent. (Tucker's 504th would not be so lucky a few days later.)

When the C-47s carrying the 505th PRCT finally approached land, the pilots, navigators and jump masters in each plane were unable to identify any of the landmarks they had thoroughly studied. Some could not even confirm that they were over Sicily.

For those few planes that were lucky enough to reach land in the vicinity of the planned route, dust and haze thrown up by the pre-invasion bombing obscured island checkpoints.

Bullets from enemy ground troops and flak from anti-aircraft fire hissed past aircraft. The C-47s pitched uncontrollably from the force of nearby explosions and high winds. Bullets and flak ripped through their thin skins, coming perilously close to gasoline tanks. A single bullet striking the vulnerable fuel container could ignite the whole plane into a ball of orange flame. To escape this hail of metal, many pilots turned on the red alert and green jump lights in quick succession to empty their planes as quickly as possible.

Pilots had been directed to slow their planes to 100 mph (near stall speed) while rising to no more than 600 feet prior to flashing the green light to maximize the chance of parachutists dropping close together. Some planes, however, were actually traveling as fast as 200 mph and as high as 1,500 feet when they released their paratroopers, causing the All Americans to fall widely separated. The wind caused parachutes to oscillate and gyrate wildly. Men landed hard in trees, in gullies, fields, rivers, streams, on roads, and within enemy positions.

Disoriented in the darkness and unable to recognize landmarks, most troopers had no idea where they were. Errant planes had dropped men more than 60 miles from their designated drop zone near Gela. Troopers "rolled up the stick," walking in the direction flown by the C-47 that dropped them, looking for companions. Those injured in the jump found the closest shelter and hoped that friends would find them before the enemy hunted them down.

Pilots towing the British Red Devils' gliders that night were no more successful in finding their targets. Out of the 144 gliders starting the mission, only 12 reached the landing zone. Sixty-seven crashed into the Mediterranean, drowning about 200 Red Devils and pilots. It was the costliest glider mission of the war.

Reports of enemy airborne activity poured into Axis head-quarters from a stretch of more than 60 miles. Italian General Alfredo Guzzoni, overall commander of the 260,000 Italian and German troops in Sicily, estimated that three or four airborne divisions, 50,000 men, had landed.

While only a small fraction of his combat team was actually dropped within a few miles of the planned drop zone, Gavin's men were successful in accomplishing most of their missions. Guerrilla-sized bands blew up bridges, planted mines in roads, and cut telephone wires. They attacked enemy couriers, pillboxes, troops and tanks heading for the Allied landing beaches.

With fewer than 100 troopers under his command, Lt. Col. Arthur "Hard Nose" Gorham captured pillboxes and blockhouses on the Piano Lupo. His handful of men then managed to delay the right wing of the elite, battle-tested Hermann Göring Division long enough to allow the American 1st Infantry Division to establish a permanent beachhead. Gorham was killed on the 11th while engaging an enemy tank.

Several miles southeast of the Piano Lupo, at Biazza Ridge, Gavin, with fewer than 300 paratroopers, mounted his own defense on July 11. Gavin's command stayed the advance of the left wing of the Hermann Göring Division long enough to allow the troops of the American 45th Infantry Division to join in the fight.

Severe pressure at Gela forced Patton to call for immediate reinforcements. Early on the morning of July 11, he directed Ridgway to call in the 504th PRCT. Although still unaware of the disposition of most of the men he had sent into Sicily 36 hours earlier, Ridgway had no choice but to dispatch his coded message to Keerans.

Patton also sent the following top priority bulletin to his unit commanders: "Notify all units, especially anti-aircraft, that parachutists of the 82nd Airborne will drop about 2330 tonight on Farello landing field."

From the moment he learned of this second airborne mission, Ridgway was concerned about the potential danger of friendly fire from Allied ships and from anti-aircraft guns on the Sicilian beachhead. The flight plan for the 504th was similar to that of the 505th two evenings before, with one notable exception. The C-47s carrying this second combat team would be flying over a larger portion of Sicily's southern coast, land now containing a vast number of Allied guns.

Patton's directive to his shore batteries did not ease Ridgway's mind. The 82nd Airborne commander decided to personally visit six anti-aircraft batteries to see what they had been told about the parachute drop that night. He found that one out of the six had not been informed of the flight. The artillery officer accompanying him promised to personally inform the officers at a meeting of all anti-aircraft units later that day.

Tucker's combat team (the remaining two battalions of the 504th PIR; the 376th PFAB; and airborne engineer, signal, and medical units) gathered around the 144 waiting C-47s early on the afternoon of the 11th. Tucker went by jeep from one group of paratroopers to another, stopping long enough to shout: "Let's give the bastards hell, men! You know what to do!"

Keerans planned to accompany the group as an observer. Since he had not yet earned his parachute wings, he would be returning to Kairouan with the empty C-47s.

The operation began as routinely as a training jump. The planes left at dusk, and the pilots had little trouble following the circuitous route most had flown two nights earlier with the 505th. The air was quiet and calm, and the quarter moon offered some illumination. They easily spotted the floodlights on Malta and turned toward Sicily.

The first formation of planes reached the drop zone without incident, five minutes ahead of schedule. The second group of C-47s was in sight of the final checkpoint when the calm was shattered by a lone machine gun. Seconds later the sky burst into a sheet of deadly missiles.

The fourth Axis air attack on Allied ships and shore batteries that day had just ended when the slow, low-flying C-47s lumbered along the Sicilian coast. Mistaking the troop carriers for Luftwaffe bombers, the Allied gunners spontaneously opened fire. The excited gunners were too carried away to notice signal flares or the blinking amber signal lights on the C-47s, identifying the craft as friendly. There was no escape for the helpless paratroopers.

One company commander, Captain Willard E. Harrison, later recalled how "guns along the coast as far as we could see... opened fire and the naval craft lying offshore... began firing."

Lieutenant John O'Malley, a platoon leader, "saw that a wide sweep of the coast was aglow with a kaleidoscope of color: yellow flares, grotesque patterns of streams of red tracers, black, acrid puffs of smoke from bursting anti-aircraft shells, puffs so thick that it appeared a person could leap from one to the other." The young lieutenant watched helplessly as a neighboring C-47 veered out of formation to escape the fire and plummeted to the earth, exploding in a ball of flame. "Oh, my God, no!" O'Malley called out, tears streaming from his eyes. The plane had carried half his platoon.

Paratroopers watched in horror as planes exploded around them. Bullets and flak ripped into the C-47s, wounding men sitting helplessly in their seats or crowding around the open doors, anxiously waiting for their chance to escape the flying coffins. Some jumped over the Mediterranean, never to be seen again. Some forgot to hook onto the static line and plummeted to their deaths. Others were shot as they floated to earth by jittery American infantry thinking they were being attacked by German paratroopers.

"Hit after hit we score," one machinist's mate observed from his ship, "until [C-47] after [C-47] bursts into flames or falls spiralling into the sea. . . . From the wounded (planes) parachutes come fluttering, some to fall in flames into the sea . . . others to billow out in slow descent. . . . Soon every gunner is firing away at the troopers, who dangle limply beneath the umbrellas of their chutes."

Captain Adam A. Komosa recalled: "It was a most uncomfortable feeling knowing that our own troops were throwing everything they had at us. Planes dropped out of formation and crashed into the sea. Others, like clumsy whales, wheeled and attempted to get beyond the flak which rose in fountains of fire, lighting the stricken faces of men as they stared through the windows."

Patton and Ridgway had gone to Farello airfield to greet the parachutists. "My God!" Patton muttered over and over as he helplessly watched. Tears streamed from Ridgway's eyes.

The firing ended as quickly as it began. An erie silence settled along the southern coast of Sicily.

Twenty-three C-47s had been shot down, among them the plane carrying General Keerans. His body was never found. The 504th suffered 81 dead, 132 wounded and 16 missing. The 52nd Troop Carrier Wing counted 7 killed, 30 wounded and 53 missing. Only 555 of the 2,304 men in the combat team were accounted for 24 hours after the jump. Of the 5,307 men of both combat teams, only 3,024 had checked in by nightfall of July 13th and 3,883 by the 16th.

Friendly fire would also pose a serious problem for the British Red Devil paratroopers northwest of Syracuse on the night of the 13th. They suffered 470 casualties, including 50 American airmen, by a combination of Allied and Axis fire.

When Eisenhower learned of the 504th's tragic flight, he

ordered an investigation. He directed Patton to "institute within your command an immediate and exhaustive investigation into allegation with a view to fixing responsibility. Report of pertinent facts is desired, and if the persons found responsible are serving in your command, I want a statement of the disciplinary action taken by you. . . . This will be expedited."

A formal hearing was held, but there was so much conflicting testimony that results were inconclusive. Although the board discovered that not all shore batteries had been notified of the flight and determined that the flight plan had been faulty, since it carried the C-47s along 35 miles of beaches filled with green troops who had been under heavy attack by Axis bombers, it was unable to find cause or fix definite blame.

Patton wrote in his diary: "As far as I can see, if anyone is blameable it must be myself, but personally I feel immune to censure. . . . Perhaps Ike is looking for an excuse to relieve me."

Years later, Ridgway stated: "Deplorable as was the loss of life which occurred, I believe that the lessons learned could have been driven home in no other way, and that these lessons provided a sound basis for the belief that recurrences could be avoided. The losses were part of the inevitable price of war in human life."

Most Allied commanders felt that the airborne missions were generally successful. Patton stated, "Despite the original miscarriage, Colonel Gavin's initial parachute assault speeded our ground advance by 48 hours."

Even the enemy praised the airborne operation. "The Allied airborne operation in Sicily," stated German General Kurt Student, "father" of German airborne forces, "was decisive despite widely scattered drops which must be expected in a night landing. It is my opinion that had it not been for the Allied airborne forces blocking the Hermann Gˆring Armored Division from reaching the beachhead, that division would have driven the initial seaborne forces back into the sea."

The inability of pilots and navigators to drop troops on target and the subsequent inability of commanders to form their men into platoons, let alone companies, battalions, or regiments, led Eisenhower to recommend that the concept of airborne divisions be abandoned for smaller fighting units. In his after-action report to General Marshall, Eisenhower stated: "I do not believe in the airborne division. I believe that airborne troops should be reorganized in self-contained units . . . about the strength of a regimental combat team. . . . To employ at any time and place a whole division would require a dropping over such an extended area that I seriously doubt that a division commander could regain control and operate the scattered forces as one unit."

If instituted, Eisenhower's suggestion would have resulted in the disbanding of five American airborne divisions (11th, 13th, 17th, 82nd and 101st). Before taking such a drastic step, Marshall made two moves that would shape the future of American airborne combat. He ordered a special board of officers, chaired by Maj. Gen. Joseph M. Swing, 11th Airborne Division commander, to make recommendations for improving airborne training and operating procedures.

Marshall also ordered a December 1943 massive airborne maneuver by Swing's division to demonstrate the effectiveness of the "Swing Board's" recommendations. The 11th was to "capture" Knollwood airport in North Carolina.

Having been in North Africa observing Operation Husky, Swing found several major errors in the airborne planning, the most serious being the inability of C-47 pilots to find the drop zones. He determined there had to be greater training and coordination between airborne and troop carrier commands. This recommendation resulted in War Department Training Circular 113, which spelled out the responsibility each command had to the other.

Swing incorporated his board's recommendations into the successful planning and execution of the Knollwood maneuver. "After the airborne operations in Africa and Sicily," Gen. Leslie McNair, commander of army ground forces, reported to Swing, "my staff and I had become convinced of the impracticality of handling large airborne units. . . . The successful performance of your division has convinced me that we were wrong. . . ."

The airborne division had survived its severest trial in Sicily. The value of large-scale airborne operations would be proved during the 1944 invasions of France and Holland.

1944

Desperate Hours on Omaha Beach

By Kevin R. Austra

As soldiers of the U.S. Army's 1st Infantry Division leaped from their landing craft into the choppy waters off Omaha Beach, many cursed the landing-craft pilots who had deposited them too far away from the invasion beach. German small-arms fire from the bluffs overlooking the approaches raked the surface of the water, while indirect artillery fire splashed amid the landing craft in the English Channel.

One the morning of D-Day, June 6, 1944, the soldiers who headed for Omaha's 4-mile-wide, crescent-shaped beach faced a 300-yard dash to the base of the bluffs. First the landing craft and soldiers had to make their way through a mixture of German obstacles, some of which protruded above the low tide. Halfway to the bluffs at the end of the tidal flat was a raised shingle ledge of sand and smooth stones. There the Germans had placed thick belts of barbed wire. That shingle was the first spot on the otherwise open beach to offer the troops any cover from the machine-gun fire. "There was still another 100 yards to go before they reached the base of the bluffs, however, where more wire and mines awaited. As the GIs struggled across the sand, the Germans poured down a steady stream of fire from their elevated positions.

The bulk of the American infantry was held up at the shingle. Some soldiers dashed back to the water to seek shelter behind the German beach obstacles. Company A of the 29th Division's 1st Battalion, 116th Infantry Regiment, hit the beach and drew such heavy fire that within 10 minutes it ceased to be an effective fighting force. Much of the unit's equipment was lost in the Channel.

The ferocity of the enemy response was due primarily to the 352nd Infantry Division, one of the few full-strength German divisions in France. Whether the Allied leadership knew of its location along the coast is the subject of debate. Some sources say that its presence was a complete surprise. Others state that Lt. Gen. Omar Bradley, commander of the U.S. First Army and all U.S. ground troops during the landings, was informed of the 352nd's relocation to Normandy, but the information came too late to alter Allied planning.

On December 14, 1941, Field Marshal Wilhelm Keitel, chief of *Oberkommando der Wehrmacht* (Armed Forces High Command), had given orders for the construction of defensive positions along the European coastline. Keitel directed, "The coastal regions of the Arctic Ocean, North Sea, and Atlantic Ocean controlled by us are ultimately to be built into a new West Wall in order that we can repel with certainty any landing attempts, even if by the strongest enemy forces, with the smallest possible number of permanently assigned field troops." Essentially, he was calling for a formidable outer rampart to replace the original West Wall (or Siegfried Line) bordering the German hinterland, but until the latter part of 1943 the Atlantic Wall was not much of an invasion obstacle. Bunkers and observation posts were scattered along 2,400 miles of coastline, with the heaviest emplacements around key ports and installations. Even the August 1942 raid on the

French port city of Dieppe did little to increase the construction efforts of the German defenders. But by 1943, with a stalemate in Russia and the collapse of Axis dominance around the Mediterranean, German attention was finally focused on the French shores.

The coastal defensive works resembled the West Wall fortifications along the German frontier, except that Atlantic Wall casemates had wider firing embrasures to accommodate heavier guns. Responsibility for construction of the coastal forts tell to Organization Todt—a construction group that was a paramilitary arm of the Nazi regime—along with additional voluntary and forced labor. At one point, 260,000 laborers were employed in the effort. Despite the construction resources pegged for the Atlantic Wall, there were shortage of material—thousands of tons of concrete were diverted for building U-boat pens, static V-1 "buzz bomb" launching sites and a V-2 rocket bunker. Because concrete was scarce, many Atlantic Wall emplacements were constructed.

The defenders, of necessity, were thinly stretched. General Erich Marcks, the one-legged commander of the German LXXXIV Corps, believed that the east coast of the Cotentin Peninsula was all too accessible to landings. Marcks' corps occupied a sector 400 kilometers wide with five divisions. The 716th Infantry covered 90 kilometers of coast and was backed by the 243rd and 352nd Infantry divisions. The 716th's coastal strongpoints were 600 to 1,000 meters apart, with gaps of up to 3[h] kilometers. To the west, the 709th Division covered 220 kilometers of shoreline, while the 319th Division sat isolated on the Channel Islands.

Major General Wilhelm Richter's 716th Infantry Division, made up of replacement units, was designated a static division whose primary purpose was to build and occupy fixed defensive positions in its assigned sector. Its soldiers were mostly non-Germans or older men from the Rhineland and Westphalia. Remarkably, the division managed to complete and man 50 fortified works spread thinly across its front. The 716th's weakest link was the 1,000-man 441st Ost Battalion, made up almost entirely of Eastern European volunteers, deployed in front of Bayeux.

The 352nd, which deployed on the coast northwest of Bayeux alongside the the 716th Division on March 19, 1944, was commanded by Maj. Gen. Dietrich Kraiss, who had served as a company commander during World War I and led the 169th Infantry Division during the June 1941 invasion of the Soviet Union.

A battalion from the 716th and the 352nd's entire 915th Infantry Regiment were held in reserve at Bayeux. Kraiss did not like the idea of his troops spending too much time in prepared defenses, and he rotated his regiments from coastal to reserve duty. Those regiments stationed on the coast were run through regular battle drills, the last of which was staged on the eve of the invasion.

During the last months of the Allied preparations to invade Normandy, the 352nd Division was not listed on any British or American rosters of the German order of battle. According to one story, their location stayed secret thanks to an isolated case of marksmanship rather than any elaborate deception. In May, a German soldier had supposedly shot down a carrier pigeon carrying a French Resistance message to London, with the information that the 352nd occupied coastal positions. Other sources say that German soldiers in Normandy shot no less than 27 carrier pigeons during the two months prior to D-Day, but that none of them carried information on the 352nd.

Organizationally, the 352nd was better off than most German divisions in 1944. At that time, as a result of severe personnel losses, German infantry divisions were generally reduced by one infantry battalion per regiment. The 352nd, however, retained its full complement of nine battalions.

The 352nd began its coastal duty by improving the beach obstacles, emplacing mined stakes and timber structures. This involved not only cutting and hauling timber from miles inland but also driving stakes and piles deep in the sand. To fully cover the sector, they needed 10 million mines, but a scant 10,000 were available.

The first band of obstacles—about 250 yards out from the waterline at high tide—consisted of "Belgian Gates," reinforced iron frames with iron supports that were built atop rollers. Next came a band of mined stakes and log ramps, meant to tear the bottoms out of landing craft or tip them over. Finally, there was a row of metal obstacles, including hedgehogs, made of iron rails. Although the Germans had attached mines to many of the obstacles, few of them were waterproofed, and corrosion had long since taken a toll on many of the explosive devices.

The soldiers of the 916th and 726th regiments occupied slit trenches, eight concrete bunkers, 35 pillboxes, six mortar pits, 35 *Nebelwerfer* (multi-barrel rocket launcher) sites and 85 machine-gun nests. The defenses were clustered in strongpoints.

The Allied invasion of Normandy's coast was the result of lengthy and exhaustive planning. Although Pas de Calais was closer both to Britain and the excellent Belgian port of Antwerp, it was more strongly defended than Normandy, which had fewer extensive coastal fortifications and more defensible inland terrain—and required more German troops to reinforce effectively. Furthermore, Normandy could be isolated from the Reich by air interdiction and by destroying the Seine bridges.

Since the Allies clearly held the initiative in selecting the invasion site, the Germans decided to spread their forces thinly along the entire coast, from Scandinavia to the Spanish frontier. The Allies took advantage of the situation, employing a series of raids and expensive deception measures to contribute to the Germans' confusion, most notably the stationing of an entire bogus invasion force, backed by inflatable tanks and trucks, ostensibly poised to invade Calais.

U.S. Army General Dwight D. Eisenhower was made the Allied supreme commander on December 24, 1943. Shortly thereafter, June 1, 1944, was targeted as the invasion date, but the schedule depended on tide and weather conditions. It had already been decided that the assault would be in daylight, to better control the monumental landings and fire support associated with the invasion.

Extensive effort went into the construction of Allied landing craft and training of troops. Soldiers practiced breaching meticulously reproduced obstacles during rehearsals on British shores. The Ninth Air Force intensively photographed German coastal defenses beginning in May 1944. Divers even went ashore on Omaha Beach to secure sand samples and inspect obstacles.

Between February and May 1944, the number of German offshore obstacles increased dramatically, and the Allies decided to schedule the invasion for one hour after low tide to allow the landing craft to maneuver around some of the beach obstacles. The decision to land at low tide proved a surprise to the Germans. Field Marshal Erwin Rommel was among many who had predicted that the landings would occur at high tide, in an attempt to pass over the obstacles and land troops closer to the bluffs.

Dependable weather forecasts were crucial to a successful invasion. The Americans and British had superior access to the North Atlantic and were able to identify high-pressure zones sandwiched between barometric lows. If the attack was properly timed, Eisenhower would be able to cloak his forces in obscuring meteorological conditions during their approach to the beaches but have the actual landings take place in clear weather.

During the first week in June the Germans, whose weather predictions were based on sparse information from U-boats and harassed weather teams on Greenland, were apprised of what appeared to be a obvious forecast—bad weather that would make an invasion unlikely. In view of that information, Rommel returned to Germany for his wife's birthday.

Selected for the assault on Omaha Beach were the U.S. 29th and 1st Infantry divisions. The 1st, known as the "Big Red One," was a Regular Army division whose distinguished history included combat in World War I. The unit had participated in the Allied landings at Oran, Algeria, and salerno, Sicily, and also fought in Tunisia. Major General Clarence R. Huebner took command of the division in August 1943. For the D-Day landings, the 1st was reinforced with elements of the 29th Division and supplemented by two Ranger battalions. The 1st Division's 16th Regimental Combat Team (RCT) and the 29th's 116th RCT would lead the first wave of the attack. Later waves would consist of the 115th RCT (29th Division) and 18th RCT (1st Division). Huebner had overall command of the landing force, while the 29th Infantry's deputy commander, Brig. Gen. Norman D. Cota, would coordinate the battle on the western edge of the beachhead.

The 29th Infantry Division, commanded by Maj. Gen. Charles H. Gerhardt, was originally a National Guard unit, with soldiers from Washington, D.C., Maryland, Virginia and Pennsylvania. It had fought in the Meuse-Argonne campaign during World War I and was one of the first U.S. divisions shipped to Europe in 1942. The 29th was part of Maj. Gen. Leonard T. Gerow's V Corps. The division consisted of the 115th, 116th and 175th infantry regiments. The 116th RCT was reinforced by an additional 500 men in expectation of high casualties.

German Major Werner Pluskat, the 352nd's artillery officer, awoke on June 6 to the drone of Allied aircraft passing overhead. At about 1 A.M., he called his regimental commander, a Lt. Col. Ocker, and a Major Block, the division Intelligence officer, to find out what was happening. Told that it was probably just an air raid, Pluskat had gone back to sleep when Ocker called back and reported that paratroops were landing.

Pluskat and two of his officers jumped into a *Kübelwagen* and sped four miles to their command bunker at Ste.-Honorine. Pluskat's cliff-side bunker, as it turned out, was perched on the eastern edge of the sector the Allies had designated as Omaha Beach.

At 2 a.m. General Marcks put his corps and the 21st Panzer Division on alert. Less than 24 hours earlier, Marcks had attended a war game where, as the "enemy" commander, he played out a seemingly unlikely scenario in which the Allies landed in Normandy. At the corps level, Marcks found himself in a situation much like that of his division commanders—he had no appreciable reserves to press into the coming fight. Allied parachutists were reportedly landing all over Normandy, and many of Marcks' subordinate headquarters reported the sound of machine-gun fire. Lance Corporal Hein Severloh, a forward artillery observer, moved into his position above the dunes of Colleville-sur-Mer when the alarm sounded. Scanning the skies, neither Severloh nor his sergeant could detect anything other than the hum of bombers in the clouds above.

As dawn approached, the inky black sky turned a murky gray. Pluskat scanned the English Channel for the next few hours without receiving a single report from his higher headquarters. Tired from his early vigil, he wondered whether the reported landing of paratroops might have been a false alarm. At about 5 a.m., the Allied invasion fleet suddenly came into view.

Inclement weather had caused Eisenhower to recall the invasion fleet after it sailed on June 4. Twenty-four hours later the fleet steamed into the Channel for a planned landing on June 6. Minesweepers had been clearing the approaches to the beaches since 9:30 on the evening of the 5th. The fleet began to drop anchor some 12 miles off Normandy's coast around 2:30 a.m. on the 6th. So far, none of this activity had been detected by the Germans, whose *Luftwaffe* was grounded by the weather. Motor torpedo boats and other patrol vessels, which usually kept watch in the Channel, had been recalled by Admiral Theodor Krancke, commander in chief of Naval Group Command West. German radar finally picked up the invasion fleet at 3:09 a.m., and Krancke belatedly dispatched his boats from Le Havre to investigate.

Allied landing craft began to depart from the transports at about 3:30 a.m. for the 12-mile run to shore. Life aboard ship had been miserable for the GIs, some of whom had been at sea since early June 4 and many of whom suffered from seasickness. By 5:30, a good portion of the first wave's 3,000 men had clambered into landing craft in the choppy seas and were on their way to the beaches. The 1st Division's 16th RCT would assault the eastern half of Omaha Beach, divided into Easy Red, Fox Green and Fox Red beaches. The 29th Division's 116th RCT would land at Charlie, Dog Green, Dog White, Dog Red and Easy Green beaches.

General Bradley observed the landings from the heavy cruiser USS *Augusta*. At 5:30 a.m., Allied Bombarding Force C, including the U.S. battleships *Texas* and *Arkansas*, British cruiser *Glasgow* and Free French cruisers *Montcalm* and *Georges Leygues*, began blasting the beaches. Meanwhile, Martin B-26 Marauders, Boeing B-17 Flying Fortresses and Consolidated B-24 Liberators began bombing the coastline. The GIs in landing craft cheered them on.

The bomber crews were concerned about hitting incoming waves of Allied troops, and were hindered by the heavy cloud cover. As General Bradley later recalled in his autobiography, "the 2.5 million pounds of bombs fell inland . . . killing some French civilians and many cattle, but few Germans." Moreover, the naval gunfire proved largely ineffective thanks to the dust thrown up by the bombardment and the low clouds.

Major Pluskat's bunker above Omaha Beach survived repeated near misses during the naval and air bombardment. His eardrums throbbing from the din, he somehow managed to find the telephone in the dust and debris. Amazingly, the phone lines were undamaged, and he was able to report the situation to division headquarters. More surprising was that none of Pluskat's guns or their crews were put out of action. Most of the artillery struck positions on the bluffs and petered out before reaching the German batteries three miles inland, but the impact of so many shells set off several concentrations of German land mines on Omaha Beach.

The landing craft were tossed about in the heavy swells, 10 of the boats sinking during their dash to the shore. Worse, 27 out of 32 canvas-enclosed DD (duplex drive) Sherman tanks, which had been specially modified to swim to the beach, foundered before reaching the shore. Three others were unable to get off their barge and had to be landed much later. The Big Red One would have to make do with only two tanks—both of which were waterlogged.

When the assault craft were 400 yards from the beach, German shells began exploding around them. At 6:36 a.m. Company A, 116th RCT, was the first to land. Three landing craft slammed into offshore sandbars. One boat took a direct hit and sank, and another simply disappeared. The water was waist-deep or deeper, and the soldiers came under a murderous cross-fire. Within 10 minutes, Company A lost all its officers and NCOs, and its overall casualties exceeded 75 percent. Company E suffered almost the same fate, largely because the German defenses were concentrated on the area where the first troops landed—above two draws, or ravines, leading inland toward Colleville-sur-Mer and Vierville.

Allied planners were aware that there were a total of five ravines, which they labeled "exits," leading from Omaha inland. It seemed likely that these exits—dotted with summer houses and roads or trails that led farther inland—would provide the easiest access to the interior of the Cotentin Peninsula. The Germans had evacuated civilians from the buildings along those routes and used the structures to house troops and create defenses. The exits were further fortified with sea walls and in some cases-boasted anti-tank ditches as well.

While troops that landed near the Colleville-sur-Mer and Vierville exits drew heavy fire, the soldiers who landed in front of the St. Laurent exit suffered only two casualties and faced an unoccupied German strongpoint. Smoke from burning buildings and grass along the shore helped screen the invading troops. That weak spot in the German defenses, however, was not immediately exploited by the drenched and exhausted Americans.

Fire from alert German troops compounded the chaos reigning just offshore. Most of the landing craft had dropped their ramps too early, and the equipment-laden troops disappeared in the water as soon as they leaped from the boats. Some bobbed back to the surface, but many others did not. Rifles, helmets, packs and other heavy equipment—as well as the bodies of dead soldiers—settled on the sandy bottom as the Big Red One doggedly continued its assault. Countless pieces of engineering equipment and explosives, meant for use in clearing beach obstacles, sank or scattered.

Units of the 16th RCT crisscrossed each other and landed on beaches assigned to other units because of heavy currents that pushed the entire flotilla eastward. The first wave suffered close to 50 percent casualties. By midmorning, more than 1,000 Americans lay dead or wounded on the sands of Omaha. On *Augusta,* General Bradley agonized over the chaotic situation: "Our communications with the forces assaulting Omaha Beach were thin to nonexistent. From the few radio messages that we overheard and the firsthand reports of observers in small craft reconnoitering close to shore, I gained the impression that our forces had suffered an irreversible catastrophe, that there was little hope we could force the beach. Privately, I considered evacuating the beachhead and directing the follow-up troops to Utah Beach or the British beaches."

German fortifications consisted of numerous small concrete bunkers beneath the sandy bluffs. The steel-reinforced casemates were designed to house field guns, normally 50 or 75mm, and were relatively open but angled to fire across the beach, and thus their crews were not directly exposed to naval gunfire from the Channel.

Farther up the bluffs the Germans had positioned concrete machine-gun pits and infantry emplacements. The undulating terrain on the slopes provided ready-made shallow trenches. In addition, there were trenches and timber-and-earthen bombproofs on top of the bluffs.

Despite slow progress in attaining the bluffs, by 7 a.m. the invasion force had opened six gaps through the German obstacles. General Cota landed at 7:30 a.m. and joined the 116th Regiment. His biggest challenge was to get his men off the beaches. The one clear path was straddled by sand dunes, rocky shingle, a stone and wooden sea wall and rolls of concertina wire. Urged on by Cota, soldiers from Company C and the 5th Ranger Battalion blew gaps in the wire and moved into a draw and on to the base of the bluffs, where they were protected from German fire. By 8:30 a.m. they had captured the German rifle pits at the crest of the cliffs. Their advance inland was then stopped by German flanking fire.

Meanwhile, the 116th's 3rd Battalion worked its way up the Les Moulins exit and moved toward St. Laurent. To the east, the 16th Infantry forced its way up the St. Laurent and Colleville-sur-Mer exits. German strongpoints were positioned on either side of the exits, but they had been built on the lower slopes of the bluffs, so their fire was limited to the beaches. At the intersection of the Les Moulins and St. Laurent exits, soldiers of the 1st and 29th Infantry divisions met just north of the village of St. Laurent. There, the Americans who reached the plateau above the beach faced much less resistance. The Germans in the bunkers and slit trenches found themselves surrounded and fought a confused two-hour battle until their commander and 20 men surrendered.

Near Colleville-sur-Mer, the 16th Infantry inched forward. When the 16th's commander, Colonel George A. Taylor, landed at 8:15 a.m. and found a group of soldiers bunched up on the beach, hesitant to go forward, he announced, "Two kinds of people are staying on this beach, the dead and those who are going to die— now let's get the hell out of here." Taylor also sent a message to General Huebner that there were too many vehicles on the beach and requested that only infantrymen be landed. Huebner immediately responded by sending the 18th RCT ashore. Upon landing, they crossed the shingle and barbed wire to the Colleville-sur-Mer exit, where the 16th RCT was in the midst of a fierce battle.

Reassured by V Corps reports that forces on Omaha were moving inland, General Bradley approved the landing of additional regiments on Omaha instead of diverting them to some other beach. The U.S. 115th and 18th Infantry regiments came ashore and assumed the follow-up missions of the 116th and 16th RCTs, moving inland toward Colleville-sur-Mer and Vierville.

As the Americans pushed forward, Hein Severloh blasted away at the 16th Infantry from his machine-gun pit. Since the landing started, he had expended 12,000 rounds. Allied gunfire had prevented reinforcement of the positions, and the Germans were running out of men and ammunition. Severloh and others held their ground until noon, when additional Sherman tanks landed on the beach below them.

At 10:30 a.m., engineers from the 37th and 146th Combat Engineer battalions landed, filled the anti-tank ditch at the St. Laurent exit, cleared minefields and bulldozed gaps through the sea wall and dunes. Naval gunfire pounded German fortifications west of the gap. By 11:30 a.m., the Germans in St. Laurent had surrendered.

General Kraiss scanned accounts of the battle from his division headquarters. Initial reports were promising, with the only bad news coming from the 716th Infantry Division, on the right. The hard-pressed 916th Regiment was standing its ground even though its own right flank was exposed. The British 50th Division had broken through the coastal defenses of Arromanches and pushed inland toward Bayeux. The 916th's 1st Battalion held out for the better part of the day, but when the 441st Ost Battalion collapsed, Bayeux was as good as lost. The 352nd's only battalion in the British zone retained the fortified Meuvaines ridge east of Arromanches until after midday.

By noon the U.S. 1st Division had cleared the Germans from the beaches and bluffs in its area, but in the 29th Division's area fire was still coming from German slit trenches and bunkers that had been bypassed or otherwise overlooked by the advancing troops.

By that time the 352nd Division was in desperate need of reinforcement. Most of its coastal positions had been lost, but some secondary positions, along with fortified command bunkers and artillery positions, were still intact. By midnight Kraiss reported to Marcks that he could hold the enemy until the next day at best. Upon learning that the only help he could hope to receive was a so-called mobile brigade equipped with bicycles, Kraiss cannibalized some of his artillery units and deployed them as infantry along the coastal road.

The Germans made one more effort to destroy the Allied beachhead. The 1st Battalion of the 914th Regiment hit the Rangers at St.-Pierre-du-Mont, just south-east of Pointe-du-Hoc. Although the Rangers suffered heavy casualties, they were able to keep the Germans at bay with mortars, and they also directed artillery fire at the attackers from a destroyer offshore. The following day Kraiss finally ordered the withdrawal of his battered division, which had suffered about 1,200 casualties.

Sixty percent of the U.S. 2nd Ranger Battalion had become

casualties in its two days of fierce fighting within a 200-yard perimeter. Overall, 1st Division losses for D-Day were estimated at 1,036, 29th Division losses at 743 and corps troops at 441.

Omaha Beach was secure, but the Americans still faced six weeks of fighting in the hedgerow country before they could escape the Cotentin Peninsula. Throughout that time, the GIs of the 1st and 29th divisions would repeatedly be in conflict with the same nemesis that first met them on Bloody Omaha—the 352nd Infantry Division.

First Superfortress Attack on Japan

By Terry M. Mays

M ajor John R. "Jack" Millar, Jr., stared through the cockpit windows at the searchlight beams in the distance.
Each one looked like a long finger of light reaching out
for one of the Boeing B-29 Superfortress bombers around him.
Millar, piloting a B-29 he had named Georgia Peach for his home
state, slipped on special dark glasses despite the night sky. If a
Japanese searchlight illuminated his cockpit, the glasses would
reduce its blinding effects.

"Everyone was very tense but stuck to his station," Millar
later wrote to his parents. Bombers on either side of Georgia
Peach appeared boxed in by the searchlights that, when combined with anti-aircraft bursts, reminded the pilot of a July
Fourth celebration. Navigator Edward Kwasniewski provided Millar with a new course heading, setting up the bomb run to the
target—the Imperial Iron and Steel Works at Yawata. The crew
opened the bomb-bay doors and initiated the bomb run. "My
knees were beating against the control column," Millar later
recalled.

Several searchlights picked up Georgia Peach as it approached the target, and anti-aircraft guns hurled a barrage at the illuminated B-29. Bright bursts lit the night sky behind and below the bomber. The Japanese were having difficulty estimating the altitude and speed of the Americans flying over their homeland. Millar noticed a flash on his instrument panel indicating the release of the bombs at the same time he heard the bombardier shout, "Bombs away!"

The pilot prepared to bank away from the target area as the bomb-bay doors closed. The cockpit crew flinched as a Japanese fighter suddenly appeared, its guns spitting flames in the darkness. The enemy plane passed over the B-29's nose and disappeared into the night without damaging the bomber. Millar completed his banking maneuver and set a course for China. The gunners called on the intercom to report that they could see bombs striking the Imperial Iron and Steel Works.

Japanese searchlights continued to illuminate other American bombers around Georgia Peach, prompting Millar to fly an evasive pattern to avoid detection and targeting by the anti-aircraft guns. After traveling some distance from the target, Millar recalled, "I did turn the plane around so the crew could get a good look at the fires that had been set at Yawata." He felt justly proud of his achievement that night in June 1944. He had participated in the first B-29 raid on the Japanese Home Islands. The only person to have flown on both the first Boeing B-17 raid against Germany and the first B-29 raid against Japan, Millar piloted Georgia Peach on three combat missions and 26 flights over the Himalaya Mountains before transferring back to the United States to assist in training new B-29 crews for the massive bombing campaign against Japan.

The B-29 began to arrive in the field in July 1943. The massive bomber boasted a wingspan of 141 feet and an unloaded weight of more than 74,000 pounds. It could carry up to 10 tons of bombs and included many state-of-the-art features. Its defensive weapons were directed by a computer-guided central fire-control system, and the 11-man crew operated in a pressurized environment that made it possible to work without oxygen masks except in emergencies. A pressurized tunnel traversed the bomb bay and connected two larger crew areas. Superchargers on the inboard engines produced the compressed air necessary for the cabins.

As part of the 58th Very Heavy Bombardment Wing, Millar and his crew arrived with Georgia Peach at a base 70 miles west of Calcutta, India, in April 1944. Georgia Peach had been built at the Bell Aircraft factory in Marietta, Ga.—within sight of the Millar home. The Army Air Forces established rear-area bases in India for stockpiling supplies to support upcoming air operations against Manchuria and the Japanese mainland. The supplies were being ferried by Consolidated C-87 and Curtiss C-46 transports across the Himalayas. Arriving B-29s, including Georgia Peach, soon joined the ferry efforts.

The planes carried gasoline, ammunition, bombs and other supplies to newly constructed airstrips in China. These stocks were subsequently used by B-29s in their raids against Japan and Manchuria. Millar and his crew became experts at storing fuel (in 5-gallon drums) and supplies on their B-29 for the trip across what was popularly called "the Hump." It took B-29 pilots two weeks of flying the Hump to haul enough fuel and supplies for one B-29 raid over Japan.

Navigating the Hump involved flying more than 1,000 miles at an altitude of over 22,000 feet in order to clear the mountains. Poor weather conditions added to the dangers of the long hauls, resulting in many aircraft losses. Millar reported, "Only once [out of 26 trips] have I seen the ground most of the way." Each crew who flew across the Himalayas earned credit for an operational mission due to the dangers involved, and the men proudly painted a camel on the fuselage of their B-29 after each trip.

The peaks of the Himalayas provided a spectacular sight, if visible, and a deadly obstacle if hidden by cloud cover. "We would rather have flown a raid over Japan than fly the Hump," Miller later confessed. On occasion, he remembered flying through cloud cover immediately after takeoff and not breaking into clear skies until he reached an altitude of more than 21,000 feet. In 1944, the peaks had not been accurately charted, and strong winds often buffeted aircraft, negating the advantages of new aviation aids. On one flight at 20,000 feet, the clouds suddenly parted to reveal two peaks directly in front of Georgia Peach. Millar managed to swerve his heavily laden bomber and fly between the two peaks. He estimated that if the clouds had broken just 30 seconds later, he would have struck the mountain.

Conditions in the China-Burma-India (CBI) Theater proved harsh for the newly arriving crews. Hot, dusty winds peppered the Indian bases during the day, hampering maintenance and making life miserable for both the air and ground crews. Daytime temperatures could soar to 140 degrees. "Even at 10,000 feet in a pressurized cabin, we were wearing just our shorts and parachutes," Millar recalled. The nights brought hot, humid air that drenched everyone. Flights to the high-altitude forward bases in China involved a 50- to 70-degree drop in temperature between takeoff and landing.

The B-29 crews flew a dress rehearsal for the Japan raid by attacking Bangkok, Thailand, a rail center for the transfer of Japanese supplies and troops in Burma. Millar and his crew joined the other raiders on this test mission. When the planes departed the bases in India on a June 5, 1944, it was a hot day, but terrible weather prohibited formation flying to the target.

Several hundred miles over the Bay of Bengal, two of Georgia

Peach's four engines suddenly shut down. Millar tried to restart them but failed. The plane began losing altitude, forcing the crew to reverse course and head back to India. The crew jettisoned the bombload, ammunition and extra equipment in an attempt to slow the steady loss of altitude. Millar managed to keep his ship aloft as they reached the coast of India and offered his men their only two options—abandon Georgia Peach and parachute into the jungle and swamps below or ride the plane in for a forced landing. The crew opted to ride down with Millar.

Millar reached his Indian base barely above treetop level and approached for an emergency landing. By now, Georgia Peach was flying on one engine, but she would lose that last engine while landing. Millar chose to delay lowering his landing gear in order to reduce the altitude loss caused by the extra drag. He knew if he waited too long, however, the plane would settle on the landing gear before it was fully extended and would end up bellying across the runway. Millar gave it his best estimate and lowered the gear just prior to touchdown. Sergeant Lyle Dickinson, the left gunner, later stated that as he watched through his blister window, the landing gear fully extended with only one foot of clearance above the runway.

The Bangkok raid was a valuable illustration of the problems faced by air and ground crews. More than 20 percent of the 98 B-29s aborted the mission due to mechanical problems. Many, like Georgia Peach, returned to India, while others ditched in the Bay of Bengal. One B-29 crashed on takeoff, killing 10 crew members. The bombing results were dismal for such a large raid—only 18 bombs fell within the primary target area.

Aviation planners set June 15, 1944, as the day for the first B-29 raid against the Japanese Home Islands. The bombers would take off from forward fields in China. Preceding the B-29s would be Consolidated B-24 Liberator bombers, which would strike airfields in Japanese-occupied portions of China. It was hoped that this initial wave of bombers would help clear a path for the B-29s' long journey. Military planners targeted the Imperial Iron and Steel Works, which produced one-quarter of Japan's rolled steel.

The crew of Georgia Peach, still smarting over the aborted mission to Thailand, prepared to make up for the lost opportunity by being among the first B-29s to drop a payload on Japan. Crew members were issued parachutes with special jungle kits, as well as Mae West life jackets, flak suits, "pointee-talkee" Chinese phrase books, and survival kits containing fishhooks, first-aid equipment and other items.

Takeoffs could be tense. Each B-29 carried a full load of bombs as well as enough fuel to get to Japan and back. With such an explosive combination, any mistake or mechanical failure during takeoff could prove fatal, as had happened during the Bangkok raid.

Aware that staying on the ground was not an option, at 3:30 p.m. on the afternoon of June 15, 70 B-29 crews prepared to bring the war to Japan's doorstep. One B-29 crashed on takeoff, but all 11 crew members managed to escape from the resulting fire. Six other planes aborted their takeoffs. Georgia Peach and the remaining 63 ships got safely aloft and set a course for Japan. One B-29 developed engine trouble approximately two hours out and returned to the base. Reports indicated that the crew members of the crippled plane openly wept and cursed at the missed opportunity to be among the first to strike Japan in a B-29. The frustrated pilot reportedly exclaimed: "Damn the engines! Damn the engines!"

The planes had taken off late in the day in order to reach their target at night. The weather prevented formation flying, and the bombers headed for Yawata in loose groups. Millar was pleased with the poor weather. "We ducked into the soup clouds and stayed there to prevent enemy fighters from attacking us," he said. "It provided excellent cover."

Japanese fighters did scramble to intercept the B-29s but were not able to catch the giant bombers. "I could see some of their planes taking off, but I knew that we were much faster than they were, and by the time they got up to our altitude, we would be long gone," explained Millar. Daylight faded before the planes departed Chinese airspace. The men donned their Mae West vests as the bombers approached the East China Sea.

Navigation was difficult during the leg across the sea. Kwasniewski, Millar's navigator, managed to make a couple of star shots through breaks in the clouds. However, a strong shift in the wind caused Georgia Peach to drift north toward the Korean Peninsula. Japanese naval vessels detected the American bombers and opened fire with anti-aircraft guns. "All of a sudden," Millar remembered, "the clouds on the left side of our plane lit up and we felt concussions. . . . I saw the first shot and called the tail gunner. About that time a dozen more shots came and all missed us. The reception was too hot and uncomfortable."

The navigator asked Millar to look at the radar screen, where several blips indicated the presence of Japanese naval vessels below them. Although the Japanese knew large planes were flying overhead, the cloud cover hindered visual identification. Kwasniewski called for a new course heading, and the pilot obliged.

Of the 63 planes that successfully launched from China, only 47 located the target. As Georgia Peach neared Yawata at approximately midnight, Millar could see the entire city was well lit, indicating they had caught the Japanese by surprise. Almost as soon as they began congratulating themselves on catching the defenders unawares, however, the city went black.

Soon the Japanese turned on their searchlights and began

working feverishly to locate the American bombers and track them while anti-aircraft guns labored to bring them down. The Japanese blackout precautions against air attack seemed to be highly effective, since few, if any, lights could be seen on the ground aside from the searchlights. Millar made sure each of his crew members was wearing a flak vest as Georgia Peach neared the target.

Sergeant Lou Stoumen, an Army correspondent with Yank magazine, accompanied the Yawata raiders as an observer in a B-29 piloted by Captain R. A. Harte. He also reported seeing the searchlights of the Yawata defenses as the bombers neared their target. Stoumen later wrote that throughout his plane's flight the No. 3 engine periodically spewed sparks for some unknown reason. This did not seem to degrade the engine's performance, so the crew continued on the mission. As the bomber approached Yawata, the chief gunner screamed, "Tracers!" They frantically searched the sky for the Japanese night fighter firing the tracers until someone called on the intercom to say it was just engine No. 3, shooting sparks into the night sky. The entire crew broke into a chorus of laughter, which eased the tension.

Japanese anti-aircraft gunners managed to down one of the American planes while it was crossing the target. Searchlights successfully locked onto the B-29 and followed it until the anti-aircraft guns scored enough hits to bring it down. Reports indicated that all four engines burned as the stricken bomber fell. The other aircraft continued on through the anti-aircraft fire, dropped their bombs and headed back for China.

Millar recalled that the clouds were dissipating over the East China Sea as the planes approached China. Intelligence personnel had briefed crews that if it became necessary to ditch, an American submarine would be on station to retrieve survivors. But Millar observed that "finding [the submarine] at midnight in the ocean would be quite a challenge."

Crew members distributed rations during this leg of the journey. Stoumen reported that every man received a large can of grapefruit juice and a chicken sandwich made with bread that was "too thick." Dessert consisted of chewing gum and cigarettes.

Having been aloft for more than nine hours, the bomber crews were now dealing with fatigue. Millar stated, "We had to fight ourselves to stay awake as the predawn set in." But the observers could afford a nap, and Stoumen took the opportunity to lie down, using a parachute as a pillow. Some others, however, were not so fortunate. The engineer and navigator on Stoumen's B-29 had taken benzedrine tablets earlier in the flight to combat fatigue.

Nearing China before dawn, the crews became more alert to possible attack by Japanese fighters. "The skies were clearing over the sea, and I knew we'd still be over enemy territory when daylight came," Millar recalled. They again encountered clouds over China, and Millar maneuvered his plane into the cloud banks. The Japanese did not attempt to intercept the bombers during their return home.

Millar instructed his radio operator to send a report that all was well as the planes closed on the American air base. The crews were hustled away for debriefing immediately upon landing at 8:30 a.m. and fed egg sandwiches and coffee in the debriefing room. Following the debriefing sessions, crew members darted for the mess hall and then to bed. Millar returned to Georgia Peach and inspected her with his crew chief. She had completed her mission without any damage other than a few minor scratches. Millar wrote his parents a long letter describing his experience and went to sleep after completing the longest bombing mission up to that point of the war.

The next day Millar received a personal radio greeting from none other than Tokyo Rose. As proof of effective Japanese intelligence gathering, Tokyo Rose read the names of several American officers on the Yawata raid, including Millar, and warned them of their fate if they ever attempted to attack the Japanese homeland again. Millar found it humorous that while Tokyo Rose also bragged of the capture of Lt. Col. Jim Edmundson during the Yawata raid, Edmundson was standing right beside him.

The Yawata raid provided a tremendous boost to American morale and offered a diversion from the operations directed against Saipan. From a practical point of view, however, the mission had dismal results. Seven B-29s were lost in the raid—one to anti-aircraft fire, five to accidents or fuel exhaustion, and one that landed at Neihsiang Airfield due to engine trouble, only to be destroyed in a Japanese air raid later that day—and the bombing results were poor. The closest bomb strikes landed three quarters of a mile from the aiming point. Other bombs hit as many as 20 miles away from the target.

Millar flew one more B-29 raid before transferring back to the United States. That mission, flown on July 29, 1944, against the industrial center of Anshan in Manchuria, proved to be his final combat operation of World War II.

Back in the States, Millar, a specialist in instrument flying, taught this skill to new B-29 pilots. His pupils included an old friend named Paul Tibbets, who would later pilot the B-29 Enola Gay, which dropped the atomic bomb on Hiroshima.

Greatest Aircraft Carrier Duel

By John F. Wukovits

Naval aviation advocates in both the United States and Japan had long argued that aircraft carriers, possessing mobility and potent air groups, would in large measure determine the outcome of the Pacific War. That prediction held true for the war's first six months as Japanese carriers recorded a stunning triumph at Pearl Harbor and supported numerous advances throughout the Pacific. American carriers redeemed Allied pride in the gigantic carrier encounters in the Coral Sea and off Midway in May–June 1942. Little, though, in the way of carrier battles occurred for two years as Japan slowly replaced its 1942 losses and waited for the opportunity to destroy the American Navy in an enormous decisive encounter.

As Japan husbanded its naval resources, its American foe moved steadily westward. Japanese naval leaders patiently waited for an opportunity to deliver that decisive defeat, and by the middle of 1944, with their carrier strength rebuilt, they saw their chance in an expected American move against either the Caroline or Palau islands north of New Guinea, or against the Marianas. In early May 1944, the commander in chief of the Combined Fleet,

Admiral Soemu Toyoda, issued a plan called A-Go in which a major portion of the Japanese navy would move against the enemy in an attempt to crush its carrier power. Commander of the First Mobile Fleet, Vice Adm. Jisaburo Ozawa, was given practically every available surface craft to throw against the Americans.

Ozawa also counted on help from at least 500 land-based aircraft, which were expected to destroy one-third of the enemy's carriers before Ozawa even steamed into battle. His lightweight carrier planes, relying on a huge 100-mile advantage in attack range that would permit the Japanese to hit American carriers before they could hit him, would then finish off any remaining American strength. This plan might have been more sensible early in the war, when skilled aviators manned the craft. But continuously worn down by combat attrition and accidents, expert fliers had become a scarce commodity. Most current Japanese pilots possessed few of the talents their predecessors carried into Pearl Harbor and into other Pacific targets in early 1942, and they logged far fewer training hours in the air than the Americans they would shortly face.

Ozawa's counterpart, Admiral Raymond A. Spruance, planned to deploy his fleet in a conservative manner. According to orders, his prime objective was to protect the Saipan invasion forces, in particular the valuable troop and supply transports, from a Japanese sea assault. He knew that enemy carriers might appear, since the Marianas represented a deep thrust toward the home islands, but he would not be lured away from protecting the Saipan invasion beaches. If he could both protect Saipan and take on Ozawa's carriersfine. But he would not endanger his prime responsibility by chasing after the enemy. The Japanese had divided their forces in other major naval engagements, such as Midway, and had reinforced their use of that tactic as recently as May, when a captured Japanese document emphasized the use of feinting to the middle while a flank attack darted around the end. Therefore, Spruance wanted to guard against being drawn away from Saipan by one force while a second group swung in on an end run.

On June 6, Task Force 58, commanded by Vice Adm. Marc Mitscher, steamed out of Majuro Harbor in the Marshall Islands on its way to the Marianas. Consisting of four carrier task groups and one fast battleship task group, the flotilla of almost 100 ships required five hours to leave the lagoon. At sea, the armada blanketed 700 square miles of ocean. Fifteen aircraft carriers bore 900 planes, including superb new Grumman F6F-3 Hellcat fighters.

Spruance's first order of business was to take out Ozawa's land-based air strength to gain local air supremacy and to remove the possibility of Ozawa's using Marianas airfields to shuttle-bomb his forces. American admirals dreaded shuttle-bombing, in which planes took off from carriers, hit their targets and landed on nearby shore bases rather than return to their carriers, because it enabled the Japanese to launch while still outside the attack range of American fighters. In two days of heavy air raids on June 11–12, American fighters and bombers tore into airfields on Guam, Rota, Saipan and Tinian, while seven carriers swerved north to blast airfields on Iwo Jima and Chichi Jima. Japanese Mitsubishi A6M Zeros rose to do battle, but the inexperienced pilots proved no match for the better-trained American fliers darting about in superior Hellcats. When the smoke had settled, Ozawa had been shorn of his much needed land-based air strength. But in an amazing display of ineptness, the commander of the decimated land squadrons, Vice Adm. Kakuji Kakuta, failed to relay that vital information to Ozawa. The Japanese admiral sailed on to meet Task Force 58, blissfully ignorant that one of his offensive arms had been hacked off.

On June 13, the same day that American battleships moved into bombardment positions to unleash a largely ineffective pre-invasion shelling of Saipan's beaches, Ozawa guided his fleet out of Tawi Tawi in the Sulu Archipelago and headed toward the Marianas. American submarines quickly reported the departure to Spruance, who later ordered the transports to continue unloading supplies on Saipan until June 17, when they were to withdraw and head east, away from the coming battle. The submarine *Cavalla* picked up Ozawa 800 miles west-southwest of Saipan on the night of June 17-18 and tracked the Japanese fleet as it churned closer to the Americans.

Both Ozawa and Spruance knew one force would sooner or later locate the other. Throughout much of June 18, both combatants cautiously moved about the Philippine Sea like boxers gingerly testing each other Ozawa wary because of Spruance's superior power, Spruance concerned about his foe's longer range and habit of slipping in an end run. Before showing his hand, Spruance intended to get a precise fix on Ozawa's location. "Until we know exactly where the enemy is," he told subordinates, "we must be positive that we are between his possible locations and those landing ships."

Ozawa split his force as he moved farther east. Admiral Takeo Kurita commanded the advance group, built around the carriers *Chitose, Chiyoda* and *Zuiho* and 88 planes protected by a lethal concentration of battleship and cruiser anti-aircraft guns. One hundred miles behind Kurita followed Ozawa's main force of two groups. Group A, commanded by Ozawa, centered on the carriers *Taiho, Shokaku* and *Zuikakau,* with 207 planes; in Group B, Rear Adm. Takaji Joshima led the carriers *Junyo, Hiyo* and *Ryuho,* with 135 planes. Ozawa hoped that Spruance's planes and ships would be lured west by Kurita's van, giving Ozawa a chance to crush him with his two lurking carrier groups. To prepare his men for the important battle, Ozawa signaled Japanese hero Admiral Togo's famous message, flashed before the Battle of Tsushima during the Russo-Japanese War early in the century: "The fate of the Empire rests on this one battle. Every man is expected to do his utmost."

Ozawa first spotted Spruance in late afternoon but refrained from sending his planes since little daylight remained. He also could not determine if Japanese airfields on Guam, where his planes would have landed after attacking Spruance, were intact or pockmarked with craters from recent American attacks.

Spruance's turn came next. Mitscher's Task Force 58 steamed west for much of the day, its search planes reaching out even farther to the west, like tentacles hunting for prey. As darkness neared, Spruance ordered Mitscher to turn eastward so the carriers would hover closer to Saipan when daylight broke on June 19 and thus guard against an end run. However, a signal intercepted when Ozawa foolishly radioed a land-based commander, placed the Japanese 355 miles west-southwest of Mitscher.

Mitscher and most aviators in Task Force 58 saw an opportunity to get in a first strike at dawn. Mitscher asked Spruance if he could again head west and close on Ozawa during the night so as to be in position for a daylight attack, but Spruance denied the request.

Spruance's orders stunned Mitscher's staff and most aviators waiting on board carriers. Instead of taking the offensive, Spruance was allowing Ozawa to steam on toward Saipan unmolested. The Japanese admiral would be within striking range of the American carriers the next day while still remaining outside the range of American planes. Captain Arleigh Burke of *Lexington* dejectedly stated: "This we did not like. It meant that the enemy could attack us at will at dawn the next morning. We could not attack the enemy."

Spruance received unjust criticism after the battle for this conservative move. Spruance had to think not only of his aviators' desire to get Ozawa's carriers but also of protecting the Saipan landings. Had he sent Mitscher's planes after the enemy, they would have flown into a tortuous series of Japanese opposition: first facing Kurita's dense concentration of anti-aircraft fire, then flying another 100 miles into Ozawa's guns and air cover to deliver their load, before finally revisiting Kurita's fire to return home. Although a number of Ozawa's planes would have been destroyed, so would a significant portion of the attacking American planes that would not have been there for the slaughter about to unfold on June 19. Spruance opted to remain near Saipan, thereby guaranteeing a full complement of air power to handle Ozawa's inexperienced pilots the next day and dish out an even more lopsided victory than Mitscher could most likely have achieved with a dawn attack.

To prepare for Ozawa, Spruance positioned his task groups so that if any Japanese pilots broke through the air screen they would have to first fly over Vice Adm. Willis A. Lee's powerful battle line of cruisers and battleships, each sporting a multitude of deadly anti-aircraft guns. Fifteen miles behind Lee steamed three of Spruance's four carrier task groups, arranged from north to south in a straight line with 12 miles separating each group. The fourth carrier group waited between Lee and the three carrier groups, three miles east and 12 miles north of the battle line. For mutual support, Spruance placed each group in circles four miles in diameter. To get at the carriers, an inexperienced enemy pilot would have to evade American combat air patrols, elude Lee's fire, and shake off carrier task group anti-aircraft fire.

Once within range, Ozawa hurled a continuous succession of Japanese fighters, bombers and torpedo planes at Spruance in a futile attempt to get his carriers. The first of his four raids departed at approximately 8:30 a.m., when 69 fighters, bombers and torpedo planes rose from Kurita's carriers and headed east toward Saipan. Expectant American radar picked up the enemy craft 90 minutes later when they were still 150 miles away. By the time American Hellcats jumped off their carriers at 10:23, only 72 miles separated the opposing forces.

A string of disastrous Japanese errors turned the raid into a fiasco. Instead of immediately pressing their attack before American fighters could reach proper intercept altitude, Japanese pilots circled at 20,000 feet to regroup. By the time they were ready, Hellcats had established a multitiered intercept formation miles in front of Lee's front-line defense. Rather than remaining in formation to take advantage of increased firepower, Japanese pilots charged alone or in small numbers at American ships or chased after Hellcats in uncoordinated attacks. They swerved away from targets before reaching effective bombing range. Veteran American pilots so easily fooled Japanese pilots with basic combat maneuvers that one is struck, in reading action reports, by how often one American flier shot down two or more enemy planes within seconds.

Spruance's fliers were assisted by superb American fighter-director officers who, having recently endured a rigorous training program that weeded out those who could not think calmly under extreme pressure, accurately deployed American fighters at proper altitudes, speed and range. They also had Lieutenant junior grade Charles A. Sims, who eavesdropped over the radio as the Japanese air coordinator sent his planes into the fray. Sims relayed this information to American fighter-director officers, who then placed their Hellcats where they could most successfully intercept the enemy. Stunning results quickly followed. Over half the planes in that first raid were shot down by waiting Hellcats before they sighted an American ship. At one point in the fray, Commander William A. Dean of *Hornet*'s fighter squadron VF-2 spotted 20 or 25 enemy parachutes floating in the Philippine Sea, a stark illustration of how hopelessly outclassed the Japanese pilots were.

On board *Lexington* Lieutenant Joseph Eggert, Mitscher's

fighter-director officer, commenced the day's slaughter by barking out the timeworn circus cry for help, "Hey Rube!" Within 15 minutes of the 10:23 a.m. launch, over 220 Hellcats raced toward the incoming enemy. Lieutenant Commander Charles W. Brewer, commander of *Essex*'s VF-15, met the Japanese 55 miles out from his ship and quickly set a pattern that would be repeated throughout the intense day. Brewer lined up the enemy leader, locked on his tail from 800 feet, and with a quick burst of machine-gun fire sent him careening toward the water. Before Brewer even emerged from the debris of this first kill, he spotted a second target and fired a rapid volley which downed that plane. A third followed in quick succession when Brewer pounced on his tail and dispatched him smoking toward the water. A fourth quarry proved more elusive and executed a string of expert maneuvers to escape, but he, too, fell victim to Brewer's accurate fire.

Twenty-seven enemy planes eluded that initial fighter screen only to encounter a second, which splashed another 16 planes. The 11 surviving craft flew on and unsuccessfully attacked the picket destroyers *Yarnell* and *Stockham.* A handful of Japanese bombers finally managed to get through to Lee's battle line and landed a direct hit on the battleship *South Dakota,* killing 27 men and wounding another 23, but not a single enemy plane reached the American carriers, their main target.

To deflect Japanese aircraft, an American pilot had to get close enough to his quarry to register a kill, but in doing so he flew perilously near a target that American surface anti-aircraft guns were simultaneously trying to destroy. An errant move by the pilot or a poorly aimed shell could bring down the wrong plane. Commander of one of the four task groups, Rear Adm. John W. Reeves, Jr., was so concerned for his pilots that he signaled all his ships during this first raid: "Try to avoid shooting down our own planes. They are our best protection."

By 10:57 a scant 34 minutes after Mitscher launched his initial fighterthe first raid had ended. While suffering minimal damage, Mitscher's force shot down 41 of Ozawa's 69 planes in a display of aerial superiority rarely witnessed in the Pacific. Lieutenant Commander Paul D. Buie, commander of *Lexington*'s VF-16, heard one of his pilots exclaim: "Why, hell, it was just like an old-time turkey shoot down home!" The phrase speedily bounced from ship to ship until most officers and men were speaking of the Great Marianas Turkey Shoot.

At 8:56 a.m., before the first raid had even located Mitscher's force, Ozawa had launched a second wave of 128 fighters, bombers and torpedo planes. Pilot Sakio Komatsu had barely lifted off from his carrier when he spotted a torpedo churning directly toward the carrier *Taiho*. Without hesitation, Komatsu reversed his course and crashed into the explosive. Komatsu's courageous self-sacrifice bought only a brief respite for Ozawa's flagship, which later fell victim to a second torpedo from the same American submarine, *Albacore*. Eight other Japanese planes experienced engine difficulties shortly after liftoff and had to return to their carriers. As the remaining 119 planes flew over Kurita's van, 100 miles out. Kurita's ships erupted in a mistaken but furious anti-aircraft barrage that downed two of their own planes and so damaged eight others that they had to turn back. Before the raid had flown out of sight of its own ships 19 planes were lost.

The rest flew on to calamity. After American radar picked up the group at 11:07 a.m., a scant 10 minutes after the first raid had retreated, Hellcats from several carriers pounced on the outclassed enemy and registered almost 70 kills in less than 30 minutes.

Commander David McCampbell of *Essex* started the slaughter at 11:39 by exploding the first Aichi D4Y2 "Judy" dive bomber he spotted. As he darted across to the other side of the enemy formation, evading a gantlet of return fire, McCampbell quickly splashed a second Judy, sped toward the front of the enemy formation to record a "probable" on a third, dispatched the formation leader's left wingman with a staccato burst, downed the leader with a steady stream of machine-gun bullets, then scored a final kill on a diving enemy craft. In minutes McCampbell, who would become the Navy's leading ace in the war, logged five kills and one probable.

During that frenetic interception, however, Lt. j.g. Alexander Vraciu of *Lexington* outperformed McCampbell, weaving his way through the enemy formation to pick off six enemy aircraft. Vraciu downed his initial quarry from a distance of only 200 feet and quickly reacted to avoid damage from the dive bomber's debris. He then crept toward a pair of dive bombers and shot down the trailing Judy before splashing the lead plane. Every minute brought the action continuously closer to *Lexington*, which meant that not only was the carrier in danger, but Vraciu and other American pilots would have to fly directly into their own ships' anti-aircraft fire to chase attacking enemy planes.

Vraciu scanned the skies, which by now were dotted with speeding Hellcats, plunging enemy planes, and hundreds of lethal bursts of anti-aircraft fire. He warned *Lexington*: "Don't see how we can possibly shoot 'em all down. Too many!" But he nevertheless chased after, and downed, a fourth dive bomber. Three other Judys zoomed into view as they began their final runs on ships below, and Vraciu followed them. He quickly downed the first but was forced into a perilous vertical dive to stop the second before it dropped its bomb on a destroyer. With anti-aircraft fire intensifying, Vraciu caught up to the enemy plane and destroyed it, then pulled out of his dive to avoid crashing into the water. Battleship anti-aircraft fire downed the final enemy dive bomber.

Vraciu headed back to *Lexington*, where he was almost killed by his own ship's fire. Shouting into his radio that he was an American, Vraciu finally landed. As he walked away from his plane, a tired Vraciu glanced toward Admiral Mitscher on the bridge and held up six fingers to indicate his success.

Other pilots experienced spectacular missions. Lieutenant William B. Lamb of *Princeton* attacked a group of 12 enemy dive bombers even though only one of his six guns operated correctly. As other Hellcats joined in, Lamb knocked down three planes. Lt. j.g. P. C. Thomas of Bataan almost latched onto more than he could handle when he charged at one enemy plane. The Japanese pilot, obviously one of the few savvy Japanese aviators in the sky, so beautifully executed a series of maneuvers to avoid Thomas that the American flier later said, "It was like trying to catch a flea on a hot griddle." He destroyed the enemy plane after other Hellcats ringed the enemy pilot on three sides and forced him to fly a straight course. *Essex* pilot Ensign C. W. Plant got on the wrong side of another skilled enemy pilot, who bounced a stream of bullets off Plant's armor plate before being destroyed by an assisting Hellcat. When Plant returned to *Essex,* amazed service personnel counted 150 bullet holes in his fighter.

Only 20 Japanese planes in that unfortunate second raid broke through the aerial intercept to approach Mitscher's ships, but they broke against a heavy anti-aircraft screen. A handful of dive bombers eluded all defenses and attacked scattered targets. Four singled out the carrier *Wasp,* but adept maneuvering by its skipper, Captain C. A. F. Sprague, avoided serious damage. Ozawa's second raid achieved little in expending itself. Of the 128 planes in this raid, 97 fell to watery graves in 30 intense minutes of action.

At least the survivors of the second raid could claim they located the American ships, something most pilots in Ozawa's third raid could not say. In the third raid, 47 planes lifted off between 10 and 10:15 a.m., but over half lost their bearings and turned back to their carriers without firing a shot. Twenty planes did spot Mitscher and forced a brief attack on Rear Adm. William

K. Harrill's three carriers of Task Group 58.4, but inflicted only minor damage while losing seven planes.

The fourth raid accomplished little more. As in the third raid, 49 of the 82 planes that launched by 11:30 a.m. failed to locate Task Force 58 and flew on to the Japanese airstrip at Guam, where waiting Hellcats shot down 30 as they attempted to land. Some pilots broke through the American intercept to deliver their loads, none of which caused serious damage.

Captain Sprague's *Wasp* received most of the fourth raid's attention. *Wasp* Hellcats intercepted a large group of enemy planes at about 2:20 p.m. and shot down three, but another eight or nine planes attacked the carrier, which was steaming at 22 knots and executing a 15-degree left turn. Sprague quickly ordered a hard right to avoid one bomb dropped by a dive bomber that crashed into the sea barely seconds after its bomb exploded. Fragments from the bomb and disintegrating dive bomber bounced off *Wasp*'s hull and across the carrier, knocking over Marine Captain R. C. Rosacker and three others as they manned a 20mm gun. Rosacker and his crew quickly jumped back up and continued firing at enemy targets. Two other near-misses sprayed more fragments about *Wasp*, wounding one sailor, while an incendiary cluster showered the ship with phosphorus.

By the time that final raid ended, Ozawa had thrown 374 planes at his enemy. Less than 100 returned to their carriers. When added to the 50 land-based craft lost by Admiral Kakuta, the Japanese had sustained an incredible defeat. While losing only 22 fighters and 60 men, Spruance had removed Japanese carriers as a factor in the war.

While Ozawa's four air raids futilely charged the American surface fleet, American submarines inflicted major damage on his fleet. Despite Japanese pilot Komatsu's heroic action of purposely crashing into a torpedo headed directly at *Taiho*, Commander James W. Blanchard of the submarine *Albacore* had aimed five other torpedoes at the same target, one of which found its quarry. Since *Taiho* used highly volatile unrefined oil from Tarakan, the crew tried to pump the oil overboard before sparks ignited. One inexperienced officer opened the ventilating ducts to remove the fumes; instead, this further spread the dangerous gases throughout the carrier. At 3:32 p.m., a spark ignited the fumes, causing an eruption that blew out both sides of the ship's hanger, warped the deck and ripped holes in the carrier's bottom. After being evacuated with his staff aboard the destroyer *Wakatsuki*, and subsequently re-establishing command aboard the heavy cruiser *Haguro*, Ozawa watched the carrier explode and capsize, taking 1,650 men to their graves.

Commander Herman J. Kossler of the submarine *Cavalla* added to Ozawa's woes. First sighting Shokaku at 11:52 a.m., Kossler moved into position and fired a spread of six torpedoes, four of which hit. For four hours the frantic crew tried to save *Shokaku*, but additional explosions doomed the carrier, which finally sank shortly before *Taiho* did. Another 1,263 men died with their carrier.

While devastation plagued Ozawa, Spruance turned his carriers north to recover jubilant, yet tired and shot-up pilots returning from the day's slaughter. Although aviators urged him to chase Ozawa and complete the destruction, Spruance held off turning west because he did not know for sure what carriers Ozawa retained, nor where they were. He would not send weary crews against an enemy of undetermined strength, especially when they most likely would have to battle at night. And he was not prepared to abandon Saipan and leave it open to that flank attack he still considered a possibility.

At 8 p.m., Spruance ordered his carriers to head west during the night. Mitscher hoped he could lessen the distance separating Task Force 58 from Ozawa for a daylight attack.

Pilots scoured the air on June 20 trying to spot Ozawa.

Finally, at 4 p.m., an *Enterprise* search plane located the enemy force in four groups 275 miles from Mitscher—just about the maximum range for American fighters. With a scant three hours of daylight left, the pilots would have to fly out, make at most two runs on the enemy, then return to their carriers before darkness or low fuel forced them into the sea. When Mitscher asked his operations officer, Commander W. J. Widhelm, if his pilots could successfully make the hazardous flight, Widhelm bluntly replied, "It's going to be tight."

Mitscher accepted the risk, and at 4:10 the order went out to launch planes. Pilots rushed from ready rooms, where chalk board messages exhorted them to "Get the carriers!" and within 20 minutes more than 200 fighters, dive bombers and torpedo planes were speeding toward Ozawa. Each aviator hoped luck went along, for the amount of fuel did not give them much room for error. One gunner hopped into his Douglas SBD on *Lexington* and saw the crew give him a thumbs-up signal. "Thumbs up, hell!" he thought. "What they mean is 'So long, sucker!' " Lieutenant Commander Robert A. Winston of Cabot doubted whether any of his squadron's planes would return.

Their unease heightened when Mitscher notified the fliers shortly after takeoff of an error in the original sighting. The Japanese fleet was actually 60 miles farther away than was first thought. As the planes neared Ozawa, pilots saw their fuel gauges dip below the halfway point, meaning they would go into battle with the certainty of ditching into the sea on the way back. With so little daylight left, Ozawa only had to hold out for 20 minutes to escape into friendly darkness. Thus a sense of urgency propelled the American fliers at their foe in uncoordinated attacks at whatever target entered their sight.

Although Mitscher's aviators had but 20 minutes to inflict their damage, they made the most of it. Sixty-five Japanese planes were shot out of the sky, and four Grumman TBM Avengers from light carrier *Belleau Wood* sank the light carrier *Hiyo,* while bombs tore into and sank three tankers, heavily damaged the carriers *Zuikaku* and *Junyo,* battleship *Haruna* and heavy cruiser *Maya.* The total cost to Mitscher was 18 planes. At the end of the day, a dejected officer penned in Ozawa's flag log what remained of the 430 aircraft Ozawa had possessed the morning of June 19, "Surviving carrier air power: 35 operational aircraft."

Now the American pilots had to worry about getting back to their carriers, 250 miles away. Most started home shortly before total darkness closed in, transforming the moonless night into a blackened shroud that eradicated the horizon. Weary pilots faced a two-hour flight in battle-scarred aircraft, to carriers that if they reached themwould be almost indistinguishable from their surroundings. One by one, planes sputtered out of fuel and swooned in guided descents to the sea. A string of phosphorescent marks, telltale signs of splashdowns, dotted the water as Mitscher's planes neared their destination.

Meanwhile, Mitscher prepared a homecoming welcome. He first spread out his task groups so that 15 miles separated each group, thereby giving the carriers ample maneuvering room to land planes or pick up downed fliers. He then ordered a daring move that could have cost him a carrier or two if any enemy submarine had lurked in the area. He ordered his ships to turn on every light so the aviators could make safer attempts at landing. All types of carrier lights flashed into brilliancetruck lights, red and green running lights, signal lights. Five-inch guns on destroyers and cruisers shot star shells into the blackened heavens, while carriers beamed searchlights straight upward as beckoning beacons for the bleary-eyed pilots.

The effect was electric. Lieutenant Commander Winston recalled the incredulity with which most men on board *Cabot* at first reacted. "They stood open-mouthed for the sheer audacity of asking the Japs to come and get us. Then a spontaneous cheer went up. To hell with the Japs around us. Our pilots were not to be expendable." From above, one ecstatic pilot stared at the lights and was reminded of a Hollywood premier, the Chinese New Year, and a Fourth of July celebration combined.

For two hectic hours, aircraft sputtered to uneasy landings near or on board anything that floated. Normal air landing procedure was abandoned, as some pilots dangerously low on fuel cut into other pilots' approaches or ignored wave-offs. Almost half of the planes landed on ships other than their own, resulting in carriers retrieving planes from as many as eight different ships.

Many made it down safely. Ensign Adam Berg circled a ship for 11 minutes, using up almost all his fuel before realizing what he thought was a carrier was, in fact, only a destroyer. Without enough fuel to hunt elsewhere, Berg stalled his plane into the sea a short distance from the destroyer and was picked up within 15 minutes. Two pilots simultaneously landed on *Enterprise* without sustaining any damage, one latching onto a forward wire while the other hooked onto a rear wire.

Other pilots landed and erupted with anger. Commander Blitch of *Wasp* stormed out of his plane after landing on board *Lexington,* drained a hefty amount of brandy, then proceeded to blast the entire operation.

Most aircraft returned in one piece. About 80 planes were lost because of low fuel or landing accidents. Fortunately, most of their crew were rescued. Altogether, about 50 aviators were either lost at sea or died in landing attempts.

The Battle of the Phillipine Sea wound to a conclusion in the next three days. On June 21, Spruance dispatched Lee's battleships and cruisers after Ozawa's retreating force, but Lee only succeeded in rescuing downed American aviators from the previous day's combat. Two days later, Spruance sent most of Task Force 58 back to Eniwetok for repairs and resupply.

Thus ended one of the U.S. Navy's most complete victories of the Pacific War. Ozawa had steamed out of Tawi Tawi on June 13, intent on destroying Spruance's carriers. He sank none. His opponent, while still fulfilling his primary duty of protecting the Saipan beachhead, so shredded Ozawa's air power that the Japanese carriers could only act as decoys for the war's remainder. Spruance's planes combined with two American submarines to sink three enemy carriers and other supporting vessels. Spruance gambled by sitting off Saipan and allowing Ozawa to come to him, but the gamble paid off handsomely.

The next month, admirals Ernest King and Chester Nimitz, commander in chief of the Pacific Fleet, visited Spruance at Saipan. Reacting to the bitter criticism Spruance was still receiving from aviators angry that he had not been more aggressive, Admiral King, the irascible chief of naval operations, pointedly told his commander, "Spruance, you did a damn fine job. No matter what other people tell you, your decision was correct."

War's Greatest Sea Fight

By John F. Wukovits

Rear Admiral Clifton A. F. Sprague, commander of Taffy 3, a unit of six thin-skinned escort carriers, could hardly believe his eyes. Only 2[h] hours earlier, he had thought his puny ships had no more than 15 minutes to survive when a powerful Japanese surface force had loomed on the horizon, taking everybody by surprise. Yet now the Japanese were turning back, just as the enemy's cruisers had lined up Sprague's carriers in their sights from close range.

After the battle, Sprague explained his miraculous escape this way: "The failure of the enemy main body and encircling light forces to wipe out completely all vessels of this task unit can be attributed to our successful smoke screen, our torpedo counterattack, continuous harassment by bomb, torpedo, and strafing air attacks, and the definite partiality of the Almighty God."

His actions formed only one although certainly the most dramatic thread of the tapestry woven during those two October 1944 days in the waters surrounding the Philippine Islands. Taken as a whole, the four separate battles constituting the Battle of Leyte Gulf produced history's grandest naval clash, one whose stage stretched across an area of the Pacific larger than France.

Army General Douglas MacArthur provided the driving impetus for the Leyte operation. Eager to return to Philippine soil since his hasty departure in early 1942, MacArthur prodded the American Joint Chiefs of Staff to approve a Philippine campaign under his control. He received opposition from the U.S. Navy, particularly the Pacific Fleet's commander, Admiral Chester W. Nimitz, who adamantly refused to let the land-oriented MacArthur control his most-valued weapon the aircraft carriers. Instead, Nimitz preferred a Navy-dominated thrust through the central Pacific to Formosa.

President Franklin D. Roosevelt listened to both commanders at a military conference in Pearl Harbor in July 1944. Rather than select one man over the other, Roosevelt compromised, as was his wont. He favored MacArthur's Philippine drive and handed control of all land units, all ships transporting those men, and all ships providing covering air support to the Army general, but left the fast carriers under Nimitz's direction. The two units would supposedly act in unison, but division of the command later haunted the operation.

Titanic amounts of men and materiel accumulated for the Philippine campaign. Vice Admiral Thomas C. Kinkaid's Seventh Fleet of 738 ships was earmarked to transport the 174,000 men of General Walter Krueger's Sixth Army and 2 million tons of equipment to the Leyte beachhead. Not far offshore, Admiral William F. Halsey's Third Fleet, including the potent Task Force 38, numbering 16 fast carriers protected by more than 80 warships, shielded the seaward approaches to Leyte Gulf in its mission of keeping the enemy fleet away from Kinkaid.

One potential flaw existed in these arrangements. While Kinkaid's Seventh Fleet answered to MacArthur, Nimitz controlled Halsey's Third Fleet. In an emergency, therefore, there would be no supreme commander ordering about both huge naval forces.

The Japanese could not afford to lose control of the resource-rich East Indies. Precious supplies, especially oil, flowed from those locations into the Japanese home islands. By seizing the Philippines, the Americans would sever the supply line and drastically reduce Japan's ability to wage war, especially through her powerful imperial fleet. To prevent that, Admiral Soemu Toyoda, commander in chief of the Combined Fleet, designed a plan to block any American attempt to seize the Philippines. Called Sho-1, the plan utilized an intricate combination of deception and daring. Japanese land-based air power would whittle away at the American forces as they approached the Philippines. Three strong naval arms would then close on the enemy, smash through any defenses, and devastate the Leyte Gulf beachhead.

To accomplish that, Toyoda had to lure away Halsey's mighty Third Fleet so his own ships could get at Leyte Gulf. He dangled an irresistible plum at the aggressive American admiral four aircraft carriers and escorting ships of Vice Adm. Jisaburo Ozawa's Northern Force. The aircraft carriers contained few airplanes because American carrier air power had decimated Japanese air strength, but Toyoda hoped the mere appearance of carriers would attract Halsey to the north.

While Ozawa lured away Halsey, Vice Adm. Shoji Nishimura's Force C of two old battleships, one heavy cruiser and four destroyers would advance northeast from the Singapore region and hustle through Surigao Strait, south of Leyte Gulf. Along the way Vice Adm. Kiyohide Shima's second striking force, comprised of two heavy cruisers, one light cruiser and four destroyers, would steam south from Formosa to form Nishimura's rear guard. Those two forces, constituting Toyoda's Southern Force, would exit the Surigao Strait and attack Kinkaid.

Simultaneously, the strongest unit of Sho-1, Vice Adm. Takeo

Kurita's First Striking Force, made up of 23 battleships, cruisers and destroyers, would depart from Singapore, head northeast across the Sibuyan Sea, and descend on Kinkaid from the north after steaming through the San Bernardino Strait.

Although dubious of the plan's success, Kurita encouraged his junior officers in a pep talk before leaving. "Would it not be a shame to have the fleet remain intact while our nation perishes? I believe that Imperial Headquarters is giving us a glorious opportunity. You must remember that there are such things as miracles."

Kurita guided his impressive fleet out of Lingga Roads near Singapore on October 18. After a brief stop at Brunei, Borneo, for refueling, he headed north for the Palawan Passage and the Sibuyan Sea. Several hours after Kurita left Lingga Roads, Nishimura's Force C debouched and steamed for the Surigao Strait. From the north, Ozawa departed Japan on October 20, followed two days later by Admiral Shima.

Initial indications that the Japanese were on the move came from American submarines *Darter* and *Dace,* stationed along the treacherous Palawan Passage. After spotting Kurita's unit shortly after midnight on October 23, the two submarines maneuvered into position for an attack. Commander David H. McClintock fired *Darter*'s six bow torpedoes at Kurita's flagship, the heavy cruiser *Atago,* then swung hard around and emptied his stern tubes at the second in line, the heavy cruiser *Takao.* As explosions rippled through the waters, McClintock took *Darter* deep to avoid the inevitable depth-charge attack.

"It looks like the Fourth of July out there!" exclaimed Commander Bladen D. Claggett, observing the aftermath through *Dace*'s periscope. "One is burning. The Japs are milling and firing all over the place. What a show! What a show!"

Within 18 minutes, the mighty *Atago* disappeared beneath the surface, while *Takao* had to limp back to Brunei, escorted by two destroyers. Another spread of torpedoes, this time from *Dace,* tore into a third heavy cruiser, *Maya,* with such force that the ship disintegrated in a tremendous explosion that sounded like "crackling cellophane" to McClintock on *Darter.* In less than a half hour, Kurita lost three heavy cruisers and two destroyers, and he still had more than half his voyage to complete before reaching Leyte Gulf.

As Kurita advanced across the Sibuyan Sea, Halsey's air power pecked away at him almost ceaselessly. Over a span of 5[h] hours on October 24, five airstrikes harassed the already bruised Kurita; the planes attacked at the rate of one per minute. Two bomb hits shook the most potent battleship afloat, *Yamato. Musashi,* her sister ship, flailed hopelessly at Halsey's aircraft as they delivered the astounding total of 19 torpedo and 17 bomb hits. *Musashi* sank at 7:35 p.m., taking with her 1,000 officers and men. A torpedo hit in her stern forced the heavy cruiser *Myoko* to return to Brunei for repairs. In two days, American submarines and aircraft sank or removed from action seven of Kurita's warships, temporarily forcing the timid admiral to reverse course.

To the south, Rear Adm. Jesse B. Oldendorf positioned his units throughout Surigao Strait in anticipation of Nishimura's arrival. Thirty-nine PT-boats nestled among numerous islands dotting the waterway, ready to hound Nishimura as he entered the narrow confines of the strait. Immediately afterward, 28 destroyers would charge from both the right and left flanks to deliver torpedo attacks, while six battleships and eight cruisers formed a double battle line at the 16-mile-wide exit to dispatch any Japanese vessels that survived Oldendorf's gantlet.

The PT-boats delivered their initial attacks one hour before midnight on October 24 and continued them until shortly after 2 a.m. on October 25. The small unit fired 34 torpedoes, only one of which hit, and did little more than pose a minor nuisance as

Nishimura steamed by. However, they did succeed in alerting Oldendorf's other units that the enemy was approaching.

Next came Oldendorf's destroyers, whose presence was hidden from Japanese radar by echoes created by the many islands. One squadron, Desron 54, approached so close to Nishimura's seven ships that the Japanese overshot them with anti-aircraft guns. As torpedoes churned through the choppy waters and gunfire illuminated the skies, Nishimura's first three destroyers in line received hits; one sank. Nishimura's flagship, the battleship *Yamashiro,* absorbed a hit that slowed her to 5 knots. About 2 a.m. the battleship Fuso took two torpedo hits; fires started that spread to her magazines. Suddenly, a tremendous explosion split the unfortunate battleship in two. The admiral's force had been reduced to his own *Yamashiro,* the heavy cruiser *Mogami* and one destroyer, *Shigure,* and he had yet to exit Surigao Strait.

Oldendorf's battleships (several of which had been raised from the mud of Pearl Harbor) and cruisers now took over. As Nishimura neared the exit, the American ships waited in a deadly line that blanketed the exit from side to side and crossed Nishimura's "T"a situation every surface commander dreams about. At 3:51 a.m., Oldendorf opened a thundering volley toward Nishimura's three hapless ships that shook the heavens with its intensity. One witness to the amazing spectacle recalled: "The devastating accuracy of this gunfire was the most beautiful sight I have ever witnessed. The arched line of tracers in the darkness looked like a continual stream of lighted railroad cars going over a hill. No target could be observed at first; then shortly there would be fires and explosions, and another ship would be accounted for."

Shells crashed down on *Yamashiro* relentlessly, finally sending her to the bottom after 4 a.m., taking Nishimura and most of her crew with her. After absorbing repeated hits, *Mogami* reversed course along with *Shigure. Mogami* and *Shigure* would be the only survivors of Force C.

Forty miles behind Nishimura, Shima guided his seven ships into Surigao Strait. Frantic messages from Nishimura and frequent gunfire flashes gave Shima an indication that all was not right. His fears were confirmed when he passed two burning hulks, which he thought were the battleships *Fuso* and *Yamashiro* but were actually the two halves of *Fuso*. After observing on radar what he thought were two American ships and ordering a torpedo attack (two of his cruisers carried out the orders and accurately hit their targetan island), Shima reversed course and headed out of Surigao Strait.

On the way out he passed the burning cruiser *Mogami*. Continuing the comedy of errors, Shima's flagship, the heavy cruiser *Nachi,* collided with the crippled *Mogami,* but both ships were able to continue the retirement joined by *Shigure.*

American ships in pursuit further pared Shima's force so that by the time it had limped back into Brunei Bay on October 27 only the destroyer *Shigure* from Nishimura's unit and one of his own heavy cruisers, *Ashigara,* and four destroyers were still operational. The Battle of Surigao Strait, the final time in naval history that a battle line was employed in action, ended with an overwhelming victory for Oldendorf and the U.S. Navy.

The final two phases of the four-tiered Battle of Leyte Gulf are closely intertwined, as the actions in one area Admiral Halsey's vitally affected events south of him, where Clifton Sprague stood guard. Had Halsey selected a different set of options, Sprague most likely would have retained a back seat to events. Instead, Halsey shoved the quiet admiral front and center.

The popular, profane Halsey had built his reputation on bold words and stout actions that garnered public adulation back home and adoration among his men in the Pacific. He loved battle and hated the Japanese, and no finer warrior could be named by an admiring press than William Halsey, particularly after his task force transported Army Lt. Col. James H. "Jimmy" Doolittle and 16 North American B-25 Mitchell bombers to within 600 miles of Japan for Doolittle's daring Tokyo raid in April 1942.

That had been more than two years earlier, however. Since then, the man who commanded the largest conglomeration of aircraft carriers in the history of warfare had only participated in one less-than-auspicious carrier duel, the Battle of Santa Cruz. For one reason or another, Halsey was elsewhere when the Coral Sea, Midway, the Eastern Solomons and the Philippine Sea battles took place. He was determined that before war's end he would command aircraft carriers in a momentous fight.

As news poured in from the Sibuyan Sea and Surigao Strait to Halsey's flagship, the battleship *New Jersey*, he searched for signs of enemy aircraft carriers. He knew they would show themselves for such an immense battle, but where were they? Leyte Gulf battle plans assigned him the mission of protecting Kinkaid's Seventh Fleet, but Nimitz had added a separate clause telling Halsey that if Japanese carriers entered the fray, their "destruction becomes the primary task" for Task Force 38.

Late in the afternoon of October 24, Halsey's search planes finally sighted the four aircraft carriers of Ozawa's Northern Force 190 miles to the north northeast. Halsey already knew two other Japanese arms had closed in, but he correctly believed that Oldendorf could handle the Southern Force and knew that Kurita's Center Force had turned back with heavy losses after being assailed by Third Fleet carrier air power.

Since he assumed no other force could threaten Leyte Gulf, Halsey concluded he could safely leave his post off the San Bernardino Strait and chase north after the carriers. Shortly before 8 p.m. on October 24, Halsey walked into "flag plot," put his finger on Ozawa's position on the wall chart, and said to his chief of staff, Rear Adm. Robert B. Carney: "Here's where we're going. Mick, start them north."

He included in his decision Task Force 34, a unit of battle-ships and cruisers under the command of Vice Adm. Willis A. Lee. Halsey had earlier radioed his own task group commanders his intention to form Task Force 34 to block Kurita should the Japan-ese admiral decide to barrel through San Bernardino Strait. Until then, the ships would remain with Halsey. As was frequently the custom, however, Kinkaid at Leyte and Nimitz at Pearl Harbor intercepted the message and inferred that Halsey was actually forming and positioning Task Force 34 off the strait.

Halsey notified Kinkaid and Nimitz at the same time that he was dashing north, but the wording led to confusion: "am pro-ceeding north with three groups to attack enemy carrier force at dawn." Halsey meant by this that he was taking his entire Third Fleet, but Nimitz and Kinkaid assumed he was taking his three carrier groups north while leaving behind Vice Adm. Lee's battle line—Task Force 34.

As Halsey steamed toward the carrier battle he had so long desired, disturbing reports rolled in that events might be heating up near San Bernardino. First he learned that Kurita had reversed course again and was now bearing directly toward the strait. But Halsey reflected upon the damage his carrier aircraft had inflicted in the Sibuyan Seaor at least the supposed damage as reported by his pilotsand concluded that Kinkaid possessed sufficient air power on board his 16 escort carriers to hold off Kurita until Old-endorf rushed to their assistance.

Then, a little before 7 a.m., a message from Kinkaid shocked Halsey. The message was actually sent at 4:12 a.m., but was delayed because of transmission difficulties inherent in the divided command set-up. The message from the Seventh Fleet commander asked if Task Force 34 was watching San Bernardino Strait. Halsey realized Kinkaid must have intercepted his earlier message; he shot back a quick reply: "Negative. Task Force 34 is with carrier groups now engaging enemy carrier force."

Halsey focused all his attention on getting Ozawa's carriers and pushed San Bernardino Strait out of his mind. At 6 a.m., the first strike was launched from the carriers of Task Force 38 and attacked Ozawa about two hours later, followed by five other strikes that succeeded in sinking all four Japanese carriers *Zuiho, Chitose, Chiyoda* and *Zuikaku,* the sole remaining carrier to have participated in the Pearl Harbor attackalong with the destroyer *Hatsuzuki.*

While his carrier airstrikes plastered Ozawa's sacrificial ships, Halsey received additional messages from Kinkaid that he needed Halsey's help off Leyte Gulf. At 8:22 a.m., Halsey learned that Kurita's Center Force stood only 15 miles from Sprague's puny screen, and eight minutes later he read a dispatch from Kinkaid urgently requesting Lee's battleships.

"There was nothing I could do except become angrier," Halsey wrote in his memoirs. He stood on the threshold of the carrier battle he had yearned for, and now another commander begged him to detach an important part of his force, a portion Halsey wanted to send in to finish what his aviators had started. Further requests for aid at 9 a.m. and again at 9:20 only raised Halsey's blood pressure.

One other officer's blood pressure was rising, as well. At Pearl Harbor, Admiral Nimitz followed the steady flow of messages with extreme interest. He also assumed Halsey had left Task Force 34 off San Bernardino, but he became worried as the morning wore on. Finally, realizing that Halsey had retained Task Force 34, Nimitz hoped his impetuous admiral would send Task Force 34 south as quickly as possible, but he hated interfering with his commanders once a battle had started. At 9:45 a.m., Nimitz sent Halsey a message that infuriated the old warhorse. Meant as a prod to send Task Force 34 to Leyte, Nimitz's message read:

"turkey trots to water rr from cincpac action com third fleet info cominch ctf seventy-seven x where is rpt where is task force thirty-four rr the world wonders." It was interpreted by Halsey as an embarrassing reprimand.

"I snatched off my cap," wrote Halsey, "threw it on the deck, and shouted something that I am ashamed to remember. Mike Carney rushed over and grabbed my arm: 'Stop it! What the hell's the matter with you? Pull yourself together!' "

The beginning and end phrases, "turkey trots to water" and "the world wonders," had been added as padding to deceive any enemy interception, but when the message arrived aboard *New Jersey,* the operator thought, in his haste, that it was part of the main signal and left it in. Halsey eventually calmed down, but he still failed to send Task Force 34 and one carrier group to Sprague's assistance for another hour.

When Halsey finally ordered Lee to turn south for Leyte Gulf, he lamented: "I turned my back on the opportunity I had dreamed of since my days as a cadet." He left three carrier groups to pursue Ozawa and headed south with Lee. By then his help was no longer needed, for off Samar, the vastly outgunned and outnumbered Sprague was participating in one of the most amazing miracles of the Pacific War.

"Now there's some screwy young aviator reporting part of our own forces," was what Sprague said to himself when first informed that Japanese ships loomed on the horizon. He asked the pilot to check again, and the flier quickly responded, "Ships have pagoda masts."

Though surprised, Sprague quickly reeled off a series of decisions as though he had practiced this scenario ahead of time. Realizing that he and his 13 ships, six escort carriers, three destroyers and four destroyer escorts armed with nothing stronger than torpedoes and 5-inch guns, (or "peashooters" as Sprague called them) were the only force between the Japanese and the American force on Leyte, he decided to throw his ships against the enemy in a sacrificial delaying act that might save the beachhead, "though obviously the end will come sooner for us."

Figuring his force would be sunk within 15 minutes, Sprague dashed off calls for aid to nearby commanders, turned his carriers away from the Japanese, launched every available plane, ordered all ships to make smoke, and then hustled toward the haven of a nearby rain squall. While the rain storm shielded him to some extent from accurate Japanese gunfire, Sprague pondered what to do next with his thin-skinned escorts, nicknamed "Kaiser Coffins" for their tendency to sink when hit and because they were constructed on Liberty ship hulls designed by Henry J. Kaiser.

Since destruction appeared inevitable, Sprague decided "we might as well give them all we've got before we go down." Exiting the rain squall, Sprague changed course to the south toward Leyte Gulf, from where he hoped help was coming. He also ordered his destroyers and destroyer escorts to charge headlong at Kurita in a David-versus-Goliath assault while aircraft from his unit and from Taffy 2 to the south pestered the enemy.

One aviator reported to Sprague that he and other pilots, forced to take off without proper ammunition, had run out of bullets and bombs. Sprague replied that they should make dry runs on the enemy ships, who would be forced to divert attention from Taffy 3's escort carriers to swat away the offending planes.

As he guided his escort carriers south, ordering each one to chase salvos veer in the direction of the last salvo in the thought that the next salvo would land elsewhere Sprague's screen boldly launched its torpedo attacks on Kurita. Led by the destroyers *Hoel, Heerman* and *Johnston,* and the destroyer escort *Samuel B. Roberts,* Sprague's screen threw Kurita into such confusion that he never truly regained control of his ships. Darting from port to starboard like little warriors fending off a group of giants, the ships aimed torpedoes, made smoke, and fired their 5-inch guns at whatever target appeared before them. One spread of torpedoes from *Hoel* forced Kurita's temporary flagship *Yamato* to reverse course, which put her and the attending battleship *Nagato* out of the battle for 10 crucial minutes.

Five-inch shells proved no match for the 14-inch and 8-inch shells that lumbered back in return, some containing various hues of dye to mark ranges for different ships. Sprague remembered that "the splashes had a kind of horrid beauty." One of the sailors yelled, "They're shooting at us in technicolor!"

The enemy shot more than pretty colors at Sprague. Large shells soon zeroed in on the small ships and whacked them with impunity. "It was like a puppy being smacked by a fire truck," remembered one man aboard *Johnston*.

In spite of the valiant efforts of the destroyers and destroyer escorts, Kurita's cruisers and destroyers closed in. Sprague again ordered his screen to attack, and when he was informed that they had no more torpedoes, a man on the escort carrier *White Plains* remarked, "The situation's getting a little tense, isn't it?"

In went the screen for another joust. Their 5-inch shells bounced futilely off Kurita's stronger hulls, but still they went in. A shell smacked *Heerman*. Hoel took as many as 14 hits and started to sink. *Johnston* single-handedly charged a column of destroyers, led by light cruiser *Yahagi,* and forced them to release their torpedoes from too great a distance, then fell prey to their combined shellfire. As *Johnston* disappeared under the surface, a Japanese officer stood at attention on board his passing destroyer, gallantly saluting the bold vessel. Pounded to ruin in an unequal duel with battleship *Kongo, Samuel B. Roberts* floated awhile in twisted agony before dropping to the depths. Enemy heavy cruisers overtook the escort carrier *Gambier Bay* and sank her.

Just as it seemed Kurita would move in for the coup de grâce, the nearest Japanese cruisers and destroyers started turning back.

"God damn it, boys, they're getting away," screamed a signalman near Sprague. The stunned American admiral "could not believe [his] eyes, but it looked as if the whole Japanese fleet was indeed retiring."

Confused by the smoke and aggressive tactics of his American counterpart and afraid that Halsey's fast carriers were actually his adversary, a timid Kurita turned away at the moment of victory. After cruising around for a time trying to determine his next move, Kurita finally abandoned the area early that afternoon.

Sprague had to face another ordeal, one that would soon haunt captains and sailors in other campaigns. About 11 a.m., Japanese aircraft led by Lt. Cmdr. Yukio Seki approached Sprague's exhausted unit. Two of the planes immediately dove for Sprague's flagship *Fanshaw Bay* and were shot down, while another peeled off toward the escort carrier *St. Lô* and a fourth selected *Kitkun Bay*. Sailors on all ships watched in horror as the planes, instead of pulling out of a bombing run, plunged straight toward their targets. The fourth plane crashed into *Kitkun Bay*'s port catwalk, exploded, then bounced into the sea, while the third smashed into *St. Lô*'s flight deck, creating fires that ignited numerous explosions through the hangar deck. *St. Lô* sank, taking 114 men with her.

Ninety minutes later, a second wave of kamikaze planes terrorized Taffy 3. Anti-aircraft fire from the damaged *Kitkun Bay* tore the wings off one plane, which splashed 50 yards off its port bow. Two others plunged toward *Kalinin Bay* and plowed into the ship's after port stack and flight deck, destroying a 20mm gun mount.

Aircraft from Taffy 3 and from Halsey's Third Fleet pursued Kurita as he retreated through the San Bernardino Strait and Sibuyan Sea, sinking light cruiser *Noshiro* and damaging one heavy cruiser. The weary Kurita departed with approximately half the force he had brought to the battle—an inglorious defeat for a man who had held victory in the palm of his hand.

The U.S. Navy delivered a devastating defeat to the Japanese at Leyte Gulf. In four separate encounters spread over two days—each action in itself a major battle—American ships and airplanes destroyed four Japanese aircraft carriers, three battleships, six cruisers and 12 destroyers, and killed more than 10,000 Japanese. American losses were comparatively light and mostly suffered by Sprague's gallant Taffy 3, whose two escort carriers, two destroyers and one destroyer escort represented five of the six ships lost at Leyte Gulf and most of the 3,000 dead. The major American casualty was the light carrier *Princeton*, hit by a Japanese bomb during the Sibuyan Sea phase and eventually scuttled after being wracked by an internal explosion that also damaged the light cruiser *Birmingham*.

The battle eliminated Japan's once-proud navy as an effective offensive force. Cut off from the vital flow of oil, the ships could do little more than remind the Japanese of past grandeur.

"After this battle," stated Admiral Ozawa, "the surface forces became strictly auxiliary, so that we relied on land forces, special [kamikaze] attack, and air power. There was no further use assigned to surface vessels, with the exception of some special ships."

Buying Time at the Battle of the Bulge

By Gary Schreckengost

August 1944 was a disastrous month for the Third Reich. In the West, American, British and Canadian armies had driven the Wehrmacht out of France and back to the Siegfried Line. In the East, the situation was even worse. Army Group Center, defending eastern Poland, was smashed by the Soviet summer offensive, and now a torrent of vengeful Red Army soldiers were pouring westward to the borders of Germany itself.

Radical action was needed if Adolf Hitler was going to have any chance to dramatically alter the course of the war. An early winter offensive in the East would be of little value. Not only would the climate and topography probably defeat such a thrust, but even if it succeeded, at most it would only result in the destruction of 25 or so Soviet divisions and limited territorial gains. In view of the size of the forces the Russians had at their disposal, such a success would have little effect on the overall situation in the East.

In Western Europe, however, things were not so bleak. An offensive launched through the wooded Ardennes region could provide the Führer with the decisive results he needed. In perhaps the Third Reich's greatest triumph, it was there in 1940 that General Heinz Guderian had punched a hole through the French lines, crossed the Meuse River below Sedan and raced to the sea in just two weeks. The Ardennes thus had a certain emotional attraction. Furthermore, the American troops who now defended the region had yet to fight in a winter campaign and, if the attack could be organized quickly and launched early enough in the winter months, the weather could markedly reduce the effectiveness of Allied air cover.

All factors seemed to point to the Ardennes as the place for the Germans to launch their last great offensive. Having decided upon his course, Hitler began to strip away badly needed units from the Eastern Front and comb the Reich for additional manpower to bring his battered formations up to strength. He also hoarded precious fuel and armored vehicles. Aware that surprise was a critical component to success, the Germans carried out these preparations with the utmost secrecy.

Through stinginess and stealth, during the fall of '44, the Führer was able to assemble a strike force whose size and strength had not been seen by German soldiers for years. As a final gesture to convince the Allies that the Germans had no plan for an offensive, Hitler's last gamble was dubbed Operation Wacht am Rhein (Watch on the Rhine).

The Führer's plan called for two panzer armies, the Fifth and Sixth—consisting of seven armored, one parachute and eight Volksgrenadier divisions-to punch through three American infantry divisions, the 99th, 106th and 28th, which were spread along the Ardennes' border with Germany.

After breaching the American line, the two panzer armies were to drive northwestward to the Belgian port of Antwerp and the sea, splitting the Allied line in two. Two other German armies, the Fifteenth and Seventh, would protect the northern and southern flanks of the principal German advance. Hitler hoped that such a blow would split the unity of the Allied alliance and cause it to crumble or, at the very least, so disrupt the Western Allies' advance that he would be able to shift badly needed forces to the East to counter the Communist threat.

One of the principal units in the operation was General Heinrich von Lüttwitz's XLVII Panzer Corps of General Hasso von Manteuffel's Fifth Panzer Army. Lüttwitz's panzer corps was to breach the American lines between the small towns of Marnach and Weiler, seize two main roads that ran east-west through those towns and cross the Clerf River on the offensive's first day. After cracking the American line, Lüttwitz's tanks were to pass through the crossroads city of Bastogne on the second day and seize the bridges over the Meuse just south of Namur and Dinant. In addition to the territorial objectives, Lüttwitz was instructed to support General Josef "Sepp" Dietrich's Sixth Panzer Army drive to Antwerp and the sea. The keys to the operation, in Hitler's mind, were speed and audacity, just as they had been in 1940.

Unlike many other formations at this late stage of the war, the XLVII Panzer Corps was made up entirely of army divisions. Lüttwitz's command consisted of the 2nd Panzer, Panzer Lehr and 26th Volksgrenadier divisions. The 2nd was highly regarded by many in the German army because it was one of the Wehrmacht's three original experimental panzer divisions. Since the start of the war it had seen extensive service in France and Russia before being removed from the maelstrom to rest and refit early in 1944.

After being reconstituted, the 2nd was assigned to the defense of the West Wall. Between June and August 1944, the 2nd took part in the fighting in Normandy's bocage country, only to be pushed back by superior Allied forces, encircled and nearly destroyed during the ensuing campaign. Following the disastrous Normandy battles, what remained of the division was judiciously pulled out of the lines and sent to Wittlich, in the Schnee-Eifel area of Germany. Once in the rear, the division received new equipment and absorbed the remains of the 352nd Infantry Division, which had also been destroyed during the brutal fighting in France.

Just two days before the operation was supposed to begin, the reconstituted division was put under the command of Colonel Meinrad von Lauchert. Although Lauchert was an able officer who had served in the Panzertruppen since 1924, he had little time to acquaint himself with his surroundings and had not even had an opportunity to meet with all of his regimental commanders prior to the attack.

Panzer Lehr was another one of the Wehrmacht's premier divisions. Officially formed on January 10, 1944, in the Nancy-Verdun area of France from various armored training and demonstration units, Panzer Lehr had received its baptism of fire against the Soviets in Hungary. After helping to temporarily slow Soviet advances in the East, the division had been rushed back to France to try to stem the tide of British and American forces rampaging across Normandy. One of the strongest armored formations of the German army, Panzer Lehr fought the Allies at Caen and St. Lô until, like the 2nd, it escaped from the Falaise Pocket and was pulled out of the lines to be reconstituted. For Wacht am Rhein, the division was put under the stewardship of its original commander, Lt. Gen. Fritz Bayerlein.

The final weapon in General Lüttwitz's arsenal was the 26th Volksgrenadier Division, which was assigned the task of infiltrating American positions and creating gaps large enough to allow Panzer Lehr to pass through to Bastogne and the Meuse unhindered. The 26th Volksgrenadier had its origins in the 26th Infantry Division. After that unit was virtually destroyed in the vicious battles in Russia in September 1944, the surviving members of the division were shipped to western Poland to the Warthelager training area to rest and refit. There, the division was reconstituted with what remained of the 582nd Infantry Division, along with new recruits and personnel combed from the ranks of the navy and air force. In order to inspire the men of this ad hoc command, as well as the many other German divisions being formed from the pieces and parts of other shattered divisions, in 1944 Hitler dubbed these new formations Volksgrenadiers (people's grenadiers). The new 12,000-man 26th Volksgrenadier Division was given to Maj. Gen. Heinz Kokott, a sturdy and meticulous veteran of many campaigns.

Over Hitler's initial objections, General Manteuffel declined the opportunity of preceding his attack with a lengthy bombardment. It was Manteuffel's intention to achieve surprise at the start of the offensive by having his infantry infiltrate through the forward American positions before sunlight. Once in place, these men could quickly take the American strongpoints and clear a path for following units. After the American positions were taken, the tanks would roll through and race to the sea unchecked. General Kokott highlighted Manteuffel's intent in his orders to his subordinate commanders: "Success or failure of the operation depends on an incessant and stubborn drive to the west and northwest. The forward waves of the attack must not be delayed or tied down by any form of resistance. . . . Bastogne should fall on the second day of the operation or at least be encircled by then."

Standing in Lüttwitz's way were the men of the U.S. Army 28th Infantry Division's 110th Regimental Combat Team (RCT). The 110th RCT consisted of the 110th Infantry Regiment and attached units. The whole team was commanded by Colonel William Hurley Fuller, a cantankerous Regular Army officer and World War I veteran who was out to redeem himself. A few months before, during the Normandy campaign, Fuller had commanded a regiment in the 2nd Infantry Division. When his regiment failed to reach its assigned objectives as ordered, Fuller was relieved of command. Once Paris was liberated, however, Fuller was able to convince his old comrade in arms, Lt. Gen. Troy Middleton, commander of the VIII Corps, to give him another chance. Middleton, who was forced to find replacement commanders for a number of regiments, gave Fuller command of the 110th Infantry Regiment in late November 1944 after its commander, Colonel Theodore Seeley, was wounded. In December the 110th RCT consisted of three rifle battalions; Company B, 109th Field Artillery Battalion; Battery C, 687th Field Artillery; Company B, 103rd Engineers; Company B, 103rd Medical Battalion; Company B, 630th Tank Destroyer Battalion; and Battery A, 447th Anti-Aircraft Artillery Battalion.

The 28th Division had formerly been a component of the Pennsylvania National Guard. After mobilization, the division had been trained for participation in the invasion of France. On July 22, 1944, six weeks after D-Day, the 28th was shipped to France and quickly sent to the front. It fought with distinction throughout the Normandy campaign and, on August 29, had the privilege of representing the United States during celebration ceremonies marking the liberation of Paris. The men of the division did not have an opportunity to enjoy the City of Light, however. After marching through Paris they were immediately sent to the front. Once outside of Paris, the 28th, now under the command of Maj. Gen. Norman D. Cota, resumed its eastward journey. On September 7 the division rolled into Luxembourg, crossed the Our River south of Clervaux and became the first Allied division to breach Germany's vaunted Siegfried Line.

The 28th was then moved to the vicinity of Rott, on the western edge of the H rtgen Forest. As it assimilated new recruits, the division was assigned the job of capturing Schmidt and the forests surrounding the town. The 9th Division had tried to secure the area a few weeks earlier and had been massacred. Following the 9th's failure, the 28th was sent into the breach and, unsupported by other First Army units, received a similar treatment from the forest's German defenders.

After its bloodletting in the Hürtgen, the 28th Division was sent to the Ardennes, which Supreme Allied Commander General Dwight D. Eisenhower considered to be a quiet area where new divisions could receive experience and battle-weary units could rest. There, what was left of the division began to take in thousands of new recruits to replace the casualties lost during the summer and fall campaigns. But although the Ardennes was considered a quiet sector, the men still held positions on the front line. The 28th's portion of the front was a 25-mile-long sector that was more than three times the area an infantry division was normally expected to defend. The 110th was assigned the vulnerable center section of the line. To make the task even more challenging, the regiment held this portion of the front with only two of its three battalions, the 1st and 3rd. The regiment's remaining battalion, the 2nd, was held behind the lines at Donnange and Wiltz, where it served as the division's only infantry reserve.

The bulk of the 110th was deployed along the St. Vith-Oiekirch Highway. Known to the Americans as "Skyline Drive," the highway was a hard-surfaced road that ran parallel to the Luxembourg-German border and overlooked the Our River and Germany to the east and the Clerf River and Luxembourg to the west. Along this road, which ran about two miles from each river, Colonel Fuller deployed his two battalions along a series of strongpoints: Company A, 110th, held Heinerscheid; three machine-gun crews from Company D held Reuler; Company B and five 57mm towed cannons from the 630th Tank Destroyer Battalion held Marnach; Companies K and B, 103rd Engineers, held Hosingen; Company L held Holzthum; and Company I held Weiler. Most of these towns, except for Hosingen, were on roads that ran east-west from the Our River and the German lines to the American rear. Believing that they were in a quiet area and that the Germans were too battered to launch an attack of their own, Fuller allowed his men to occupy their positions during the daylight hours and to retire to warmer quarters in the evening. During the hours of darkness, the forward American positions were only lightly held.

Behind these strongpoints were Fuller's reserves. At the resort town of Clervaux was the 110th's command post, Headquarters Company, Supply Company, some of Cannon Company and Companies D and B of the 103rd Medical Battalion. Company C was in Munshausen, Companies M and A of the 447th Anti-Aircraft Artillery were in Consthum, and the 109th Field Artillery and Battery C of the 687th Field Artillery were deployed along the reverse slope of the ridge between Clervaux and Consthum.

All told, the 110th RCT numbered about 5,000 men on the evening of December 15, 1945. Across the Our River was Heinrich von Lüttwitz's entire XLVII Panzer Corps, with 27,000 infantrymen and 216 tanks, assault guns or tank destroyers, which intended to smash through the 110th's positions in one day, seize the Clerf River bridges intact and drive on to reach the Meuse two or three days later.

To seize control of the Our River, Manteuffel ordered his infantry battalions to go in first, crossing the Our in rubber boats in the early morning hours of December 16, when the American positions were manned by the fewest men. Once across the river, German soldiers would surround the forward American positions and attack soon after dawn. After these forward positions were seized, Manteuffel's engineers would build a series of bridges over the Our to allow the mechanized units to cross. If all went according to plan, the armored battalions of the 2nd Panzer and Panzer Lehr would be across the Clerf River by the end of the first day and on their way to Bastogne and the Meuse by December 17 or 18.

GARY SCHRECKENGOST

Lüttwitz and his division commanders were confident that they could satisfy Manteuffel. They knew that their defenders across the river were spread thin. So weakly held was the American front that several reconnaissance patrols, unchallenged by sentries, had already crossed the Our, pinpointed enemy positions and marked infiltration lanes around them.

Soon after 1 a.m. on December 16, 1944, elements of the 304th Panzergrenadier Regiment from the 2nd Panzer Division and the 39th and 77th Volksgrenadiers from the 26th Volksgrenadier Division began their 20-yard crossing of the Our in small rubber boats. By 2 a.m., the Germans were across and headed west through the snow-covered, forested draws of the Our River valley toward their objectives. Quietly, skillfully, they approached to within 300 yards of the American defenses at Marnach, Hosingen, Holzthum, Weiler, Munshausen and Clervaux, surrounding them with squads, platoons, companies or—in Hosingen's case—an entire battalion. Once they had worked themselves into position, the German formations sought cover and waited for the first shots of the artillery bombardment that signaled the beginning of the attack.

Just before dawn, the Germans began their artillery bombardment. Then around 7 a.m., after a brief period of calm, the German infantry who had infiltrated through the front lines began their assault. Well-coordinated attacks began to hit all of the 110th's positions almost simultaneously.

Shivering lookouts from Company K, posted in a water tower in Hosingen, were startled to see an entire company of white-clad Germans from the 77th Volksgrenadiers charging across an open field to their front and trying to force their way into the town. Despite their surprise, the lookouts were able to alert their fellow GIs in positions around Hosingen. Soon the Americans were firing a .30-caliber machine gun, a Browning Automatic Rifle (BAR) and M-1 rifles at the advancing enemy. The firing lasted only a few minutes before the Germans were forced to retreat back to the shelter of the woods.

It was the same across the 110th's entire front. The Germans spilled out from cover, "coming out of the ground from all directions," as one American veteran put it. Most of those attacks, however, were quickly repulsed by the quick reaction of startled GIs along the front.

Despite their initial setback, however, the advancing Germans had been able to surround the 110th. Soon additional German infantrymen were coming to the front, increasing the pressure on the now isolated American positions. All along Skyline Drive the fighting was becoming more intense. So close had the action come that some artillerymen in batteries positioned between Munshausen and Consthum were engaged in close-quarter fighting. Although the artillerymen were able to successfully defend their positions, the distraction caused by the German attacks prevented them from supporting other hard-pressed American units. It was becoming clear to the American commanders that if the Germans could maintain the intensity of their attacks, there was no way the Americans' strongpoints could continue to hold.

Back at regimental headquarters in Clervaux, Fuller was in a sour mood. His lines of communications to his forward outposts had been cut, and his headquarters was now under fire. Desperate for news of what was happening, Fuller quickly dispatched his executive officer, Lt. Col. Daniel Strickler, to get down to Consthum or Holzthum to find out what was going on in the 3rd Battalion's sector. Fuller also managed to get word to General Cota that the Germans were making a major push against his command and that reinforcements were needed immediately. Cota informed Fuller that the division's other regiments were also being hit and that he was reluctant to dispatch his few reserves until the situation became clearer.

Despite the shock of the early morning attack, the GIs of the

110th had been able to considerably slow the German advance. As a result, Lüttwitz's soldiers failed to seize their assigned objectives on the morning of December 16 as expected. At that point 12 infantry companies from the 2nd Panzer Division were pinned down at Marnach by the 110th's Company B and five 57mm cannons from the 630th Tank Destroyer Battalion. Twelve other companies from the 26th Volksgrenadier Division had been stopped at Hosingen by the 110th's Company K and Company B, 103rd Engineers.

In the southern sector, meanwhile, Company I was holding out against five companies from the 26th Volksgrenadier Division at Weiler and Holzthum, and along the route assigned to Panzer Lehr the men of Company L were somehow managing to hold out against seven companies of attacking Volksgrenadiers.

After four more hours of desperate fighting, Cota determined that the main German effort was indeed aimed at Fuller's units. He then decided to dispatch 16 Sherman tanks from the 707th Tank Battalion to help relieve Marnach, Hosingen and Holzthum. Aware that all that stood between the Germans and a potentially critical rupture of American lines was the 110th RCT, Cota passed down a chilling order to the officers and men of his—"Hold your position at all costs."

Departing Wiltz a little after 1 p.m., the Shermans from the 707th Tank Battalion rumbled toward the front in a staggered column. About a mile from the Clerf, at a slushy fork in the road, the first four tanks were ordered to bear to the right and head for Holzthum to reinforce Company L. Once this platoon crossed the Clerf, it was forced to run a gantlet of fire from a half dozen squads of the 39th Volksgrenadiers, which had set up along the tree-lined road with MG42s. Fighting their way through to Consthum, the tank platoon was ordered to continue on to Holzthum. In the confusion of battle the lead tank mistook an anti-tank gun from Company M, which was posted near a cafe on the western side of Holzthum, for a German gun and fired on it, killing or wounding most of its crew.

Meanwhile, the rest of the tank column had taken the left fork out of Wiltz and had crossed the Clerf at Drauffelt. After going another mile and a half, the column once again split at a fork in the road. The first four tanks headed down the right fork and fought their way into Hosingen; the remainder took the left fork and headed north to Munshausen and Marnach. Of these, half stayed in Munshausen to reinforce Company C, some anti-tank guns from Company D and the 1st Battalion's headquarters. The other four tanks went on to Marnach, fighting their way through the surrounding German infantry.

Soon after dusk, the engineer battalions from the 2nd Panzer and Panzer Lehr divisions had, after considerable confusion and delay, finally completed the bridges over the Our at Dasburg and Gemund, and the assault guns began to cross. However, the delay caused by the slow construction of the bridges meant that, instead of making a 15-minute drive to the captured bridges over the Clerf as originally planned, the 216 tanks, assault guns and tank destroyers of Lüttwitz's corps were now diverted to aid their infantry brethren in clearing the roads to Bastogne of the resolute men of the 110th Infantry.

General Manteuffel was not happy when he attempted to sum up the situation on the evening of December 16 to his superiors: "The Clerf was not reached at any point. The enemy was unquestionably surprised by the attack. He offered, however, in many places tenacious and brave resistance in delaying by skillfully fought combat tactics. His counterattacks, which started at once, partly supported by small armored groups, resulted in many points in critical situations. . . . The tenacious resistance of the enemy, together with the road blocks placed . . . were the most essential reasons for the slowing of the attack whose timing was not going according to plan."

Determined to regain lost time, the Germans did not cease their attacks when darkness came. At Marnach, the lead elements of the 2nd Panzer Regiment rolled in to support the stymied 304th Panzergrenadier Regiment with tanks and halftracks. The subsequent combined arms assault was fast, furious and decisive. The Germans attacked the town with the help of artificial moonlight—tanks mounting spotlights, which bounced their beams off the low-lying clouds, illuminating the battlefield. Four Shermans from the 707th Tank Battalion and five towed guns from the 630th Tank Destroyer Battalion were quickly knocked out. In addition, all of the infantrymen in Marnach were killed, captured or driven from the town.

Farther south at Hosingen, the stymied 77th Panzergrenadier Regiment was relieved by the 78th Panzergrenadiers and its assault guns so the 77th could push on to Drauffelt and secure the bridge over the Clerf as originally intended. In the dark, the 78th made a few probes but was unable to organize a full-scale attack until the next day.

As the Germans licked their wounds at Marnach and Holzthum, Cota decided to give Fuller the last of his available reserves. Companies F and H, 110th Infantry, and the last company from the 707th Tank Battalion, 18 Stuart light tanks, were dispatched to join the four remaining Shermans in Munshausen.

Fuller believed that Marnach was still holding out, and he assembled a force to relieve the beleaguered members of Company B on December 17. Four Shermans from the 707th and a hundred or so infantrymen from Company C were directed to attack Marnach from the south. Companies E and F, supported by machine guns from Company H, were to attack directly east up the road from Clervaux, and the 18 Stuart tanks from Company A were to swing down from the north from Heinerscheid.

Although Fuller began his counterattack with high hopes, the assault was a complete failure. The Stuarts were almost wiped out by ferocious German anti-tank fire. Only seven of the lightly armored tanks were able to escape, retreating back into Heiner-scheid and into the arms of Company A. The infantry attack of Companies E, F and H was quickly repulsed by well-placed machine-gun fire, and the four Shermans coming up from Mun-shausen were driven back by German Mark IVs.

Once this local counterattack was thrown back, Lauchert ordered the 2nd Panzer forward to take Clervaux and the bridge across the Clerf. The Germans were now becoming impatient to get the operation moving again.

Lauchert's reconnaissance battalion sped down the road first, followed by 10 Mark IVs and a few assault guns. Hanging onto the sides of the vehicle were infantrymen who had not become tangled up in the fierce small actions of the previous day. While the reconnaissance battalion pinned down the American force in Clervaux, Lauchert readied another, much more powerful force, to encircle the town and prevent the garrison from escaping. This second force was assembled on the western side of Marnach and consisted of the remainder of Lauchert's Mark IVs, his 49 Pan-thers and the balance of his Panzergrenadiers.

Clervaux was not well situated for defense. It rested at the bottom of the Clerf River valley and was overlooked by a wooded ridgeline. The main north-south road bisected the town, and it was straddled on both sides by two- or three-story buildings and a few churches. The most prominent feature of Clervaux, on its northern edge, was a chateau with thick walls, which was strate-gically situated on a spur that ran off a wooded ridge that encir-cled the town.

Companies E, F and H, 110th Infantry, were the town's princi-pal defenders. Aware of the desperate nature of the situation, however, Fuller had also directed Headquarters Company—scouts, cooks and clerks, plus men from other units of the division who had been trapped in Clervaux when the offensive began—to grab whatever weapons were available and take up positions in the buildings throughout the town. The 707th Tank Battalion's three remaining Shermans were deployed just outside of town. This gave Fuller, who was headquartered in the Hotel Claravallis on the northern edge of the twon, about 450 men, three tanks and a few anti-tank guns to defend against Lauchert's 5,000 infantry and 120 tanks and assault guns.

The battle for Clervaux could clearly become a bloody affair. Not wanting to become entangled in a vicious urban battle, the Germans hoped that, once encircled, the Americans would simply surrender. If they did not, however, the Germans knew that the town would have to be stormed, a costly proposition and one that the 2nd Panzer Division could ill afford. Fuller and the men of the 110th trapped in Clervaux, knew that surrender was not an option.

By the morning of the 17th, the leading vehicles of Lauchert's reconnaissance battalion crested the ridge that overlooked Clervaux. After a quick review of the situation, the 2nd Panzer's commander decided to bombard the low-lying town from the ridge while the 2nd Panzergrenadier Regiment conducted a dismounted double envelopment, capturing the crucial bridge and suppressing any enemy anti-tank fire.

While this force occupied the defenders, 16 armored vehicles would charge down the road to the bridge over the Clerf. From there, the tanks would continue on to the critically important crossroads town of Bastogne, with the reconnaissance battalion once again in the lead. Lauchert directed that while his forces moved in and around the town, artillery and mortar fire would rain down upon American strongpoints, especially upon the fortress-like chateau that dominated the landscape.

Soon German shells were raining down on the town. Instead of quickly surrendering as Lauchert hoped under this massive bombardment, however, Fuller's command held out as best it could. Covered by direct and indirect artillery fire, Lauchert's Panzergrenadiers were able to swing around both sides of the town, taking the ridge that overlooked the chateau. By 10 o'clock, they had secured the crossing for Lauchert's tanks.

Desperate, Fuller called in what artillery he could from the division and ordered his four Shermans to come forward from the backside of the town to try to silence at least some of the assault guns, which were now among the buildings of the town and were cutting down his nearly defenseless men.

As the Shermans advanced through Clervaux, Sergeant Frank Kushnir exacted some revenge from the Germans who were now firing point-blank into American positions. Armed with a bolt-action M1903 Springfield sniper rifle in a tower of the chateau, Kushnir took the opportunity to kill a few careless Germans who were "smoking and joking" outside their armored vehicles instead of safely inside with the hatches shut.

When the Shermans arrived on the eastern edge of the town, they fired a few times at the German tanks that were deployed along the ridge and then moved astride the road up through a snowy field. Their effort was of little value. Soon after moving into the field they were smashed by the combined fire of dozens of 75mm guns, which were posted on the heights above.

With the Shermans dispatched and the town in flames, Lauchert now ordered his main attack. The American position became even more tenuous as several German armored vehicles with supporting infantry charged down the road and invested the town from the east.

The struggle was becoming more intense. The Americans, however, refused to surrender, and the fighting moved like a tidal wave from street to street, house to house, room to room. While tanks clanked down the street, blasting American strong-points at close range, dismounted Panzergrenadiers followed, pointing out targets to the tankers, guarding the flanks and rear of the armored vehicles and spraying the houses with rifle and machine-gun fire.

What the Germans had hoped would be a lightning-swift attack had now turned into a desperate slow-moving fight where advances were measured in inches. The American soldiers fought desperately, but with so much enemy infantry now swarming through the town, they were unable to take out any of the tanks or assault guns that were destroying Clervaux one building at a time.

The fighting continued off and on all day. Still the Americans held the town. The Germans would push down a block, and the Americans would respond with a withering fire that would slow the advancing German infantry. The Germans would then call up supporting armored vehicles and push back the Americans. Although the Germans were slowly gaining the upper hand, they knew that by this time Lauchert's Panthers were supposed to be moving out of Bastongne and heading north toward the Meuse. Instead of restoring the initiative to the German offensive, the 2nd Panzer was slugging it out with an ad hoc infantry battalion in Clervaux.

At 6:45, after fighting the Germans all day, Fuller sent his last message back to division. He requested that what remained of his battalion be allowed to retreat. Upon being told that this was not permissible and that he should fight on, Fuller responded that his command post was under direct enemy fire from German tanks and that he was going to try to get back to the division head-quarters at Wiltz.

Totally cut off, overwhelmed and out of ammunition, the defenders of Clervaux now tried to escape from the battle area using the wooded draws around the town for cover. Fuller was forced to leave his second-story command post when a German tank began pumping artillery rounds into the first floor. There was no formal order of retreat. Fuller, what was left of his staff, and some wounded riflemen went out a back window of the hotel and climbed a cold steel ladder up the face of the windblown cliff that overlooked Clervaux. As they were exiting the building, they could hear the thud of German jackboots on the floor below.

The few GIs who had escaped the struggle now began to make their way westward as best they could. As the American defense disintegrated, Lauchert's Panther Battalion, now two days behind schedule, began to roll through town and across the Clerf River. Fuller, without a command, tried to make his way westward. After a harrowing period of avoiding various German detachments, the unfortunate colonel was eventually captured. Unable to locate Fuller, Colonel Theodore Seeley returned to command what remained of the regiment.

Clervaux, however, was not yet completely in German hands. The chateau was still held by 50 or so stalwart souls under Captain Clark Mackey, commander of the 110th's Headquarters Company, and Captain John Aiken, Fuller's signal officer. All night long, as tanks of the 2nd Panzer Division raced west toward Bastogne, the Americans continued to fight.

Although the manpower was badly needed elsewhere, Lauchert was forced to leave an entire battalion behind to mop up opposition at the chateau. By the afternoon of December 18, totally out of ammunition and with the chateau burning and crumbling around them, the gallant defenders of "Fort Clervaux" finally surrendered.

Kushnir volunteered to exit the building first. He held a prisoner in front of him to ensure that a vengeful German would not shoot him as he left the chateau. When he was not fired on, the rest of the Americans followed the sergeant out to surrender. Soon after surrendering, Kushnir remembered, "a German colonel asked the German sergeant who we had held as prisoner, 'What was the treatment?' 'Well,' the sergeant said, 'they didn't mistreat us, they

fed us good, they took care of our wounded, and they also protected us within the chateau so we wouldn't be under our own
fire, you know.' And then the colonel comes out in perfect English:
'You men are so lucky. My intention was to shoot all of you for
the dead comrades [who] are strung throughout the compound.' "

Farther south, Panzer Lehr was now finally crossing the Clerf
at Drauffelt. The long since bypassed American garrisons of
Holzxthum and Hosingenn, still battling German formations left
behind to finish them off, fought stubbornly from house to house
before making the individual decision to either flee the battle
area on the evening of December 17 or surrendered late on the
morning of the 18th.

By the evening of the second day of the offensive, the only
organized resistance east of the Clerf was in Consthum, where the
110th's executive officer, Colonel Daniel Strickler, had assembled
the scattered remnants of the 110th's 3rd Battalion, the 447th
Anti-Aircraft Battalion, and some 105mm howitzers from the
109th and 687th Field Artillery battalions along the ridges that
flanked the town. With help from the rest of the 687th Field
Artillery back at Wiltz, Strickler's force now pounded the tanks
and infantry of Panzer Lehr.

Strickler called in massive amounts of artillery fire on Bayerlein's tanks as they passed through the town. "We killed off practically all of their infantry," Strickler later proudly recalled. "We just
slaughtered their infantry who were with the tanks and following
the tanks . . . we then brought up our artillery to the front lines and
had them fire directly at the tanks coming down the road."

Aware that he could not simply ignore this determined American force, Bayerlein was forced to detach badly needed tanks
and men to subdue Strickler's force. After a good deal of close-
quarters fighting and many additional casualties, the Germans
were finally able to subdue the Americans by nightfall.

With the fall of Consthum, the last strongpoint held by the 110th RCT was finally eliminated. Unlike Fuller, however, Strickler was somehow able to avoid German patrols and make it back to Wiltz, where he was ordered by Cota to gather what troops remained and hold the enemy back as long as possible.

By December 19, the 28th Division had been swept from the map by the XLVII Panzer Corps. However, the unit's demise had not been in vain. Lüttwitz's panzers were now three days behind schedule. The time that the Allies gained by the sacrifice of the 110th and the other elements of the 28th Infantry Division had allowed Eisenhower to rush reinforcements to the Ardennes. General Middleton could be happy with his decision to appoint Fuller to command the 110th. He later commented that "The 110th Infantry of the 28th Division, which was overrun by the attack, did a splendid job. . . . It put up very stiff resistance for the three days. Had not this regiment put up the fight it did the Germans would have been in Bastogne long before the 101st Airborne reached that town." Colonel Fuller had been redeemed. Appropriately enough, when the XLVII Panzer Corps finally did reach Bastogne, fighting alongside the 101st in Bastogne was Team SNAFU, which was composed of individual members of the 28th Division who had been able to make their way back to American lines after their positions had been taken during the first three days of the German offensive.

Of the 5,000 officers and men of the 110th RCT who manned positions along Skyline Drive on the morning of December 16, only 532 officers and men were fit for duty after Hitler's last great offensive had been defeated. Once the German offensive had been blunted and the Americans had a chance to catch their breath, the widely scattered elements of the 28th Division, including the 110th, which was now commanded by Strickler, were gathered together to reconstitute the division. In the spring of

1945, as the Allies went on the offensive all along the Western Front, the 28th was brought back up to strength with thousands of new replacements and sent to fight in the rugged Colmar Pocket. The division remained in combat until Germany surrendered in May 1945.

1945

Remagen: The Allies' Bridge to Victory

By Flint Whitlock

Second Lieutenant Karl Timmermann could scarcely believe his eyes. From his vantage point atop a hill north of Remagen, Germany, the officer studied the structure, that military logic said should not exist—a still standing bridge over the Rhine River. Through his binoculars, he could see thousands of panicked German soldiers and civilians fleeing eastward, away from the American forces that were descending on Remagen.

It was March 7, 1945 a gray, chilly day. The previous day Timmermann a native of West Point, Neb., had been promoted to commanding officer of Company A, 1st Battalion, 27th Armored Infantry Regiment, 9th Armored Division, because of heavy casualties among the higher ranking officers.

Timmermann's company was the vanguard of the entire American drive to the Rhine and had just arrived at a high point above the ancient resort town located on the scenic west bank of Germany's most important river, midway between Köln and Koblenz.

The 9th Armored had been fighting against determined resistance since it had crossed the border farther north a few weeks earlier. The men in Timmermann's company were cold, tired, worn-out, fed up, and just a little bit scared. They had seen far too many of their friends wounded, maimed and killed. The war seemed to be slowly grinding to a victorious conclusion, there was little point in sticking one's neck out now and getting killed, what with the end of the war almost in sight.

After all, many of the men reasoned, they had already seen more than their fair share of combat. In August 1944, Maj. Gen. John W. Leonard's 9th Armored Division had left Fort Riley, Kan, crossed the Atlantic Ocean on the luxury liner *Queen Mary,* spent the month of September training in England, and then crossed the English Channel to lend its armored weight to the Allied drive rushing eastward across France.

Elements of the 9th Armored had been used to plug gaps in the American front lines when the Germans launched their ferocious counterattack toward Antwerp—an action that became known as the Battle of the Bulge. It was also men from Timmermann's company who were found massacred in the snow near the village of Malmedy.

The 9th Armored was part of Lt. Gen. Courtney Hodges' First Army, which itself was part of Omar Bradley's 12th Army Group, sandwiched between Field Marshal Bernard Law Montgomery's 21st Army Group to the north and Maj. Gen. George Patton's Third Army to the south. All were driving eastward like enormous spears, their combat units forming the points, their supply trains trailing behind like shafts hundreds of miles long, all aiming at one thing: the heart of Germany.

The First Army was headed for Köln, just below the heavily industrialized Ruhr area. After Adolf Hitler's last great counteroffensive had been broken in the Ardennes in January 1945, Western Allies were faced with the daunting task of assaulting the Siegfried Line defenses and crossing the great natural barrier, the Rhine. Under the master plan, Montgomery's troops were given the task of forging a Rhine crossing north of the Ruhr, beginning in February, with the Americans playing a supporting role.

Bradley's forces were to support Montgomery's thrust by capturing dams on the Roer River and then squeezing the Germans into a trap formed by Hodges' and Patton's armies west of the Rhine. The 9th Armored's assignment was to push across the Roer in the 78th Infantry Division's sector and support the attack toward the Rhine. But the Germans confounded those plans by demolishing the Roer dams and flooding the valley, making the Americans' progress slow and dangerous.

Capturing a bridge over the Rhine had been a dream of the Allied forces for many months. Indeed, the whole purpose of Montgomery's Operation Market Garden in September 1944—an operation that ended disastrously for the Allies—had been to seize bridges over the Rhine, as well as other rivers. While some officers continued to hope that an intact bridge might be found, most had given up on the dream.

In February 1945, Maj. Gen. John Milliken's III Corps, part of Hodges' army group, moved forward to take control of the area from XVIII Airborne Corps. At a First Army briefing, Milliken asked, "What about bridges over the Rhine?" He was informed that by the time he got to the Rhine there would be no bridges because the Germans were blowing them up before they could fall into Allied hands. Indeed, on March 2, two Rhine bridges—one at Oberkassel, near Düsseldorf, and the other just south of Ürdingen—exploded virtually in their would-be captors' faces.

The timing for the demolition of a bridge was a very tricky thing. No bridge was to be destroyed too soon, since Germans fleeing eastward would be cut off on the wrong side of the river. Those in charge of the demolitions also could not wait too long, lest they risk having the bridge fall into enemy hands.

It was discovered that two bridges in III Corp's zone—at Bonn and 12 miles south of Remagen—had not yet been destroyed, and plans were swiftly drawn up to try and capture at least one of the spans intact. On March 6, III Corps issued a field order directing 9th Armored's Combat Command B to head for the Remagen area. No mention was made, however, of the bridge as an objective. No one really believed it would still be standing.

Called Ricomagus by the Romans who had settled there 2,000 years earlier, Remagen was a town of some 5,000 inhabitants. It had been battled over, destroyed and rebuilt many times during its long history. Soldiers from Spain, Sweden, France and Russia had all occupied Remagen at one time or another.

The swiftly flowing Rhine, the cliffs on the opposite bank, the fine hotels and restaurants and the streets that wound their way through the quaint old sections had brought tourists to Remagen for many years. The prime attraction was the Church of St. Apollinaris, which was built on the ruins of a Roman fort during the Middle Ages and held the bones of the martyred saint in its reliquary.

A railroad bridge on the southeastern edge of town—the Ludendorff Bridge—was Remagen's other major point of civic pride. Begun in 1916 as a link between the armaments factories in the Ruhr and the World War I battlefields of the Western Front, the bridge was named in honor of General Erich Ludendorff, a member of Field Marshal Count von Schlieffen's general staff and a strong proponent of building more Rhine bridges.

Few potential crossing sites on the Rhine were more formidable than Remagen. Here the river is swift and wide—about 300 yards across. A tributary, the Ahr, flows into the Rhine about a mile above the town, adding to the turbulence. On the far bank, a 600-foot cliff, known as the Erpeler Ley after the nearby town of Erpel, rises sharply from the eastern bank.

The handsome bridge was a three-span design, more than 1,000 feet long, that rested on two stone piers in the river and was anchored on either end by two fortresslike stone towers.

Gun ports in each three-story tower gave the impression that this was a bridge that could, and would, be heavily defended if it were ever threatened. A pair of railroad tracks ran across the structure, along with narrow catwalks along its outer edges for foot traffic. The tracks disappeared into a tunnel in the cliff on the eastern bank.

As handsome as the bridge was, it was also deadly, primed for self-destruction. Sixty boxes were strategically located along the structure's length; if the span was threatened with capture, explosives could be installed in the boxes and detonated. An electric ignition fuze system, with its control switch located safely inside the tunnel's entrance, had been installed, along with a primer cord backup system. Additional charges could be installed beneath the approach road on the western side of the bridge to crater the road and prevent (or at least slow down) any motorized enemy columns from reaching the span.

While the Allies were hammering closer to Germany's western frontier in the fall of 1944, the Ludendorff Bridge had come under increasing aerial attack to cut off the trainloads of vital supplies and reinforcements being rushed to the front. A heavy air attack on December 29 had caused considerable damage to the bridge, and for several more weeks the bridge continued to attract Allied bombers like a magnet.

In charge of the small group of German army engineers whose job it was to destroy the bridge at the right moment was Captain Karl Friesenhahn, who was generally regarded as a likeable sort, even if he was a bit of a hard-line Nazi.

Another captain, Willi Bratge, twice the recipient of the Iron Cross, was detailed as combat commander of the Remagen area. It was the duty of his troops, many of whom were either Russian "volunteers" or convalescing wounded soldiers with unreliable captured weapons, to guard the bridge and its approaches. A hodgepodge of other units of varying quality (mostly poor), and with no allegiance to either Bratge or Friesenhahn, were also in the area. The heaviest armament locally available was a few 20mm flak batteries on or near the Erpeler Ley. The number of German combatants totaled about 500, about 90 percent of whom, according to their commanders, were likely to be unreliable in a fight.

In the early hours of March 7, 1945, with the Americans just 10 miles from Remagen, German LXVII Corps, under whose jurisdiction the bridgehead had recently been placed, appointed Major Hans Scheller to organize the defenses at Remagen and, if necessary, personally supervise the destruction of the bridge. Scheller was completely unfamiliar with the bridge, its demolition system, the men stationed there, and the confusing command structure, which seemed to change from day to day. In spite of these drawbacks, Scheller set out from his headquarters for Remagen, some 40 miles away. Getting through on roads clogged with fleeing men, machinery, horse-drawn wagons and frightened civilians was anything but easy.

While Scheller was beginning his journey, Lieutenant Timmermann was being summoned to a meeting of company commanders at the 14th Tank Battalion's headquarters. Lieutenant Colonel Leonard Engeman, the 1st Battalion commanding officer, informed Timmermann that his company would be leading the charge into Remagen. Company A would ride in halftracks, accompanied by a platoon of new Pershing tanks.

At 7 a.m., under a cold, gray, drizzling sky, Timmermann's advance force roared off to the south, toward Remagen. Fighting their way through roadblocks and ambushes, the force passed through one village after another. Where bright Nazi banners had once waved triumphantly from windows, now white flags hung sullenly in the damp, misty morning.

That afternoon, Timmermann, his jeep leading the entire American army, emerged from a wooded area, rounded a bend, and there, laid out below him, was an incredible sight—the three spans of a bridge, intact, almost beckoning him onward, like the mythical Lorelei who charmed boatmen to their doom along the banks of the Rhine, just a few miles south of Remagen.

In the last few days before Timmermann's column arrived above the town, German troops had worked feverishly to lay planks over the bridge's railroad tracks so that vehicles pulling back from the front could regroup east of the Rhine. The narrow streets of the town were choked with German trucks, tanks and troops, all trying to escape to fight another day. The congestion around the western end of the bridge became so acute that in the early hours of March 7 Captain Bratge took personal control of the traffic situation to ensure an orderly progression across the bridge. Playing traffic cop was something he could ill afford to do, for it took him away from the all important task of organizing his defenses to meet the growing threat. Unfortunately for Bratge, many of the anti-aircraft guns that had been situated on top of the Erpeler Ley, which would have provided excellent observation and firepower against the Americans, had been relocated to other areas.

Early on the morning of March 7, the stream of German troops heading eastward through Remagen had become a torrent. The Americans were nipping at their heels just a few miles back. Friesenhahn and his engineers put the finishing touches on the demolitions and tested the circuits. Everything was in order. Mines and barbed wire had been placed in strategic spots, and last-minute arrangements were made to crater the approach road leading to the western side of the bridge.

Shortly after 11 a.m., while Bratge was directing traffic, he was approached by Major Hans Scheller, who informed Bratge that he had orders to assume command of the combat troops in the Remagen area. Bratge breathed a sigh of relief; perhaps his hitherto ignored cries for help had finally been answered by higher headquarters, and reinforcements soon would be arriving. The major dashed Bratge's hopes; there would be no reinforcements. The sounds of battle announced to both officers that the Americans were getting closer.

The Americans were by now less than two miles north of Remagen and smashing their way through what insignificant opposition stood in their way. The less-than-fanatic German defenders were giving up or changing into civilian attire and going AWOL. Lieutenant Timmermann and his Company A, forming the tip of a very long American spear, were using binoculars to study the bridge teeming with soldiers, civilians, vehicles and livestock. Timmermann sent a runner off to Colonel Engeman with a request for tanks and artillery, but the request was turned down. Instead, the battalion was ordered to assault the town.

General Hodges' operations officer, who happened to be in the area, noticed the still-standing bridge and realized he had to tell his commanding general about it. Hodges raced to the scene, arriving shortly after 1 p.m., and saw his prize spanning the Rhine. "Get those men moving into town," Hodges ordered, unaware that, even then, Timmermann's company and a handful of tanks were already moving cautiously through Remagen's nearly deserted streets, heading toward the bridge. Suddenly an ear-splitting blast ripped through the air and a geyser of dirt and rocks shot skyward. From the other side of the river, Friesenhahn had set off his first charge, blowing a crater 30 feet wide in the approach road. Through his binoculars, Timmermann could see the German engineers making their last-minute preparations to add the Ludendorff Bridge to the long list of ruptured spans that littered the Rhine.

The lieutenant and his men took up ringside seats near the crater, waiting for the big fireworks show, directed by Captain Friesenhahn, that they expected to begin at any moment.

The respite was short-lived. Orders came down from General Hodges: Take the bridge.

Timmermann took another look at the Germans' frantic preparations to blow the structure and asked his battalion commander, "What if the bridge blows up in my face?" The commanding officer didn't bother to reply, for there was no answer to that question. Believing it was a suicide mission, Timmermann probably gave a brief thought to his baby daughter, born the previous week, then growled to his platoon leader, "All right, we're going across." His men grumbled but rose from their positions and advanced, crouching, toward the structure that suddenly looked many times longer than its 1,000 feet.

American tanks and artillery pumped fire across the river toward the tunnel entrance in the Erpeler Ley, where several hundred German soldiers and civilians were huddled in fear. Smoke shells also crashed onto the far bank, wrapping the bridge in a gauzy haze and shielding the operation from German eyes. Seeing that the Americans were about to make their assault, Scheller, Bratge and Friesenhahn decided the time had come to blow the bridge.

Friesenhahn took the firing mechanism in hand, connected the wires, and twisted the handle.

Nothing happened.

Instead of a huge blast, all that was heard was the sound of American tank rounds exploding on the cliff face and the metallic ping of bullets hitting the bridge's girders.

Realizing that shellfire must have cut the circuit, Friesenhahn ordered his emergency repair team out into the hail of lead and shrapnel to find and fix the problem. But the captain rescinded the order when he realized there was not enough time for such a complex operation. He asked for a volunteer to light the primer cord by hand. At first there were no volunteers; but then Sergeant

Faust said he would go. The sergeant managed to make it out, light the cord, and rush back to safety. A few seconds later, a tremendous blast shook the riverfront. Eyewitnesses said they saw the bridge literally jump into the air.

Timmermann and his men had been just about to dash onto the bridge when the charge went off. A feeling of relief passed through the company. Now we won't have to cross that damned thing, seemed to be the shared thought.

When the smoke cleared, however, men on both sides of the river were dumbfounded: the bridge was still standing. Timmermann stood up and looked down the length of the bridge. Although there was a gaping hole in the timbers that had been laid over the tracks to create a roadbed, he could see that the catwalks still seemed to be in place. He also could see the German engineers scurrying about, preparing for a second blast. There would be no reprieve from the hazardous undertaking.

Company A had again begun moving toward the bridge when a machine gun in one of the nearby western towers opened up on them. American tanks quickly silenced the enemy fire. Timmermann and his company were now on the bridge, joined by the engineers who located the wires running to the demolition charges and severed them. Small-arms fire from the far bank ricocheted among the girders but failed to stop the Yanks.

Sniper fire from a half-submerged barge located about 200 yards upriver prompted Timmermann to call for the tanks, which were still on shore, to direct their 75mm guns at the target. A few well-placed rounds eliminated the threat.

The American advance had halted, however; fear had overtaken the company, and the men seemed unwilling to budge in the face of mounting enemy fire, a lack of cover, and the real possibility that the structure might go up at any moment.

Timmermann urged one of his platoon leaders, Sergeant Joe

DeLisio, to get his men moving. DeLisio led by example. Bobbing and weaving, with bullets splattering all around him, the sergeant dashed forward. "There goes a guy with more guts than sense," one of the men muttered, but the stalled column began to move again. Right behind DeLisio was Timmermann, yelling, ordering, and encouraging the rest of the unit.

DeLisio rushed to the base of one of the towers, kicked in a wall of hay bales that was blocking the doorway, and climbed the stairs. Surprising a group of three Germans who were trying to unjam their machine gun, DeLisio captured the men and threw their gun out the window. This prompted the GIs to rush the other tower and clean it out. DeLisio then captured a German lieutenant and another soldier and herded all five of his captives to the tower's ground level.

American soldiers were now dashing across the bridge and fanning out to form a defensive perimeter, and the engineers were still disabling the German demolitions, cutting the wires and throwing the charges into the river. As he stepped onto the eastern bank, Lieutenant Timmermann became the first officer of an invading army since Napoleon to cross the Rhine. But Timmermann had a few more immediate things on his mind than his moment in the spotlight of history. The first was clearing out whoever might still be alive inside the tunnel.

DeLisio and four other men crawled to the tunnel's entrance, fired a few shots inside, and captured several more German soldiers. The Americans, however, were unaware that in the black recesses of the tunnel hundreds of others, including Bratge, Scheller and Friesenhahn, were crouching in fear and apprehension. Shortly after 4 p.m., Timmermann ordered the 2nd Platoon to climb the Erpeler Ley and secure the high ground overlooking the bridge and the river. Lieutenant Emmet Burrows and his men, scaling the rocky face of the cliff, quickly came under 20mm anti-aircraft fire from nearby German batteries. Burrows lost many men on the climb, but the platoon made it to the top and clung to its precarious perch.

By dark, most of the 1st Battalion had crossed the bridge, but Timmermann worried that he still had too few men to hold off any determined German attack. Headquarters was worried, too, and was working hard to bring reinforcements to the far side. Engineers were filling the huge crater in the approach road while other soldiers were planking over the hole in the middle of the bridge. But it was painfully obvious that American armor would not be rumbling across the structure for several more hours.

Meanwhile, inside the tunnel, Major Scheller tried to organize his meager forces for a counterattack, but discipline was nonexistent. No one was willing to risk his life for a Reich that was obviously in its death throes. Unable to contact headquarters by radio, Scheller set out for headquarters from the rear of the tunnel on a bicycle. Shortly thereafter, Bratge sent a messenger out the main entrance on a motorcycle; the courier was blasted from his cycle moments after exiting the tunnel.

Unable to stir his men to action against the Americans, Bratge began herding the soldiers and civilians toward the tunnel's rear exit, only to be forced back inside by a handful of GIs who had gotten around the Erpeler Ley to cover the exit. Further resistance was hopeless, Bratge decided. He saw a small group of civilians and soldiers escape from the main entrance, carrying a white flag. The time had come to give up.

Bratge announced to those still within the tunnel: "The white flag was raised against our will. To continue fighting now would constitute a brazen violation of the Geneva Convention and would make us responsible for the deaths of innocent women and children. For this reason, I order that all fighting cease immediately! Please disable your weapons, and, soldiers, be the last to leave the tunnel." The frightened group emerged with hands held high, and within minutes the contingent was headed west, across the bridge that was now one long stream of olive-drab uniformed soldiers traveling in the opposite direction.

At General Bradley's headquarters, word of the intact bridge across the Rhine was electrifying.

Bradley wrote in his autobiography: "Suddenly my phone rang. It was Hodges.

" 'Brad,' Courtney called, with more composure than the good news warranted, 'Brad, we've gotten a bridge.'

" 'A bridge? You mean you've got one intact on the Rhine?'

" 'Yep,' Hodges replied, '[Maj. Gen. John] Leonard nabbed one at Remagen before they blew it up.'

" 'Hot dog, Courtney,' I said."

Even Eisenhower was elated. "Hold on to it, Brad," said Ike from his headquarters in Reims. "Get across with whatever you need, but make certain you hold that bridgehead."

On the western bank, it was clear to General Hodges that the Germans would not wait long before launching a massive counterattack. Higher headquarters was quick to respond to his call for reinforcements; additional troops were already being diverted to reinforce the tenuous bridgehead. The First Army began pouring all its available troops toward Remagen. One regiment each from the 9th and 78th Infantry divisions were motorized and were joined by a number of artillery and anti-aircraft units. American forces were not going to allow their unexpected gift— which, if properly exploited, would materially shorten the war—to be taken away.

Shortly before midnight, the bridge was deemed safe enough to bring armor across, and a platoon of 35-ton Shermans was sent over without incident. Nine tanks crossed that night, followed by several tank destroyers. One of the latter, however, broke through the planks and slipped into the hole in the flooring. Attempts to either extract the vehicle or push it over the side failed, but it was pushed far enough out of the way to allow other vehicles to pass. The bridge, however, was blocked for more than five hours.

During the night, the Germans brought up their reserves and mounted a number of serious counterattacks in a determined effort to break through and destroy the bridge. In some cases, American tank crews were forced to toss grenades out of their hatches to kill Germans who were swarming on and around them. The order to the tank platoon leader was, "Hold your place until the last tank is shot out from under you."

Despite the fury of the German attacks, the Americans held, and by daybreak the crisis was over. The next day, March 8, the 9th Infantry Division's 47th Infantry Regiment stopped a number of determined attempts by two German panzer divisions to break through the lines and attack the bridge.

In the 24 hours since Timmermann and his men had made the crossing, nearly 8,000 troops, along with scores of pieces of armor and artillery, had reached the eastern bank. In the days to follow, the remainder of the 9th Armored and the 9th and 78th Infantry divisions, along with the 99th Infantry Division, would cross the river and expand the bridgehead.

To relieve the pressure on the Ludendorff Bridge, which was straining under the tremendous weight of the American traffic, a decision was made to build temporary bridges a few hundred yards upriver.

On March 10, under German observation and harassing fire, as well as air attacks from the *Luftwaffe,* men of the 51st and 291st Combat Engineer battalions began assembling both a pontoon and a treadway bridge—tasks they completed in just over a day.

Unable to push the Americans away from the Ludendorff Bridge and destroy it with conventional explosives, a furious Hitler was determined to wreck it by unconventional means. The area was bombarded by one of the Germans' huge 17cm railroad guns, by 11 extremely powerful but highly inaccurate V-2 rockets and even by the Luftwaffe's latest jets—the Arado Ar-234B bomber and Messerschmitt Me-262A-2a fighter-bomber. Through it all, the bridge remained standing, but the concussions weakened it.

On the afternoon of March 17, 10 days after the Ludendorff Bridge had fallen into American hands, some 200 engineers from the 267th Combat Engineer Battalion and the 1058th Bridge Construction and Repair Group were working on the structure, trying to shore up its tired, damaged framework. At 3 p.m., the sound of popping rivets was the only overture to the bridge's sudden death knell. The entire framework began to tremble, and frantic men dropped their tools and began sprinting toward either end of the bridge. With a sickening screech of twisting steel, mingled with the screams of doomed men, the structure collapsed into the icy, fast-rushing waters of the Rhine. The final casualty toll was 28 dead and 63 injured.

The bridge finally gone, Hitler turned his rage on those thought to be responsible for allowing the Americans to cross the Rhine. Hitler's tribunal, presided over by Maj. Gen. Rudolf Huebner, who ignored the code of German military law, swiftly tried and, without proper counsel or the faintest nod toward justice, sentenced four scapegoats to death: Majors Hans Scheller (for deserting his post), August Kraft (commander of engineer troops at the bridge), Herbert Stroebel (commander of an engineer regimental staff responsible for protecting Rhine River crossing sites) and Lieutenant Karl-Heinz Peters (commander of an anti-aircraft battery with the top-secret *Flakwerfer 44* weapon that had fallen into American hands). All four were executed by firing squads. Bratge and Friesenhahn, now both American POWs, were tried in absentia; Bratge was sentenced to death, while Friesenhahn was acquitted for some unexplained reason.

In addition, Hitler sacked Gerd von Rundstedt, commander in

chief of the Western Front, and replaced him with Field Marshal Albert Kesselring, who had done a masterful defensive job in Italy.

On the American side, honors were in great abundance for those who had captured the bridge, fought to keep the Germans at bay, and kept it usable until it collapsed. Thirteen soldiers, including Timmermann and DeLisio, received the nation's second-highest medal, the Distinguished Service Cross, while 152 received the Silver Star. Three others received Distinguished Service Crosses for gallantry in combat after the bridge had been crossed. The units that constituted Combat Command B of the 9th Armored Division received Presidential Unit Citations.

After the war, while on a visit to Remagen and the site of the old bridge, Karl Friesenhahn reflected for a moment on the Americans who had braved tremendous fire to cross a bridge that they expected to be blown out from under them at any moment. He called them the greatest heroes in the whole war.

Perhaps their former enemy's words will always remain the greatest monument to 2nd Lt. Karl Timmermann and the Americans who captured the bridge at Remagen.

Sulfur Island Seized

By Joseph H. Alexander

The Japanese defending Iwo Jima on D-day displayed superb tactical discipline. As Lieutenant Colonel Justus M. "Jumpin' Joe" Chambers led his 3rd Battalion, 25th Marines, across the first terrace on the right flank of the landing beaches, he encountered interlocking bands of automatic-weapons fire unlike anything he had faced in Tulagi or Saipan. "You could've held up a cigarette and lit it on the stuff going by," he recalled. "I knew immediately we were in for one hell of a time."

The Battle of Iwo Jima represented to the Americans the pinnacle of forcible entry from the sea. This particular amphibious assault was the ultimate "storm landing," the Japanese phrase describing the American propensity for concentrating overwhelming force at the point of attack. The huge striking force was more experienced, better armed and more powerfully supported than any other offensive campaign to date in the Pacific War. Vice Admiral Raymond A. Spruance's Fifth Fleet enjoyed total domination of air and sea around the small, sulfuric island, and the 74,000 Marines in the landing force would muster a healthy 3-to-1 preponderance over the garrison. Seizing Iwo Jima would be tough, planners admitted, but the operation should be over in a week, maybe less.

By all logic, the force invading Iwo Jima should have prevailed, quickly and violently. But the Japanese had also benefited from the prolonged island campaigns in the Pacific. Lieutenant General Tadamichi Kuribayashi commanded the 21,000 troops on the island. Formerly a cavalry officer, Kuribayashi was a savvy fighter, one who could glean realistic lessons from previous combat disasters. He decided to junk the defensive tactics used by his predecessors in the ill-fated campaigns in the Gilberts, Marshalls and Marianas. Significantly, Japanese forces on Iwo Jima would defend the island in depth from hidden interior positions, not at the water's edge and they would eschew the massive, suicidal banzai attacks. Kuribayashi figured if the garrison could maintain camouflage and fire discipline, husband its resources and exact disproportionate losses on the invaders, maybe the Americans would lose heart. His senior subordinates may have grumbled at this departure from tradition, but Kuribayashi's plan made intelligent use of Iwo's forbidding terrain and his troops' fighting skills.

Two well-armed antagonists had thereby set the stage for a violent confrontation close to Japan's home waters. The ensuing battle produced memorable results:

- Thirty-six days of unremitting hell on a small, wretched, reeking island.
- The only major battle in the Pacific War in which the U.S. Marines suffered greater casualties than they inflicted on the Japanese defenders.
- Lingering controversies over the high costs and disputed dividends of the Pyrrhic victory.
- An enduring tributenow embodied in the world's largest bronze sculptureto the fortitude of young Americans of all

services who surpassed themselves under conditions we today can hardly imagine.

Iwo Jima means "Sulfur Island" in Japanese. It is one of the Volcano Islands that extend east of Okinawa and roughly south of Japan itself. The island is about 12 square miles, larger than Tarawa, but much smaller than Saipan or Guam. Hilly, rocky, and generally barren, the island did not figure in the grand strategy of the Pacific for the first several years of the war. Formosa was the longtime goal of the Americans' Central Pacific drive, once General Douglas MacArthur had recaptured the Philippines. But Formosa was huge, stoutly defended, and still a long stretch for bombing runs against the empire. Meanwhile, the Japanese built airstrips for their own bombers and fighters on previously unoccupied Iwo Jima. Planners on both sides could see the geographic reality. Iwo Jima was almost exactly halfway between the Marianas and the Japanese home island of Honshu.

Operational airfields represented valuable rungs in the strategic ladder leading to Tokyo. The American seizure of the Marianas in mid-1944 brought the main Japanese home islands within range of the newly developed Boeing B-29 Superfortress of the Army Air Forces. B-29s based in Saipan and Tinian began striking targets in Japan in late 1944, but the strikes were not yet truly effective. The thorn in the side was Iwo Jima.

Since no American fighters had the "legs" to escort the Superfortresses to and from Japan, the B-29s were often at the mercy of fighter interceptors launched from Iwo's airstrips. And Japanese bombers based on Iwo were an even graver threat. In fact, the Twentieth Air Force lost more B-29s to enemy bomber raids from Iwo Jima than it did on any of its long-range forays over the Japanese homeland. The absence of an emergency landing or refueling field for B-29s along the return route from Tokyo was yet another problem for strategic planners. In American hands, Iwo Jima would provide fighter escorts and a suitable divert base; the threat from Japanese bombers would be erased. These were compelling reasons to seize the island. On October 3, 1944, the Joint Chiefs of Staff (JCS) ordered Admiral Chester W. Nimitz, Commander in Chief Pacific, to prepare for the seizure of Iwo Jima early in the coming year.

The JCS orders contained a contingency clause: Nimitz must continue providing covering and support forces for General MacArthur's liberation of Luzon. Japanese defense of the Philippines proved tougher than anticipated, and the Iwo Jima invasion slipped a month. General Kuribayashi took maximum advantage of this grace period. The Japanese army's general staff sent Japan's best fortifications engineers, men with combat experience in China and Manchuria. Iwo Jima's soft rock lent itself to swift digging. Japanese artillery pieces and command centers moved underground. A labyrinth of tunnels connected many positions, especially in the north. Engineers and laborers built five levels of underground defenses within some hills.

Mount Suribachi, dominating the island at 556 feet, eventually contained a seven-story interior structure. Kuribayashi had plenty of weapons, ammunition, radios, fuel and rations, everything but fresh water, always at a premium on that sulfuric rock. Indeed, American intelligence experts concluded that the island could support no more than 13,000 defenders because of the acute water shortage. Kuribayashi had many more men than that, but all of them were on half-rations of water for weeks before the invasion even began.

Admiral Spruance picked veterans of amphibious operations to command the major subordinate forces of the Fifth Fleet for the seizure of Iwo Jima. Vice Admiral Richmond Kelly Turner commanded Task Force 51, the joint expeditionary force, which included nearly 500 ships. Rear Admiral Harry Hill commanded

Task Force 53, the attack force. Marine Maj. Gen. Harry Schmidt commanded the V Amphibious Corps, comprised principally of the 3rd, 4th and 5th Marine divisions. Operation Detachment, the code name for the invasion of Iwo Jima, would be the largest combat employment of U.S. Marines in history. Spruance and Turner asked the old warhorse Lt. Gen. Holland M. "Howlin' Mad" Smith, U.S. Marine Corps, to come along as commander of expeditionary troops. This was a contrived billet. Unlike the preceding operations in the Central Pacific, Operation Detachment would focus on a single island. General Smith, the amphibious pioneer, had enough strength of character to keep out of Harry Schmidt's way.

Roughly half the Marines in the three assault divisions had experienced previous combat. Some, like Gunnery Sgt. "Manila John" Basilone, were veterans of the first offensive, years earlier, at Guadalcanal. Basilone had received the Medal of Honor for his actions as a machine-gunner on "Starvation Island," but he had since refused a commission and volunteered to return to the Pacific for more action. Other veterans were younger. Private First Class Anthony Muscarella had joined the Corps illegally at age 14. Two years later, a veteran of heavy fighting in the Marianas, he was one of the best machine-gunners in the 4th Marine Division.

General Schmidt planned to land on Iwo Jima's southeast beaches with two divisions abreast, the 4th Division on the right and the 5th on the left, next to Mount Suribachi. Schmidt kept the 3rd Marine Division in reserve initially. The amphibious assault of Iwo was a classic in its own right, favorably reflecting the lessons learned at such high cost starting with Tarawa 14 months earlier. The preliminary naval and aerial bombardment, however, disappointed most Marines. By D-day, the Americans had hit the island with 6,800 tons of bombs and 22,000 Naval shells. But the issue was accuracy, not volume. General Kuribayashi's well-built, artfully camouflaged gun positions were hardly affected by the bombardment.

Some of Kuribayashi's subordinate commanders lacked his iron will. When American underwater demolition teams approached the landing beaches in lightly armed LCIs (landing craft, infantry) during a daring daylight reconnaissance on D-minus-2, the defenders hiding in prepared positions along the slopes of Mount Suribachi were unable to resist opening fire. The frogmen and landing craft took grievous casualties but accomplished the job, finding no mines or underwater obstacles offshore. More important, many of the Japanese gun positions on Suribachi were revealed for the first time to Navy spotters. The fire-support ships had a field day.

D-day for the assault on Iwo Jima was February 19, 1945. The ship-to-shore movement worked to perfection. Sixty-eight armored LVT (landing vehicle, tracked) amphibians led the way, firing their snub-nosed 75mm howitzers from the moment they crossed the line of departure. Hundreds of troop-carrying LVT-4s and LVT-2s carried the assault waves ashore. Admiral Turner carefully orchestrated naval gunfire support, adjusting it just ahead of the first waves and then creating a rolling barrage further inland. Carrier-based fighters, including two squadrons of Marine Corps Vought F4U Corsairs, swooped in low, "dragging their bellies on the beach." And for once, there was no barrier coral reef, no killer neap tide to worry about. Eight thousand troops stormed ashore on their designated beaches right at H-hour. Light enemy fire gave fleeting hopes of a cakewalk. Then things became difficult.

The first opponent was not the Japanese but the beach itself. A volcanic island, Iwo Jima has few beaches worthy of the name; all of them are extremely steep. With deep water so close to shore, the surf zone is narrow but violent. The soft black sand immobilized all wheeled vehicles and bellied up some of the tracked amphibians. In short order, a succession of towering waves hit the stalled vehicles before they could completely unload, filling their sterns with water and sand and broaching them broadside. The beach soon resembled a salvage yard. And once the beaches were choked with landing craft and the steep terraces clogged with infantry, Kuribayashi fired signal flares. At that point, the Japanese opened up with their heavy ordnance-hidden mortars and artillery batteriesexecuting a masterful rolling barrage of their own.

Survivors of this rain of steel marveled that the entire landing force was not knocked out. "I just didn't see how anybody could live through such heavy fire barrages," recalled one veteran. Navy fire-support ships moved in closer, notably the battleship Nevada and the cruiser Santa Fe, which took out some of the nearest Japanese firing positions with deadly accuracy.

Despite the counterbattery fire, Japanese gunners ensured no Americans crossed the terraces with impunity. Sergeant Basilone tried to rally his shocked mortar platoon, yelling, "Come on, you bastards, we've got to get these mortars off the beach!" An exploding shell killed him instantly. The troops moved on. Private Muscarella survived the initial dash to the first airfield, then looked back. "The beach was a pile of wreckage," he recalled. "Tanks and amtracs were stuck in the heavy sand everywhere. Some had been flipped over on their backs by exploding mines and shells."

The Marines suffered and bled but kept moving forward. Enterprising troops organized LVTs to haul heavy equipment off the beach. More Sherman tanks hustled ashore. Beachmasters landed early to establish order. Engineers blew up wrecked boats and LVTs to clear lanes for subsequent waves. Communications remained surprisingly good. Offloading continued, despite the slaughter and destruction. Thirty thousand combat troops had landed by nightfall, the assault elements of six regimental landing teams. Each team brought ashore an assigned artillery battalion. The cannoneers caught hell moving their 75mm and 105mm howitzers across the soft beaches under fire, and casualties were substantial. By dusk, however, both division commanders could report that their organic artillery was in place and delivering close fire support.

The news was enough to give Admiral Turner and General Schmidt grounds for cautious optimism the night of D-day. True, the beach gradient had been an unpleasant shock and Japanese artillery fire had been uncommonly effective, but even with 2,400 casualties the landing force was still proportionally better off than it had been at the end of the first day on Tarawa or Saipan.

Both officers expected Kuribayashi to launch a major banzai attack that night, which would afford the opportunity to cut down several thousand of the empire's most ardent warriors. Then, it would be a matter of simply mopping up. But Kuribayashi foiled this logic, refusing to allow any of his subordinates to make vainglorious final charges. Some small-scale banzai attacks occurred later in the battle, but for the most part the Americans never really had a target. Each night, small parties of Japanese would conduct intelligence probes, seeking gaps between units, and quietly exacting a toll on American outposts. By day, they hunkered down and waited for the invaders to enter their pre-registered killing zones. Such enforced discipline made the battle both prolonged and costly. Before long, the Americans knew that this battle was different; this enemy commander was resourceful, crafty.

Mount Suribachi, its defenses fatally weakened by the fire-support ships during the early stages of the assault, fell early to elements of the 28th Marines on D-plus-4. Associated Press photographer Joe Rosenthal captured the achievement with his classic photo of the second flag raising—truly a magical moment—but the battle still had a bloody month to run. The troops in their attack positions down below cheered when they saw the Stars and Stripes, then continued their swing to the north. General Schmidt ordered the 3rd Marine Division ashore and into line.

The fight for the northern half of the embattled island was a toe-to-toe slugging match, with the Americans possessing the advantage of superior firepower and the Japanese using their prepared positions and good concealment to their advantage. General "Howlin' Mad" Smith came ashore a couple of times to see for himself just how ugly the fight was. "It was the most savage and the most costly battle in the history of the Marine Corps," he would later state. An artillery officer on the staff of the 4th Marine Division could only shake his head in despair: "We still didn't have an effective method of either destroying or neutralizing the defenders in a very restricted area, so it fell to the thin green line to get in there and dig them out in hand-to-hand combat. There must be a better way."

The convoluted ravines in the north made flat-trajectory naval gunfire less effective. Worse, Admiral Spruance deployed the fast carriers north for a series of strikes around Tokyo, removing eight Marine fighter squadrons trained in close air support operations. Navy fighters flying off the remaining escort carriers tried to pick up the slack, but they could not carry large bombs, nor were they allowed to descend below 1,500 feet. The Americans used some napalm bombs, but those were disappointing. At that stage of the war, the "bombs" were still primitive old wing tanks with improvised detonators. Half did not explode. Nor did the troops appreciate such area weapons being dropped from high altitudes.

Marianas-based Consolidated B-24 Liberator bombers of the Seventh Air Force continued to pound the island daily. Some of the best close air support, after the initial week, came from a squadron of Army Air Force North American P-51 Mustangs that flew into the first captured airfield below Suribachi. It was not at all a dive bomber squadron, but the pilots were good at glide bombing, plus they were enthusiastic. Marine Colonel Vernon E. McGee, commanding the experimental Landing Force Air Support Control Unit ashore, instructed the pilots to arm their 1,000-pound bombs with 12-second fuzes, and directed them against the cliffs and bluffs along the flanks of the attacking Marines. Sometimes those bombs achieved spectacular results, dropping a cliff face into the sea, exposing the tunnel system, and causing smoke to roll out of hidden entrances. The Marines loved this improvised support.

Both sides unveiled new weapons for the close-in fighting. The Japanese had enormous 320mm "spigot" mortars, firing shells bigger than most Marines had ever seen. Kuribayashi also used aerial bombs lofted from crude rocket launchers. These were grossly inaccurate, but their psychological effect was awesome. No American who survived Iwo has ever forgotten the sight of those huge bombs, the size of a 55-gallon drum, tumbling end over end, seemingly headed right for the viewer's foxhole. For their part, the Americans introduced the Mark I flamethrower built into the Sherman M4A3 medium tank. The days of using thin-skinned light tanks or LVTs for assaulting fortified positions were finally over. The Mark I system could spew burning napalm at a range of 150 yards with a duration of more than a minute. Unfortunately, despite the deployment of three tank battalions ashore, the Marines could only muster eight vehicles equipped with the Mark I for Iwo Jima. These were in constant demand.

Not surprisingly, most casualties in the first three weeks of the battle resulted from high explosives mortars, artillery, mines, grenades and the hellacious rocket bombs. Time magazine combat correspondent Robert Sherrod, a veteran of earlier landings in the Aleutians, Gilberts and Marianas, reported that the dead at Iwo Jima, whether Japanese or American, had one thing in common: "They all died with the greatest possible violence. Nowhere in the Pacific war had I seen such badly mangled bodies. Many were cut squarely in half."

"Jumpin' Joe" Chambers' exclamation on D-day had been prophetic. Landing Team 3/25 was indeed "in for one hell of a time." Chambers' mission was to seize the rock quarries on the right flank, then act as a hinge as the entire expedition swung around to the north. The team accomplished this at staggering cost. Chambers reported the loss of 22 officers and 500 men in the first day alone. Three days later, a Japanese machine-gunner shot Chambers through the chest. The battalion surgeon pulled him out of the line of fire at great risk and saved his life. Chambers' war was over. He received the Medal of Honor, one of 24 Marines and attached Navy corpsmen to be so recognized for courage "above and beyond" during the battle for Iwo Jima.

Including Colonel Chambers, 14 of the 24 Marine infantry battalion commanders engaged on Iwo Jima were killed or wounded. Higher losses occurred among company and platoon commanders. One company commander who miraculously survived unscathed reported 100 percent casualties in his unit every man in the outfit had been hit at least once. Japanese gunners destroyed one-third of the Sherman tanks and one-fourth of the LVTs. More LVTs sank in the rough seas while shuttling casualties out to ships or delivering ammunition ashore.

During the pre-dawn hours of D-plus-16, maneuver elements of the 3rd Marine Division executed one of the few battalion-size night attacks in the Pacific war. At 5 a.m., the 3rd Battalion, 9th Marines, moved silently across the line of departure, foregoing the telltale artillery barrage, and advanced toward Hill 362C, a particularly vexing objective 500 yards away. Surprise was complete. The battalion moved gingerly across open ground for 35 minutes before attracting a few rounds from startled Japanese sentries. By the time stiff resistance materialized, the Marines seemed to be on the hill. Then it was the Americans' turn to be surprised. In the darkness they had seized the wrong hill. Their real objective lay another 250 yards away, and now it was fully daylight. But such was the momentum of their surprise attack that the battalion pressed on, reaching the crest by early afternoon. "Although nearly all the basic dope was bad," the commander reported, "the strategy proved very sound." In a battle marked by painstakingly slow progress, this advance was a real breakthrough.

On March 4, two weeks after D-day, a shot-up B-29 made an emergency landing on the captured bomber strip while the fighting still raged. Thirty-five more crippled Superfortresses made emergency landings on Iwo Jima during the battle. The troops had almost daily reminders of what the fighting was all about. On March 16, Schmidt declared the island secure. His salty veterans snickered at this premature euphemism and continued dueling die-hard Japanese soldiers. Finally, advance elements reached Kitano Point on the north coast. Kuribayashi and his chief of staff died at the end, either in a final charge or by suicide. On March 26, a full 34 days after the landing, Schmidt announced that the operation was over. Yet just a few hours earlier, a well-armed force of 350 Japanese had infiltrated Marine lines and fallen upon a rear encampment of support troops, inflicting 200 casualties in the confusion of darkness before being overwhelmed and snuffed out. Schmidt turned the island over to Army garrison forces of the 147th Infantry and began re-embarkation. It was time to start thinking about the next assault landing.

The Marines and their multiservice supporting arms killed about 20,000 Japanese on the island during the battle, and the troops captured nearly 1,100 prisoners. That success came at an appalling cost to the Marines. Altogether, the V Amphibious Corps sustained 24,053 casualties in the fight. Over 6,000 men died. The total casualty count represented the equivalent loss of 1[T] standard divisions. The overall casualty rate was about 30 percent of forces employed, but many rifle battalions surpassed 75 percent. As Private Muscarella recalled, "There were no good days, and we lost a hell of a lot of people. Hell, I didn't know who the company skipper was, or who the battalion commander was." By D-plus-35, few Marines did.

News of the casualties and savagery of Iwo Jima shocked the American public. The Hearst newspapers demanded that Nimitz and Spruance be replaced by General MacArthur, "a general who looks after his troops." But there was hardly time to indulge in recrimination. The invasion of Okinawa began four days after Iwo Jima fell. That campaign was equally bloody and savage. Ahead, presumably, lay the assault on the Japanese home islands themselves. The long, bloody road to Tokyo looked costlier than ever.

Seizing Iwo Jima achieved all the strategic goals desired by the Joint Chiefs of Staff. American B-29s could henceforth fly with less reserve fuel and a greater bomb payload, knowing Iwo Jima would be available as an emergency field. Iwo-based fighters escorted the Superfortresses to and from Honshu. For the first time, all the Japanese islands were within bomber range, including Hokkaido. Was all this worth the cost? One surviving Marine Corps officer thinks the question is still moot: "We saved a lot of airplanes, but whether it was worth the Marine lives to save Air Force planes, I don't know."

The 2,400 Army Air Force pilots who were forced to land at Iwo Jima between its capture and V-J Day had no doubts. Said one, "Whenever I land on this island, I thank God and the men who fought for it."

Liberating Dachau

By Flint Whitlock

The existence of German concentration camps was common knowledge among Allied political and military leaders for years, and the camp at Dachau, the Nazi regime's earliest such camp, was particularly notorious. About 10 miles northwest of Munich, Dachau had been an ordinary, peaceful suburb until March 1933, when the Nazis converted a gunpowder factory there into a prison camp to house their political opponents. At first, it was nothing more than a normal detention facility. But once the Nazi regime became more ruthless, the Konzentrationslager, or KL, acquired a much more sinister persona. Hundreds of camps and subcamps based on the Dachau model were built, followed by the construction of the horrendous extermination camps.

At Dachau, in addition to the internment camp, there was also a huge SS training complex, where guards were schooled in their brutal craft; the finance offices for the entire SS; living quarters for the guards and officers; a military hospital; a camp headquarters building; a variety of factories that relied on the camp's slave labor; and storerooms bulging with clothing, shoes and eyeglasses confiscated from the inmates. An electrified fence separated the prisoners' compound from the SS camp, as did a deep dry moat with steep concrete sides, and a swiftly flowing canal—the Würm River.

Seven watchtowers manned by armed guards were strategically placed around the enclosure, and armed guards with dogs patrolled the fence line. A 10-foot-high masonry wall enclosed the entire complex, shielding the nefarious activities within from prying eyes. A sign on the Jourhaus—the camp's guardhouse, which enclosed the only entrance into the prisoners' compound—ingenuously proclaimed, "Arbeit macht frei" ("Work makes one free"). Behind the high walls, unspeakable cruelties were carried out by the SS guards on the helpless inmate population.

While Dachau was never one of the Nazis' "death factories," more than 30,000 of the 200,000-plus prisoners incarcerated there died during its 12 years of existence. Many of the inmates died from being overworked and underfed. Many more died at the hands of guards while being tortured, while others died from disease, in front of firing squads, or after they were used as human guinea pigs for the pseudoscientific experiments carried out by the camp's medical personnel.

In March 1945, as the Allied armies were squeezing Germany from the east and west, the Germans were either trying frantically to evacuate the concentration and death camps and hide the evidence or making last-ditch efforts to exterminate as many Jews and other political prisoners as possible before the Reich was defeated.

Because of reports from escapees, Lt. Gen. Wade H. Haislip's advancing XV Corps (consisting of the 3rd, 42th, 45th and 86th Infantry divisions, the 20th Armored Division and the 106th Cavalry Group, all heading for Munich) was prepared to deal with horrific conditions when it reached Dachau at the end of April.

Much had already been learned about what had gone on at concentration camps after Buchenwald—some 220 miles north of Dachau—had been discovered by the U.S. 6th Armored Division on April 11. The unanswered questions were: How many—if any—of the camp's inmates would still be alive and which unit would liberate the camp? It was the latter question that would fuel the flames of an interdivisional dispute between veterans of the 45th and 42nd Infantry divisions that continues to this day.

Poring over maps, officers at XV Corps headquarters saw that the 45th was in the best position to reach Dachau first. On April 28, a call was made to Maj. Gen. Robert T. Frederick, former commander of the elite 1st Special Service Force and now commanding general of the war-weary 45th "Thunderbird" Division, setting the wheels in motion for the 45th to liberate Dachau.

The 45th had already seen more than 500 days of combat—including four amphibious assaults, months of brutal warfare in the snowy mountains of Italy, the saving of both the Salerno and Anzio beachheads, and the punishing drive through German-occupied France and the Siegfried Line. When Lt. Col. Felix Sparks, commanding the 3rd Battalion, 157th Infantry Regiment, 45th Infantry Division, received orders diverting him from the drive on Munich to the liberation of KL Dachau, he was not happy. He felt the change of orders would slow his battalion down. "I didn't consider the concentration camp a military objective," he said.

The message to Sparks read, "Dachau may be very important, both militarily and politically. Be especially careful of operations in this sector." At 0922 hours on the 29th, Sparks received another message: "Upon capture of Dachau by any battalion, post air-tight guard and allow no one to enter or leave."

Sparks was also told that, once the camp was secured, nothing was to be disturbed. The evidence of atrocities was to be left for an international prisoners committee to investigate. Most of the men of the 157th knew little or nothing about concentration camps and had no idea what these orders meant or what lay ahead. They received a grim education on the unseasonably cold day of Sunday, April 29, as they cautiously advanced through the town, looking for snipers. All was unnervingly silent. In the center of the city, Sparks' men came to an intact railroad bridge and crossed the river, then followed a set of tracks that led toward the southwestern corner of the SS complex about one kilometer away. The time was approximately 1215.

"We went along the south side of the camp and I saw the main entrance and decided to avoid it; if the Germans were going to defend it, I figured that's where they'd do it," Colonel Sparks later said. "So we found a railroad track that went into the camp on the southwest side." Sparks' decision to avoid approaching the main gate would result in much confusion and controversy for decades to come. Inside that main gate, the Germans had been waiting, ready to surrender.

Sparks conferred briefly with 1st Lt. William P. Walsh, commanding officer of I Company, the battalion's lead element. Sparks told Walsh his orders were to seize the camp, seal it and let no one in or out.

The men of I Company moved out, unprepared for what they were about to encounter. Between the town and the camp, the Thunderbirds saw a string of 39 boxcars and open gondola cars standing on the track. If ever the American soldier needed confirmation as to why he was at war, why he was required to put his life on the line day after day, it was contained in those 39 railroad cars.

As the GIs cautiously approached the boxcars, the sickening stench of death grew ever stronger. In each railroad car were piles of rotting human corpses—a total of 2,310 men, women and children—either totally naked or partially clad in blue-and-white-striped concentration camp uniforms. Most of them had starved to death while being evacuated from Buchenwald 22 days earlier in an effort to keep them from falling into the hands of the approaching Allies. A few with enough strength to attempt escape had been shot down by the SS guards or brutally beaten with rifle butts.

Private First Class John Lee was one of the first men on the scene. "Most of the GIs just stood there in silence and disbelief," he later remembered. "We had seen men in battle blown apart, burnt to death, and die many different ways, but we were never prepared for this. Several of the dead lay there with their eyes open. It seemed they were looking at us and saying, 'What took you so long?'"

To a man, I Company was seething with anger at what they had discovered on the railroad tracks. "Tears were in everyone's eyes from the sight and smell," Lee recalled. "Suddenly, GIs started swearing and crying with such rage and remarked, 'Let's kill every one of those bastards,' and 'Don't take any SS alive!' Never had I seen men so fighting mad willing to throw caution to the wind."

I Company continued grimly on, many of the men stunned and sickened at what they had encountered, others bent on avenging the mass killing. Suddenly, four SS men, their hands held high, emerged from a hiding place and tried to surrender to Walsh's party. But Walsh was not having it. He had heard stories of the notorious SS atrocities, and he had just seen firsthand the awful fruits of their labor. Filled with rage, Walsh herded the four men into one of the railroad cars and emptied his pistol into them. They were lying there moaning when Private Albert Pruitt came up and finished them off with his rifle.

The killing of unarmed German POWs did not trouble many of the men in I Company that day. Lieutenant Harold Moyer, a platoon commander in I Company, later testified: "I heard every man, or a lot of men, who said we should take no prisoners. I felt the same way myself. I believe every man in the outfit who saw those boxcars prior to the entrance to Dachau felt he was justified in meting out death as a punishment to the Germans who were responsible."

As I Company neared the SS infirmary, Private Lee recalled: "My buddy and I heard a loud scream and commotion around the side of one of the buildings. We went to investigate and there were two inmates beating a [German] medic in a white coat with shovels. By the time we got there, he was a bloody mess. We ordered them to halt. They said they were Poles, and one of them dropped his pants to show he had been castrated in the hospital and this German was somehow involved in the operation."

Near the camp's infirmary, Walsh's men were rounding up a number of German soldiers and separating the SS men from the ordinary Wehrmacht troops. The SS men were then herded into a large, enclosed area and lined up against a high stucco wall that formed part of a coal yard for the camp's nearby power plant.

Several of the SS prisoners in the coal yard refused to keep their hands up, and others began muttering to each other in German. At that point, the handful of GIs guarding them were getting nervous. Lee recalled that the GIs "shouted for the SS to keep their Goddamned hands up and stay back."

Lieutenant Walsh ordered the others to set up a machine gun facing the prisoners and to fire if they didn't stay back. The gunner, Private William C. Curtin, loaded the belt in the machine gun and pulled back on the cocking lever so the gun would be ready to fire if necessary. The SS men, seeing the machine gun being cocked, apparently thought they were about to be shot. They panicked and started toward the Americans. Someone yelled "Fire!" and the machine gun opened up with a short burst of fire. Three or four riflemen also fired.

Shortly before the firing began, Sparks, who had been observing the roundup of Germans in the coal yard, had been distracted by a soldier approaching him. Sparks recalled: "He said, 'Colonel, you should see what we found,' so I started to go off with him. I hadn't gotten more than 10 yards away when all of a sudden the machine gun opened up. I wheeled around. The gunner had fired one burst—maybe 10 or 12 shots—at the guards." The SS guards dived for the ground, but in the hail of gunfire, 17 of them were killed. Sparks said: "I ran back and kicked the gunner in the back and knocked him forward onto the gun, then grabbed him by the collar and yelled, 'What the hell are you doing?' He said they were trying to get away, and then he started crying. I pulled out my .45 and fired several shots into the air and said there would be no more firing unless I gave the order. I told them I was taking over command of the company."

Sparks said: "I never like to see people killed unnecessarily, no matter what they have done. We did kill some people there that I consider [were killed] unnecessarily. However, given the circumstances, well, I'm sorry about it. It was just one of those things that no one could control. We tried to take prisoners and treat them honorably. But that was one situation that I was just unable to control for a short time."

Inwardly boiling at what had just taken place but understanding the motivation behind the troops' actions, Sparks directed that the wounded men should be taken to the infirmary, then remembered the enlisted man who had wanted to show him what new horrors I Company had uncovered. Sparks soon arrived at the crematorium, where he saw piles of emaciated corpses, stacked nearly to the ceiling. A count later revealed approximately 200 bodies.

The corpses found there and throughout the camp, including the bodies of the SS men in the coal yard, were left undisturbed for several days while investigators did their work and photographers recorded the scene. A stunned Corporal James Bird later came upon the horrors in the crematorium. After that experience, he found that his mind was forever etched with nightmarish images. "I recall seeing the ovens used to burn bodies and recollect there were still some partly consumed bodies in some of them," Bird said. "One of my buddies photographed many scenes there, and later provided us with copies. I do not have them now because I think my mother destroyed them, since they were beyond her belief."

By now, I Company was only a few yards from the northwest corner of the prison compound. At least 31,000 inmates were huddled in the barracks there, not knowing if the next few minutes would bring liberation or death. Many feared that as the Americans neared, the SS men would carry out Reichsführer Heinrich Himmler's orders to dispose of them all.

Unknown to Sparks, a small advance party from the U.S. Army's 42nd "Rainbow" Infantry Division was rapidly closing in on the camp from the south at that point. As with all of the other American units dashing through Bavaria, the prize those GIs had in view was Munich. At 0220 hours on the 29th, the 42nd's commander, Maj. Gen. Harry J. Collins, sent a message to his 222nd Infantry Regiment: "Combat battalion to be moved as soon as possible, regiment to follow thereafter as desired. Case of champagne to first battalion to enter Munich." Collins made no mention of Dachau because he knew his division had not been authorized by the Seventh Army to attempt entering KL Dachau—that was the 45th's assignment. But a contingent of American and foreign war correspondents had heard the 42nd was close to the camp and were evidently pressing the division to move toward it—and take them along. There were also the humanitarian concerns. How could he say no? He ordered Brig. Gen. Henning Linden, the assistant division commander, to take a small patrol into the camp.

According to Linden's later testimony to the inspector general, at approximately 1530 the 42nd's advance party, following on the heels of the 45th, came upon the ghastly scene at the railroad siding. Technician Fifth Grade John R. Veitch, who was driving a jeep, recalled: "I had no idea where we were going or what we were going to see. Then we encountered the train with all the bodies. It was terrible."

Linden's party entered the camp at the railroad gate, then turned east toward the main gate. Leading the group were two generals—Linden and Brig. Gen. Charles Y. Banfill, deputy commander for operations, U.S. Eighth Air Force, who was accompanying the 42nd to observe the effects of supporting aerial operations. Others in the entourage included three junior officers and a number of enlisted drivers and bodyguards. Two jeeps carrying members of the press also tagged along, with a Belgian reporter and a photographer in one and Sergeant Peter Furst, a writer with *Stars and Stripes,* and war correspondent Marguerite Higgins in the other.

Higgins was a 25-year-old fledgling war reporter from the *New York Herald Tribune* who had been in Europe only since March but was determined to make a name for herself. Two weeks earlier, at Buchenwald, she had received a quick introduction to the horrors of the SS camps. But Buchenwald was yesterday's news. Higgins wanted to be in on the liberation of a camp. While at Buchenwald, she teamed up with Furst, who had a jeep, and the two of them pressed forward toward Dachau along the same general route used by the 45th and 42nd divisions. Furst and Higgins arrived at the main gate about the same time as Linden's party.

John Veitch recalled, "We got to the outskirts of the camp and heard a lot of small-arms fire." Not knowing if enemy fire was being directed at them, Linden's party, along with Furst and Higgins, scrambled out of the jeeps and took cover in a drainage ditch near the camp's main gate. "The small-arms fire let up. The firing was coming from the 45th, already inside the camp, and then, out of the gate area, came this SS officer. I think there was another man with him. I ended up going up to this SS officer and stuck my .45 in his ribs and told him to put his hands on his head. I'm hitting him in the ribs, trying to get his hands up, but he saw I was just a GI and he was an officer. I brought him back to the general and Linden said to me, 'Tell him to put his hands up.' I said, 'Sir, he won't do it.' Well, General Linden always carried a little stick, kind of a hickory stick with a knob on the end, and he hauled off and hit this guy up the side of the head and said, 'Put your hands up' and he immediately did. He saw that Linden was a general officer."

A brief surrender ceremony took place near the main gate, with the German detachment under the protection of a white flag on a broomstick held by Victor Maurer, a Swiss Red Cross representative. Unaware that the 45th had arrived at Dachau first and was, at that very moment, clearing out the SS camp's buildings, SS Untersturmführer Heinrich Wicker officially surrendered the camp to the 42nd, thereby fueling a debate between the two divisions that lasts to this day regarding which was the true liberator of Dachau.

In his testimony to the Seventh Army assistant inspector general, Linden recounted his version of the events: "The interpreter stated that he and the SS troopers and one or two others had been sent into the camp the night before to take over and surrender the camp to the American forces, and asked me if I was an American officer. I replied, 'I am assistant division commander of the 42nd Division.' Linden then dispatched one of his jeeps to the town of Dachau with a message to Colonel Lucien E. Bolduc, the acting commanding officer of the 222nd Infantry Regiment, asking him to bring up some men to secure the camp.

Linden told the assistant inspector general, "At this time,

small-arms fire broke out to the west of us in the camp area"—evidently shots fired by the 45th. He sent his aide, Lieutenant William Cowling, into the camp to find out what was going on.

In the meantime, Lieutenant William Walsh of the 157th had evidently reached the prisoner enclosure. In a video documentary, The Liberation of KZ Dachau, Walsh said of the incident: "We finally get up to the main gate. This is the gate that says 'Work makes you free.' And when I get to the gate, I ask if anybody spoke English, and there was an Englishman there [Albert Guerisse, in reality a Belgian, also known as Patrick O'Leary]. I think he was a naval officer . . . and I say to him, "Are there any Americans in there?" And he says, 'I don't know . . . I think so, but there may be only one or two.' And then I said, ' . . . I can't open the gates, but I want you to know there's all kinds of medical supplies and doctors and food and stuff like this coming behind us, and they're going to take care of you.' And then he said, 'I want you to come in here first . . . I want you to see what was going on.' And then he finally prevailed on me. I said, 'okay, I'll go in.' And I went in with [Lieutenant Jack] Busheyhead and a sergeant. Of course, we had to squeeze through the gate because they're all inside, screaming and hollering."

Following Guerisse toward some buildings, Walsh was astounded by the hellish scenes that unfolded before him. "There's two or three guys in uniform that are being hammered to death with shovels . . . by the inmates. They're the kapos or the . . . trustees, or whatever. They have them in every camp, and there they are, they're being beaten to death. And he takes us up into an area where they had been experimenting on high-altitude stuff . . . there were a lot of bodies on this boardwalk outside this building . . . where they used to take these high-altitude tests . . . used to put these guys in this thing and drain the air out . . . I get to another barracks and the bunks are roughly four feet high, and they're all full of straw. There's no mattresses or anything. . . .

There's an old guy in the second bunk and he's reached out and he's got a cigarette in hand. A German cigarette, I think and it's water stained, a little yellow color on it, and he's offering it to me. The Englishman's right behind me and, of course, everybody is staring out of their bunks at us . . . and I say, 'Oh, no, you keep it.' "

Guerisse understood the significance of that gesture—by offering to give away his only worldly possession, the prisoner was showing his deep gratitude for the arrival of the Americans. Guerisse whispered in Walsh's ear: "Take it. That's the only thing that guy owns in this whole world. That's his everything . . . a cigarette. Take it."

Meanwhile, at the main gate, Linden and the small knot of Rainbowmen were champing at the bit. They had heard sporadic gunshots and were anxiously waiting to enter the camp. At last a jeep with Lt. Col. Lucien Buldoc in it roared into view. It was decided to send Lieutenant Cowling on another scouting mission inside the camp. Cowling, possibly accompanied by an enlisted man, moved in cautiously. He went about two blocks north, then turned east and discovered the Jourhaus gate 150 yards ahead of him. Seeing a crowd of inmates beginning to form at the Jourhaus, Cowling tried to tell them help was on the way. He then returned to Linden's group at the main gate and told them to come see what he had found.

The advance party from the 42nd Division arrived at the Jourhaus, where a group of SS guards emerged and surrendered to Linden's men without incident. In his testimony to the assistant inspector general, Linden said: "I moved in with my guards into [the military part of the camp], and I found the inmates—having seen the American uniform of my guards there, and those of the 45th Division—approaching the main stockade [i.e., the Jourhaus and the western side of the prisoner enclosure] from the east, had stormed to the fence in riotous joy. This seething mass increased in intensity until the surge against the steel barbed-wire fence was such that it broke in several places, and inmates poured out into the roadway between the fence and the moat [canal]. In this process, several were electrocuted on the charged fence."

In his testimony, Lt. Col. Walter Fellenz, commanding officer of the 222nd's 1st Battalion, said: "We were warned by the inmates that there were other German troops manning one of the towers to the left of us [Tower B]. This tower was approximately 200 yards away from us at this time. On the ground in front of the door to the tower, I saw a man who appeared to be in German uniform. With my field glasses, I identified him as a German soldier and I also saw several other German soldiers in the tower itself. By this time, bodyguards of the above-mentioned officers also saw the German soldiers. Part of the soldiers immediately rushed toward the tower going by the trail near the barbed-wire fence. Others of the bodyguards moved by the road opposite the fence." After he crossed a small bridge that spanned the canal near Tower B, Fellenz said, firing broke out. "Several more shots were fired inside the tower," he added, "and when these shots were fired, the men guarding the prisoners outside the tower shot through the windows of the tower and apparently the German soldiers outside the tower attempted to free themselves from the custody of our troops and were shot in the struggle."

The shooting began some minutes after Tech. 3rd Grade Henry J. Wells, the interpreter accompanying the 42nd's party, proceeded to the tower and fired a burst at the door with his .45-caliber M-3 "grease gun." Once all the guards had been flushed from the tower, Wells formed the group, numbering 16 men, into two ranks with their backs to the canal. A group of 42nd and 45th Division men held the captives under armed guard, and one of the Americans began disarming the Germans. It is not known whether one of the SS men made a move for a weapon, but suddenly the Americans began firing into the group.

When the firing stopped, seven SS guards lay dead on the bank of the Würm River canal. If the count of 16 Germans rousted from the tower is correct, the bodies of nine other guards fell into the canal and were washed downstream, for only seven bodies were accounted for in the inspector general's report. Linden's men then apparently withdrew from Tower B and the Jourhaus and returned to the main gate.

Shortly after the shooting, Sparks, along with a number of I Company men, arrived at Tower B from the crematorium. Seeing only his Thunderbirds in the area, with no 42nd Division personnel around, Sparks assumed the I Company men had killed the Germans who were lying in a neat row at the base of Tower B. Continuing on to the Jourhaus, Sparks still saw no one from the Rainbow Division and did not even realize the men of the 42nd were inside the camp. Decades after the incident Sparks surmised, "Linden's group panicked after the shooting, took the German guards they had taken prisoner at the Jourhaus, and returned with them to the main gate."

On his way to the Jourhaus, Sparks saw prisoners streaming from their barracks by the thousands and rushing toward the wire that enclosed them. "Walking along the canal almost to the Jourhaus, I saw a large number of naked bodies stretched out along the ends of the barracks," Sparks recalled. "I estimated there were about 200 bodies there. I also spotted quite a few of my men at the Jourhaus. About this time, the camp erupted. The prisoners came out of the barracks shouting and screaming."

Thousands of inmates dashed to the wire enclosure, emitting an unearthly howl—a howl of rage at what had befallen them, and a howl of joy at their redemption. Sparks said: "I told Karl Mann, my interpreter, to yell at them and tell them that we couldn't let them out, but that food and medicine would be arriving soon. Then I saw bodies flying through the air, with the prisoners tearing at them with their hands. I had Karl ask what was going on. The prisoners told him that they were killing the informers among them. They actually tore them to pieces with their bare hands. This went on for about five minutes until they wore themselves out. I had Karl tell them to send their leaders to the fence, where I told them to keep calm, that medicine and food would be coming soon. This seemed to settle them down."

Sparks recalled what he saw when he reached the Jourhaus: "A beautiful iron gate to the concentration camp itself . . . that had a sign on it that said in German, 'Work makes you free.' Of course, they worked those prisoners to death. I was standing there at the gate, talking to one of my officers about security when, all of a sudden, I saw three jeeps coming up and they stopped at the end of the little bridge that spanned the canal [at the Jourhaus]." In the jeeps were Generals Linden and Banfill, Colonels Bolduc and Fellenz, along with several others, including journalist Higgins and photographer Furst.

The jeeps stopped at the western end of the bridge that spanned the canal, and Sparks talked briefly with Linden. Sparks said Linden told him that Higgins wanted to enter the camp to interview the inmates. Sparks replied that his orders prohibited anyone but his men from entering the camp. Higgins then spoke up, demanding to be allowed inside the enclosure. She said, "Colonel, there are some famous people in there," and rattled off a list of names, including the deposed Austrian Chancellor Kurt von Schuschnigg with his wife and daughter, Pastor Martin Niemöller, an anti-Nazi theologian, Hitler's former chief of staff Franz Halder—and many others.

Sparks reiterated his orders. Undeterred, Higgins ran to the gate and began to open it. She was nearly trampled by prisoners trying to get out. Sparks recalled that his men were forced to fire warning shots over the heads of the prisoners to achieve order before they could reclose the gate. "When the firing started," Sparks said, "it scared this woman and she ran back to her jeep."

At this point, a violent argument broke out between Sparks and Linden—an argument remembered clearly more than 50 years later by men from both divisions. Exactly what touched off the argument has never been conclusively determined. Sparks said it was because he refused to abdicate his responsibility to secure the camp and turn it over to an American general from a division that was not supposed to be there. It also may have concerned an I Company soldier whom General Linden had hit or "tapped" on the head with his stick. Sparks' recollection is that he ordered one of his men to escort the general and his party from the area, and that Linden struck the soldier on the helmet with his stick when he approached the jeep. The catalyst may have been Marguerite Higgins, who tried to intervene in the tense situation. Certainly Sparks' war weariness, brought on by nearly two years of almost continuous combat, could have played a significant role in the incident. Or the outburst could have been attributable to the incredible events of the day—the discovery of the death train and the corpses at the crematorium, Walsh's rampage, the killing by I Company men of the SS guards at the coal yard, and the line of German corpses at Tower B. Whatever the catalyst, Sparks admitted that he briefly lost his composure and threatened the general with his .45-caliber pistol.

Corporal Henry "Hank" Mills, of 3rd Battalion's Intelligence and Reconnaissance Platoon, said, "I remember distinctly that Sparks put a gun to that guy's head and said, 'If you don't get the f—out of here, I'm going to blow your brains out.' "

John Lee related, "The general, who was not in charge there, was upset and told the colonel he would be court-martialed. The general was so upset, he struck Sergeant Brumlow on the helmet."

Sparks confirmed that he advised the general and his party to leave. The general shook his fist at Sparks and told him that he was relieved of his command. "That's when Colonel Fellenz came running up," said Sparks. The two lieutenant colonels exchanged threats.

According to Sparks, Fellenz said, "I'll see you after the war." Sparks responded, "You son-of-a-bitch—what's the matter with right now?" Fuming, Fellenz returned to his jeep and the group departed.

Once Linden and his group departed, Sparks saw no one from that group again. "After they left, I placed security around the camp," Sparks said. "Walsh and some of his men went into camp kitchens to see if there was any food, but there wasn't much."

The 45th's chief of staff, Colonel Kenneth Wickham, commented: "I heard of the various discussions of the assistant division commander of the 42nd being there and the argument with one of our lieutenant colonels. At that moment, it didn't seem very important. General Frederick wasn't very concerned one way or the other—he thought the 42nd general was kind of out of line." Evidently, however, word reached Frederick that Linden had struck one of the 45th's enlisted men, and he phoned General Collins on the evening of April 29 to inform him that he intended to prefer court-martial charges against Linden. After hearing versions of the incident from Linden and Cowling, and learning that Brigadier General Banfill was an eyewitness and would corroborate the other two officers' stories—and perhaps realizing there was some dispute as to whether Linden had struck the soldier or merely tapped him with his walking stick—Frederick let the matter drop.

By now, Sparks and I Company were totally confused as to what the 42nd was doing there and who was supposed to be in charge. Wanting some clarification as to exactly in whose zone of responsibility the camp lay, the 45th Division operations officer queried XV Corps headquarters. The response was: "With reference to your TWX stating that Fury [code-name for the 42nd Division] was attempting to relieve your guards at the Dachau PW camp (Y765700), the guarding of this camp is your responsibility as it is in your zone." That order was later changed, and the 42nd was put in temporary charge of the prisoner compound, with the 45th assigned to secure the SS complex and the area outside the prisoner compound.

Many of the soldiers were thankful they had reached the camp in time to save the lives of many of the inmates, but they discovered it was virtually impossible not to be repelled by the awful conditions in the camp. Sidney C. Horn, a member of I Company, 157th, recalled the terrible overcrowding and the lack of proper sanitation: "The people wanted to hug you and love you for what you were doing, but the stench was so bad, you couldn't keep from running from them."

As the gray, sunless day settled into a cold night, a sense of relief spread within the inmates of KL Dachau. From the barracks came sounds of laughter, singing and prayers of thanksgiving. There was little joy, however, among the American liberators. Although they had undoubtedly helped save thousands of lives, many of the men of I Company felt sick and depressed over what they had seen and heard that day. For some, it was a delayed reaction.

John Lee recalled: "That night was when the realization really hit. We had to guard the bakery, our squad. No one ate chow that night . . . everyone was sick. I was sick constantly all night long. I don't think there was a guy who slept that night, and I don't think there was a guy who didn't cry openly that night." He added: "I really didn't feel good about what happened there, but also I have to admit there was a certain amount of revenge and, in a way, I felt that even though these [guards] may not have been the men who perpetrated this sort of thing, at least you paid back a little bit for these people, what happened to them. I realized you can't resolve it by doing that—it was wrong, what happened there, but you had to have been there to see what we saw."

The 222nd remained in the Dachau area until the next day, April 30, when it pushed forward and opened a new command post in Munich.

An artillery battalion relieved Sparks' 3rd Battalion of the 157th at Dachau, and his troops followed the rest of the division into Munich, where the anticipated German "fight to the last man" failed to materialize. The 45th and other units were placed in charge of maintaining order in the city where the Nazi system had been born.

On May 1, Sparks was relieved of command of the 3rd Battalion—apparently, he thought, the result of his having threatened a general officer. "On May 1st, General Frederick came to see me in Munich," Sparks recalled. "He said, 'Things are getting hot. General Linden is raising a stink. I'm going to send you back to the States immediately. Our division is scheduled to invade Japan and I'm sending you back. You can take a leave and rejoin us when we come back to the States.' " Sparks called his company commanders together, told them he was going to the States and said goodbye.

Lieutenant Colonel Joseph Whitaker, the Seventh Army's assistant inspector general, spent several weeks interviewing as many participants and witnesses to the events of April 29 as he could reach, then wrote up his findings. Once his report, stamped "Secret," was complete, it was sent to the office of the Seventh Army judge advocate general, who recommended that Lieutenants Walsh and Busheyhead, Tech. 3rd Class Wells, and Private Albert Pruitt—who had finished off the four Germans Walsh had herded into the railroad car—should be charged with murder and tried by court-martial. Other men were charged with lesser crimes.

Lieutenant General Wade Haislip, who had succeeded Alexander Patch as commander of the Seventh Army, however, refused to proceed with the recommended courts-martial, saying that the inspector general had failed to take into account the emotional state of the troops, who had been in nearly continuous combat for more than a month. Haislip approved only of charging Walsh and Pruitt with shooting the four SS soldiers in the boxcar, but he stalled long enough for his Seventh Army to be reorganized and ordered to push on into Austria. Patton's Third Army, relocating its headquarters from Regensburg to Bad Tölz, south of Munich, would take control of Bavaria. Because the 45th Division was reassigned to become part of the Third Army, the matter was handed over to the Third Army for disposition.

Patton, not uncharacteristically, also chose to take no disciplinary action. His position, no doubt, was that it was the Germans who were the enemy. The SS had run the concentration camps, and, if some of them got killed in the process of liberation, that was just too damn bad. Furthermore, the surviving leaders of the Nazi regime were being rounded up and imprisoned in anticipation of war-crimes trials that were to take place in the upcoming months in Nüremberg. To conduct a court-martial of Americans involved in the Dachau massacre would not only besmirch the honor of the American fighting man but could also seriously weaken the Allies' case against the Germans accused of atrocities. According to Sparks, Patton—in his presence—destroyed Whitaker's report, and no courts-martial were ever conducted. Only a single copy of the inspector general's report survived, and it lay undetected within the bowels of the National Archives for half a century.

The civilians living in or near Dachau, who claimed that they knew nothing of the horrors being committed in their backyard, were given a lesson in the brutality of their countrymen. Medic Peter Galary recalled that once the camp was in American hands, "We made the civilians who lived around there parade past the boxcars full of dead bodies, and they said, 'We never knew about it.' They cried, but what good is crying going to do?—it wouldn't bring any of those people back to life."

Half a century after the incident, Walsh said, "I don't think there was any SS guy that was shot or killed in the defense of Dachau that wondered why he was killed." While some accounts have claimed that upward of 500 guards were killed during the liberation of Dachau, according to the inspector general's report, the official bodycount was 24 dead SS men.

And what of the prisoners—all 31,432 of them? Whether their redeemers wore a thunderbird patch or a rainbow was of absolutely no concern to them. Medical teams from the XV Corps tried to save as many of the critically ill former inmates as possible, but an additional 2,466 died between April 29 and June 16. Because the danger of typhus was high, the inmates had to remain quarantined inside the camp for several weeks before they were repatriated to their former homelands.

One of the Polish inmates told the inspector general about the joy felt by the liberated inmates: "Prisoners swarmed over the wire and grabbed the American soldiers and lifted them to their shoulders amid many cries. I helped to lift the soldiers. . . . All that could were crowding in to kiss their hands and clothes. . . . For the past six years we had waited for the Americans, and at this moment the SS were nothing."

Greatest Battle Never Fought

By Ansil L. Walker

In the late spring of 1945, the arc of American military might was fast closing around Japan. U.S. Marines had captured the island of Iwo Jima, providing another airfield within striking distance of the home islands and adding to the awesome power of warplanes based on Tinian and Saipan in the Marianas. General Douglas MacArthur had made good on his promise to return to the Philippines; the island of Leyte had fallen, Manila had been recaptured, and by the end of March the soldiers of General Tomoyuki Yamashita—the "Tiger of Malaya"—had been defeated at mountainous Baguio, the summer capital of the Philippine island of Luzon. In disarray and short of supplies, thousands of Japanese soldiers were in headlong flight to the north and northeast, trying to escape the stalking U.S. 33rd Infantry Division and other Sixth Army forces by hunkering down in the primitive, uncharted wilds of the Cordillera Central and Sierra Madre. Whether they knew it or not, their war was over. By July, all islands of the Philippines were liberated.

The island of Okinawa, which had belonged to Japan since 1879, was invaded on April 1, 1945. In late June, after the bloodiest campaign of the Pacific War, the Thirty-Second Japanese Army surrendered. Okinawa was only 400 miles from Kyushu, southernmost of the four home islands.

Japanese cities on Honshu Island were then ravaged, one after another, by General Curtis LeMay's 20th Bombardment Group, striking from the Marianas. Adding to the devastation, U.S. warships cruised along coastlines, blasting port cities, interfering with fishing fleets, and blockading the shipping lanes. On March 9 the first low-level night raid, carried out by a force of 325 Marianas-based Boeing B-29 Superfortresses, unloaded 2,000 tons of incendiaries in a three-hour punishment of Tokyo. The raid unleashed an appalling firestorm rivaling those produced by the Allied bombing of Dresden and Hamburg in Germany. In the inferno more than 80,000 terrified citizens perished, and bodies choked the Sumida River as masses vainly sought relief from the holocaust. One million became homeless, and a 15-mile swath of eastern Tokyo lay smoldering and obliterated.

Next to suffer from the Superfortress attacks were the great Honshu industrial cities of Nagoya, Osaka, Kobe, and Yokohama. They were struck four times in 10 days, leaving factories, steel plants and shipping docks smashed and burned. By early June, 50 percent of Honshu's industrial capacity had been destroyed or damaged by LeMay's marauding B-29s; and General George C. Kenney's Far Eastern Air Force began to soften up the major cities, airfields, and military bases of Kyushu.

Defeat was inevitable. Japan was being systematically destroyed, and this grim truth became more and more difficult to conceal from the people. Surrender was the sensible alternative in early summer 1945, and peace terms would hopefully ensure the survival of the Japanese nation, its people, and the emperor. But to the Japanese at least four major points seemed to require rejection of the surrender terms that had been issued in the Potsdam Declaration of late July 1945:

- The ultimatum of "unconditional surrender or face prompt and utter destruction" was unacceptable. The language was too harsh, and no direct reference was included as to the future status of Emperor Hirohito.
- The Japanese government had no experience, no precedent, in defining the implications of national surrender and little understanding about the importance of unity in such a time of crisis. Aggressive debate, arguments, and the pursuit of power in the cabinet between the "hawks" and "doves" were creating a paralysis in governmental decision making.
- The government might not understand surrender, but in the face of national peril, it understood its people; in case of invasion, the millions of civilian volunteers in the National Force would stand ready. Boys and men, aged 15 to 60, and girls and women, 17 to 40, armed only with sharpened bamboo spears, pitchforks, rusty bayonets, and dynamite charges strapped to their bodies, anticipated a fight to the death. Their efforts, augmenting the defensive capabilities of the regular combat divisions, should result in American combat losses so costly and unacceptable that a negotiated cessation of hostilities more favorable than unconditional surrender could be arranged.
- High-level meetings in Moscow were hoped for and could result in agreement for continuation of Russo-Japanese neutrality. The Soviets, although a wartime member of the Allied powers, had not fired a shot against Japan except for minor clashes along the borders of Manchuria. Now, in the summer of 1945, they had massed a mighty army on the same periphery, poised for attack. During this time, the Americans were pressuring Stalin to abandon the Russo-Japanese neutrality pact, in effect since 1905, and participate in the final stages of the war. Conversely, the Japanese

prepared to offer real estate and other concessions to Stalin in return for a continuation of neutrality. If the Soviets were agreeable, part of the Japanese Kwantung Army would be freed from Manchuria for a return home to reinforce the regulars already in place on the four main islands.

As early as May 1945, the Joint Chiefs of Staff (JCS) in Washington, D.C., in spite of an initial lack of unanimity among the U.S. Army, Air Force, and Navy leaders, had reached a conclusion. Continued air assaults, even when coordinated with naval gunfire and a blockade of the Japanese coastline, were not going to force the Japanese nation to her knees. Japan would be forced to surrender unconditionally only through a continuation of the bombing, the blockade and a massive, concomitant amphibious invasion. The early plans at the JCS level included the appointment of General Douglas MacArthur as commander in chief, U.S. Army Forces, Pacific, with the overall responsibility for invasions and ensuing campaigns. Fleet Admiral Chester W. Nimitz was designated as commander of all naval participation, consisting of the Third Fleet (Admiral William F. Halsey) and Fifth Fleet (Admiral Raymond A. Spruance). General Carl A. Spaatz was to command the Strategic Air Force during future operations.

General MacArthur and Lt. Gen. Walter Krueger, commanding the Sixth Army, began specific plans and preparations in late May for the anticipated invasion of Japan. A two-step assault was envisioned and code-named Operation Downfall. The first phase, designated Operation Olympic and later renamed Majestic for a time in the summer because of a suspected security leak, called for the invasion of Kyushu by Krueger's veteran army on November 1, 1945.

If Japan did not capitulate during the Kyushu campaign or during the winter, the second step, Operation Coronet, was projected for March 1946, with an amphibious assault upon the beaches of the broad, sweeping Kanto Plain before Tokyo. In combination, Olympic and Coronet would be carried out by an awe-inspiring naval, air, and land force greater than any other ever before assembled. A total force of 5 million men, all American except for the inclusion of three British Commonwealth infantry divisions, a contingent of air support, and the British Pacific Fleet, would be engaged in the land campaigns and on the waters around the Japanese homeland.

Preparations for Olympic accelerated in the summer. Eleven Army divisions, three Marine divisions, and two Army regimental combat teams, totaling almost 550,000 combat troops, were targeted for the invasion of Kyushu. These men were veterans of two to three years of fighting in the jungles and on islands of the Southwest and Central Pacific. After undergoing amphibious training and making practice landings on secured islands on the way to Kyushu, they were going in again. Preliminary estimates of casualties indicated that the killed and wounded might total a staggering 35 percent of their number.

As the Kyushu campaign progressed in November, 250,000 additional troops were scheduled as reinforcements, including support and service elements and naval and air force personnel assigned to operate the captured bases and newly constructed installations. This augmentation swelled the planned total participation to nearly 800,000 men.

Admiral Spruance's Fifth Fleet comprised approximately 3,000 amphibious craft, troop transports and warships charged with landing and covering the assault forces, sweeping the waters of Japanese mines, and supporting the troops ashore with naval and aircraft gunfire.

Admiral Halsey's Third Fleet included 20 aircraft carriers, 10 battleships, 20 cruisers and 75 destroyers. The carrier planes would range far and wide over Kyushu, Shikoku, and Honshu, targeting communications, troop concentrations, installations, airfields, aircraft, naval bases and shipping. An additional task would be softening up the landing areas with pre-invasion naval bombardment and airstrikes. Adding to the fire power, General Kenney's Far Eastern Air Force (FEAF), now based within striking distance of Kyushu, would concentrate the attacks of its Fifth, Seventh, and Thirteenth air forces in an isolation strategy of disrupting and destroying communications, rail lines, transportation facilities, roads and avenues of approach from north and south. As the campaign progressed, the FEAF counted on moving to the captured and newly constructed air bases in southern Kyushu in order to furnish both tactical and strategic air support.

General MacArthur reviewed the physical geography of Kyushu and studied its relationship to the strategic military aspects of the operation. The island lies between 31 and 34 degrees north latitude, and the East China Sea and Korean Strait wash its western and northwestern shores respectively. Directly eastward is the island of Shikoku, narrowly separated from Kyushu by the Inland Sea. The other two main islands, Honshu and Hokkaido, are positioned to the northeast, with Kyushu and Honshu separated by the narrowest of straits.

From north to south, Kyushu covers about 180 miles. East to west, the island varies in width from 80 to 120 miles. The island's latitudinal location, the relatively warm ocean currents nearby, and temperate winds blowing across the island combine to provide a mild climate. Kyushu is indented by numerous bays, coves and inlets. A half-dozen hilly and rugged peninsulas stretch like fingers into the sea. A major mountain range, centrally placed and extending northeast to southwest almost the full length of the island, is heavily forested. The range includes lower hills and plateaus, at least three major active, fuming volcanoes, and rugged, deep, almost impenetrable ravines. Coastal plains circle the island and infiltrate the highlands as upland plains and negotiable valleys.

Three assigned military objectives faced MacArthur and Sixth Army planners in Manila. First, they must isolate and cut off Kyushu from the main island, Honshu. Second, it was essential to destroy the Japanese forces on Kyushu. Third, they must seize existing air and naval bases and construct additional installations and facilities on Kyushu. Accomplishment of the third military objective would provide support for the massive second phase of Operation Downfall, the Coronet invasion of Honshu scheduled for March 1946.

The strategies for achieving the three objectives were pure MacArthur and typical of his disdain for costly frontal assault, especially when envelopment, end runs, bypassing, and leapfrogging tactics had effected a successful march toward Japan through the Southwest Pacific and the Philippines with limited casualties. So MacArthur drew his line in the sand across southern Kyushu, from coastal cities Sendai, just north of Kushikino, to Tsuno. He had no aspirations for land beyond this, believing that all three objectives were attainable within the modest land confines south of the line. This area of Kyushu was to be seized and held.

On X-Day, November 1, 1945, three separate and widely dispersed amphibious assaults were scheduled for the invasion of Kyushu. On the east coast, the 33rd, 25th, and 41st Infantry divisions of Maj. Gen. Innis P. Swift's I Corps would pour ashore along the sandy, idyllic coastline at Miyazaki City. A popular resort area, Miyazaki's beaches were part of an extensive north-south coastal plain that widened considerably in the region. A major seaplane base and airfield were the main targets for seizure; its accessible landing beaches and spreading plains offered ample room for armor and infantry maneuver.

Fifty miles south, Lt. Gen. Charles P. Hall's XI Corps was

slated to invade Ariake-Wan and the beaches at the head of the bay in the Shibushi City area. The XI Corps was comprised of the 43rd, 1st Cavalry and Americal divisions, and the 112th Cavalry Regimental Combat Team. Prior to the landings, General Kenney's FEAF would destroy the Japanese gun batteries and seaplane bases ringing the 18-mile-wide bay, as well as the suicide boats and midget submarines along the shoreline.

The V Amphibious Corps, commanded by Marine Maj. Gen. Harry Schmidt and consisting of the 2nd, 3rd, and 5th Marine divisions, was to assault the long, narrow beaches south of Kushikino City on the west coast.

Four days before X-Day, Brig. Gen. Donald J. Myer's 40th Infantry Division was to seize the small islands west of Kushikino and Sendai, set up radar and air-warning facilities, and keep the sea lanes open to the landing beaches. Also on X-minus-4, the 158th Regimental Combat Team, led by Brig. Gen. Hanford Mac-Nider, was given practically the same mission—to capture the southernmost islands of Yaku and Tanega in the Osumi-Kaikyo Strait. Later, both the 40th and 158th would be available as reinforcements on Kyushu.

Two days before X-Day, the 81st and 98th Infantry divisions of Maj. Gen. Charles W. Ryder's IX Corps planned to demonstrate off the east coast of Shikoku, diverting attention and confusing the enemy about X-Day landing sites. Afterward, sailing south, the corps expected to add the 77th Division to its convoy, and on X-plus-4, strike the southern beaches of Satsuma Peninsula. The 11th Airborne Division, Maj. Gen. Joseph M. Swing commanding, was afloat near Okinawa as a reserve force during this time. That brought the planned total of invading Sixth Army troops to 14 infantry divisions and two regimental combat teams, all battle-tested and intensely trained for combat.

The prize was Kagoshima, a scenic port city at the head of

vast Kagoshima-Wan in southern Kyushu. Sometimes called the "Naples of Japan" because it was dominated by an active, towering volcano, the city featured important air, navy, seaplane bases, installations and supply depots. With natural approaches and a physical setting resembling Pearl Harbor, Kagoshima City and the bay provided the rehearsal site for the attack on Pearl Harbor.

After consolidating beachheads in the Kushikino area, the Marines of the V Amphibious Corps planned to detach units to block enemy movement from north to south down the coast from Sendai. The main force, meanwhile, would be driving eastward, aiming primarily for Kagoshima, and isolating the Japanese forces in the Satsuma Peninsula. During this time, the divisions of the IX Corps proposed to push northward from their landings along the southern coastline, destroy the enemy in the Satsuma Peninsula, and strike for Kagoshima in a dual effort with the V Amphibious Corps. Of serious concern for the IX Corps was the intelligence report that the southern coastline was alive with nests of suicide surface and underwater craft loaded with explosives and eager to seek out and crash into American convoys and troopships in the darkness. Pre-invasion saturation bombardment of the coastline and bay areas by Kenney's FEAF and naval warships carried the highest priority.

Following the capture of Kagoshima by the combat forces, U.S. Navy, Air Force, and Army personnel would be responsible for rehabilitating existing air and naval bases, supply depots, and other installations as well as constructing new facilities. Kagoshima would become the major port for the continuing Kyushu campaign and the principal advance base for the massive Coronet invasion. From Kagoshima, the plan called for continuing the attack northward to the headlands of Kagoshima Wan, then eastward as far as Kokubu.

Miyakonojo was the focal point in southeast Kyushu. The city was a road, rail, and communications center with nearby supply depots, ammunition dumps, and an important air base. Extensive plains around Miyakonojo favored infantry and armor assembly and offered offensive maneuverability.

Similar to the V Corps strategy on the west coast, the I Corps plan at Miyazaki called for a force to block any Japanese reaction down the eastern coast from Beppu, Nobeoka and Tsuno. The 33rd Division would be alert for any Japanese response from the Kobayashi/Kirishima Mountain strongholds, to the east. The ensuing primary mission called for the I Corps to strike out for Miyakonojo, 25 miles away, and link up with the XI Corps, which was pushing north from the Shibushi beaches on Ariake Bay. Highlands, some impenetrable defiles and valleys, and heavy forests—all favoring defense—had to be confronted much of the way before Miyakonojo. Along the route, elements of the I Corps planned to establish a line or front isolating Japanese forces in southeastern Kyushu.

The XI Corps would be closer to Miyakonojo, and the terrain there would provide a more expedient route of advance than the route proposed for the I Corps elements.

After attacking and seizing the Miyakonojo region and establishing the line from Miyazaki to Miyakonojo, the two corps intended to push westward and team up with the columns moving from Kagoshima in the Kokobu region. The 10-mile, relatively open corridor between Miyakonojo and Kokobu encouraged armor, tank and infantry maneuverability.

Sixth Army planners envisioned an unbroken front extending from Miyazaki westward through Miyakonojo and Kokobu to Kushikino on the west coast, serving as an initial phase line for an all-out, concerted Sixth Army drive northward to MacArthur's limit of advance. Along that limit, Operation Olympic would close, and troops would await orders for any future operations. Isolated enemy forces to the south could only die on the vine or be subject to clean-up operations by reserve combat forces making new landings.

Planning for Coronet was only in its preliminary stages. There was a strong feeling that the second invasion might not be necessary, that Japan would surrender before March 1, 1946. A general design called for nine infantry divisions, three Marine divisions, and two armored divisions to land on the Nagoya-Hamamatsu-Tokyo-Chosi coastline of Honshu Island. Formed into an Eighth Army and a supporting Tenth Army, under Lt. Gen. Robert Eichelberger, their assignment included the control of the vast Kanto Plain, the capture and occupation of the Tokyo-Yokohama complex, and the preparation for a continuing campaign on this main island. Ten infantry divisions and one airborne division brought from Europe would follow from Pacific staging areas. General Courtney H. Hodges was designated to lead this First Army. Should the Japanese continue to resist in an act of ultimate national suicide, a mighty redeployment of up to 30 infantry divisions might be expected as American reinforcement.

The Japanese code name for defense of the homeland was Ketsu-Go, or Operation Decision. Time was of the essence. A chain of command was organized, listing two great general armies at the top and, in descending order, area armies, armies, corps, divisions with their regiments, and independent brigades.

More than 21$\frac{1}{2}$ million regular army soldiers comprised Japan's two general armies. First General Army, with headquarters near Tokyo, was charged with the defense of eastern Honshu and Hokkaido Island. Thirty infantry divisions, two armored divisions, and a number of brigades made up the initial land force. Western Honshu and all of Kyushu and Shikoku were the defensive responsibilities of Second General Army, headquartered at Hiroshima. Four infantry divisions and scattered brigades were located in western Honshu, and three divisions were on Shikoku. Fourteen infantry divisions and five brigades, including two tank brigades, settled in Kyushu. Elements of the Kwantung Army in China were on the way, and immense manpower conscriptions were in long-range planning.

A shortage of steel, cement and other construction materials created difficulties in defensive preparations. Caches of food, ammunition and fuel, as well as command posts, kitchens, billets, medical facilities and power installations, were going underground on both Kyushu and Honshu. A honeycomb network of natural and man-made caves, corridors and tunnels connected and protected them. In-depth lines of defense were devised. Along the coastal areas, suicidal riflemen manned crudely fortified pits. Although they would certainly be severely decimated in the pre-invasion bombardment, some might survive and be put to use as ambushers. Farther back, concentrations of heavily fortified strongholds, machine-gun nests and mortar positions were sited. On high ground and in the mountains, artillery pieces on wheels and railway tracks traveled inside enormous cement tunnels from one firing port to another, the mouths of the tunnels hidden and protected by camouflaged sliding steel doors. Other artillery positions were strategically emplaced on high ground to deliver both direct and enfilading fire on troop transports and landing craft as they came within range and approached the beaches. At the same time, the 25 million nonmilitary men, women, and children of the National Volunteer Force waited, armed with their primitive weapons.

MacArthur and Nimitz were greatly concerned about the effect of kamikaze attacks against ships standing off the invasion beaches. The Japanese general staff proclaimed that more than 30 percent of the landing troops would be sunk with the ships. The keys to victory, the Japanese reasoned, were the kamikaze attacks and the surprise night raids of both surface and underwater suicide craft. Ten thousand aircraft, including obsolete trainers, would be piloted by young men who were looking forward to glorious self-destruction. Six thousand planes were directed for attacks against Operation Olympic, with the remainder reserved for Operation Coronet.

Japanese intelligence predicted the Kyushu invasion would occur in late September. With the further expectation that Coronet was a winter away, the development of defensive works on Kyushu progressed at top speed. By August the stage was set, the actors in final readiness.

In the pre-dawn darkness of August 6, 1945, an American B-29 lifted into the sky off Tinian in the Marianas, headed for Hiroshima. At 8:15 a.m. the Superfortress released an atomic bomb, which detonated over the city and annihilated 100,000 people, radiated as many more, and completely obliterated one of Honshu's important cities.

On August 8, the Soviet Union entered the war against Japan. In a dawn offensive along the Manchurian frontier, its armies overwhelmed the Japanese Kwantung Army and rushed into North Korea, bent on seizing as much territory as possible before Japan surrendered.

At noon on August 9, another B-29 dropped an atomic bomb on historic Nagasaki, the Madame Butterfly city and a busy industrial port on a northeastern peninsula of Kyushu.

With his nation in a most distressed state, his cabinet resigning, and a wave of senior officers and leaders committing ritual suicide with their sacred disemboweling knives, Emperor Hirohito began a broadcast of an imperial rescript to a sobbing, distraught populace. His voice trembling, he stated: "The enemy has begun to employ a new, cruel bomb...." He went on to announce an end to all hostilities. Loudspeakers and radios on Allied ships all over the Pacific passed along the news of capitulation to a relieved and thankful audience.

The American war with Japan was over. The Allied landing forces were "going in again," but not against hostile beaches. The new duty would be called occupation, and then, finally, the fighting men of the Pacific would be going home. In an eloquent overseas broadcast, MacArthur asked his nation to "take care of them."

Related Websites on World War II

In addition to the hundreds of new books published each year, leading magazines such as *World War II, Military History, Aviation History and MHQ: The Journal of Military History,* bring the stories of World War II alive month after month.

The World Wide Web has opened up a whole new universe of outstanding resources providing an immense amount of information on World War II. Some of the best of the Web include:

www.thehistorynet.com *—Where History Lives on the Web*
Among the Web's largest and most popular history sites TheHistoryNet presents hundreds of in-depth articles and vivid images about World War II.

www.nara.gov
The Web site of the National Archives is the repository of unit histories, a vast still and motion picture collection and sound recordings of historical figures.

www.loc.gov
The Library of Congress site houses a large collection of rare documents and books, and is also the home of the American Memories collection, which has a huge number of images that can be downloaded for free.

www.history.navy.mil
The Naval Historical Center has a large collection of ship's histories as well as other material related to the history of the U.S. Navy.

www.army.mil/usamhi
The United States Army Military History Institute houses a large collection of unit histories and manuals as well as a photographic collection. It is also the repository of several large collections of personal papers and is actively involved in collecting oral histories of World War II veterans.

www.army.mil/cmh-pg/default.htm
The Center of Military History is the official historical branch of the United States Army. It also maintains the Army's impressive art collection.

www.airforcehistory.hq.af.mil
The United States Air Force Historical Branch is the official historical branch of the USAF. In addition to publishing original research on the history of the USAF, the historical branch also maintains the Air Force art collection.

www.marineheritage.org
The Marine Corps Heritage Foundation helps coordinate efforts on behalf of those working on projects that promote Marine Corps' history. In addition, they are working to construct an enlarged Marine Corps Heritage Center at Quantico, Va.

www.ddaymuseum.org/home.htm
Opened in 2000, The National D-Day Museum is dedicated to telling the story of every amphibious operation of World War II, starting with Operation Overlord in 1944.

www.iwm.org.uk
The Imperial War Museum is dedicated to preserving the memory of all of the conflicts of the 20th Century. It is rightly regarded as Europe's premier military museum. In addition to its huge collec-

tion, the IWM also houses a large collection of personal papers, original artwork and photographs pertaining to World War II.

www.cwgc.org
In addition to maintaining hundreds of cemeteries around the world, the Commonwealth War Graves also provide an electronic database of every British or Commonwealth casualty of the two World Wars, and, where possible, their final resting place.

www.pro.gov.uk
The Public Record Office houses a wide variety of official British government documents and personal papers, many of which pertain to World War II.

www.awm.gov.au
The Australian War Memorial displays a large collection of military memorabilia in a variety of exhibits. In addition to its displays, the memorial maintains an enormous collection of art, photographs and personal papers.

www.civilization.ca/cwm/cwmeng/cwmeng.html
In addition to its displays, the Canadian War Museum the museum houses a large collection of personal papers, artwork and photographs.